# Homeward Bound

---

## WHY WOMEN ARE EMBRACING
## THE NEW DOMESTICITY

---

Emily Matchar

SIMON & SCHUSTER

New York   Toronto   London   Sydney   New Delhi

Some names and identifying characteristics have been changed.

Simon & Schuster
1230 Avenue of the Americas
New York, NY 10020

First Simon & Schuster hardcover edition May 2013

SIMON & SCHUSTER and colophon are trademarks of Simon & Schuster, Inc.

For information about special discounts for bulk purchases, please contact Simon & Schuster Special Sales at 1-866-506-1949 or business@simonandschuster.com.

The Simon & Schuster Speakers Bureau can bring authors to your live event. For more information or to book an event contact the Simon & Schuster Speakers Bureau at 1-866-248-3049 or visit our website at www.simonspeakers.com.

Designed by Maura Fadden Rosenthal

Manufactured in the United States of America

1   3   5   7   9   10   8   6   4   2

Library of Congress Cataloging-in-Publication Data
Matchar, Emily.
Homeward bound : why women are embracing the new domesticity / by Emily Matchar.
pages cm
Includes bibliographical references and index.
1. Homemakers—United States. 2. Women—United States—Psychology. 3. Home economics—Social aspects—United States. I. Title.
HQ536.M346 2013
640.92—dc23
2013005815

ISBN 978-1-4516-6544-4
ISBN 978-1-4516-6546-8 (ebook)

*For Jamin*

*A baked potato is not as big as the world.*
—Betty Friedan, *The Feminine Mystique*

# Contents

# Introduction

In the immortal words of Buffalo Springfield: there's something happening here.

Here is a thoroughly noncomprehensive list of some of the memoirs released by major publishers in the past few years:

> *My Life from Scratch: A Sweet Journey of Starting Over, One Cake at a Time* by Gesine Bullock-Prado: A young Hollywood exec flees Los Angeles to open a bakery in small-town Vermont.
>
> *The Pioneer Woman: Black Heels to Tractor Wheels* by Ree Drummond: A young career woman quits her "spoiled city girl" life in Los Angeles to marry an Oklahoma rancher and become a "domestic country wife."
>
> *Rurally Screwed: My Life off the Grid with the Cowboy I Love* by Jessie Knadler: A young type-A magazine editor in New York meets a Montana cowboy and moves to rural Virginia to farm chickens and raise a baby.
>
> *The Dirty Life: A Memoir of Farming, Food, and Love* by Kristin Kimball: A young, female Manhattan journalist ditches the city to start a farm in upstate New York.
>
> *Made from Scratch: Discovering the Pleasures of a Handmade Life* by Jenna Woginrich: A young female Web designer quits city life to raise goats on a farm in rural Vermont.

I could keep going (and going and going), but you get the picture: the career girl—gone—*Green Acres* memoir is the new chick lit. Our new collective escapist fantasy is more likely to involve a Vermont farmhouse and a cute Anthropologie apron than a SoHo loft and a pair of Manolos.

Just step outside of the bookstore and look around. The fashion of the early twenty-first century is a whiplash-inducing 180-degree turn from the androgyny of the 1990s. Today, on the streets of Brooklyn and San Francisco and Austin and Chicago, fashionable twenty- and thirtysomethings walk around looking like they popped out of a cosmic wormhole from 1963 or 1944 or 1922, or even 1890 (any further back and you might wind up in Renaissance Faire territory). In are A-line dresses, dotted-Swiss aprons, prairie skirts, gingham. For men, lumberjack beards, classic Red Wing work boots, and vintage denim are de rigueur.

Makers of midcentury vintage-reproduction clothing report sales increases of 25 to 30 percent over the past four years, a period where most other clothing retailers have seen a downturn. "Designers are cranking out housewife-homage looks for spring that would have June Cleaver bursting her girdle with pride," enthuses one fashion writer.[1] "Retro fabulousness!" chirps *Glamour*.

"People used to laugh at me when I tried to sell these kinds of clothes when I started 13 years ago," says the owner of a vintage-style clothing company. "Now my clothes are sold in 40 countries and more than 1,000 boutiques."[2]

Our nostalgia for old-fashioned home and hearth has transformed our food culture as well. Who hasn't tried canning jam or making their own pickles? Young women who, had they been of age in the 1990s, might have been boozing it up in the Meatpacking District are now spending Saturday nights baking cupcakes and photographing them for their food blogs. The kinds of kitchen work once associated with Depression-era farmwives—making curds and whey, preserving sauerkraut, grinding flour—are now thoroughly unremarkable pastimes for young people flush with today's DIY back-to-basics spirit.

Walk through the streets of a hip neighborhood in any American city, and you're likely to spy something that hasn't been seen in urban areas in a hundred years: vegetable gardens. Gardening, once the domain of the suburban middle-aged, is now a mark of cool among the kind of urban young people who, in a less domestic era, wouldn't have met their first trowel until they had their second kid and moved to Connecticut. And raising your own farm animals is now a completely acceptable activity for city-dwelling architects and lawyers and publishing assistants, with cities passing ordinances to legalize backyard chicken coops. It is now normal—normal!—to hear roosters crowing in Williamsburg or Silver Lake.

The trendiest restaurants of today aim to replicate your meemaw's 1930s Georgia kitchen, their menus a nostalgic tribute to the "handcrafted," the "heritage," and the "heirloom." The pickled beets aren't just pickled beets; they're "Aunt Janey's pickled beets." The meat is from a small family farm; the farmer's name is written on the back of the menu. Read some of today's popular food writers and count the number of times "old-fashioned" or "like our grandmothers might have made" is used—"Don't eat anything your great-great-grandmother wouldn't recognize as food" is foodie guru Michael Pollan's oft-quoted cri de coeur.

Our longing for the handmade, the old-fashioned, the authentic has launched crafting out of the sewing room and into the mainstream. Activities like knitting, crocheting, quilting, and sewing, long associated with eighty-year-old grannies, are now deeply hip among their twenty- and thirtysomething granddaughters. The tinny click of knitting needles has become soothing background noise in the coffee shops of Chicago and Seattle and Los Angeles, where people talk of "reclaiming" lost domestic arts and "getting back to basics." Yarn sales have shot through the roof, knitting circles have popped up like mushrooms after a rain, and crafting-based social-networking sites are being called the new Facebook.

Nowhere is the new domestic chic so apparent as in the blogosphere. If you're a young woman, chances are you already know all about the "domestic porn" blog phenomenon, which is overwhelmingly female dominated and overwhelmingly enamored of a cozy vintage aesthetic. You'll find young women in retro dresses showing off their knitting projects, pictures of steamy apple pies and overexposed shots of wildflowers in Mason jars, musings on one's love of rainy days and iced tea and vintage KitchenAids. If the bloggers have children, expect moony, angelic pictures of toddlers in hand-knitted striped sweaters and arty, backlit close-ups of infants' downy little ears. Some of these women will refer to themselves, in a cheeky but serious spirit, as "homemakers" or "housewives"—"I'm a modern-day homemaker" or "Just call me a 'hipster housewife.'" If "housewife" was a dirty word in the seventies, eighties, and nineties, it's now dirty in the good sense, electric with the shivery delight of taboo-breaking.

Motherhood itself is being venerated in a way not seen since the hypernatalist 1950s. If you've spent any time eyeing the tabloids in the supermarket checkout line, you know what I'm talking about, of course—"Bump Watch! A Baby for Jen: The Ultimate Fulfillment!" But it's not just in Hollywood that parenthood is cool again—the yummy mummy/boho domestic goddess has become an enduring icon for the 2000s, the double-wide stroller a signifier of urban affluence. "The old-fashioned, full-time mother at home is being celebrated—as fashion icon, as status symbol, as sex symbol," crows the *Daily Telegraph,* while the Huffington Post asks, "Is 'career woman' the new 'spinster'?"

And today's parenthood is itself nostalgic, aiming to recapture the simplicity and goodness of a rose-tinted past. "Natural" and "instinctual" and "traditional" are buzzwords among today's young moms and dads; the wisdom of our grandmothers and/or indigenous tribes is invoked with regularity in the playgroups and birthing centers of the twenty-first century. From home births to diaper-free infants to hand-mashed baby food to extended breast-feeding, today's parenthood often seems to take its cues from *Little House on the Prairie.*

Clearly, something has been shifting in our culture over the past decade or so. The various pieces—the urban chickens, the domestic-porn blogs, the retro cookery, the attachment parenting—are beginning to come together to reveal a larger whole. To say that these phenomena are "just trends" or to snark on them as the whims of privileged hipsters is to ignore this emerging bigger picture. Fashion is fashion, but our current collective nostalgia and domesticity-mania speak to deep cultural longings and a profound shift in the way Americans view life. I call this phenomenon "New Domesticity."

## NEW DOMESTICITY

Devotees of New Domesticity are everywhere. Chances are, you know one. If not, you've probably read her blog.

She's the Brooklyn hipster who quit her PR job to sell hand-knitted scarves at craft fairs. He's the dreadlocked "urban homesteader" who raises his own chickens to reduce his carbon footprint. She's the thirty-one-year-old new mom who starts an artisan cupcake company from her home kitchen rather than return to her law firm. He's the hard-driven Ivy

Leaguer fleeing corporate life for a Vermont farm. She's the food blogger writing winsome odes to the simple pleasures of slow-roasted pork and homemade applesauce.

The type of lifestyle these people embrace is a 180-degree turnaround from the consumerist fantasies of the late 1990s and early 2000s, when the media's much-flogged feminine ideal was a *Sex and the City*-style urban careerist who used her oven for storing extra copies of *Vogue*.

Now we're all baking brownies again. What gives? Why are women (and more than a few men) of my generation, the children of post–Betty Friedan feminists, embracing the domestic tasks that our mothers and grandmothers so eagerly shrugged off?

The motivations behind New Domesticity are varied: an interest in self-sustainability; concern for the environment; the need for flexible, child-friendly work; the desire to remain connected to older generations. But the common thread seems to be this: my generation—those of us in our twenties and thirties—is longing for a more authentic, meaningful life in an economically and environmentally uncertain world.

Our parents—stressed-out, divorced baby boomers—haven't provided us with much of a road map for balanced living. All-out careerism certainly didn't seem to make our parents happy. Is it entirely surprising, then, that we're looking toward a rose-tinted past for tips on how to have a more meaningful, happy life?

## A GROWING PHENOMENON

When I started tentatively investigating New Domesticity, I didn't have to look far. Within an hour or two of my home in the small college town of Chapel Hill, North Carolina, New Domesticity types were popping out of the woodwork.

Alana, thirty-three, is a PhD student in environmental science and public policy at Duke. But while other stressed-out grad students suck down ramen noodles and unwind by playing pool and drinking far too much beer, Alana spends her free time picking and canning fruit, making cheese, baking, teaching knitting classes, and growing vegetables on the roof of her downtown Durham apartment. These are not just hobbies for her. She has a deep and committed belief that homemaking is central to a sustainable, socially just society. She believes that traditional "women's work" like cooking, crafting, and raising children has been devalued and sees restoring this work to its rightful place of honor as one of her most important goals.

"I'm a feminist," says Alana, a petite woman with white-blond hair whose outfit of a 1970s-style T-shirt and sneakers makes her look a decade younger. "But I also feel like there has to be a space where you can embrace the life-giving stuff that comes with being a woman. My appreciation for tradition is puzzling to older women, who clearly 'fought the fight.'"

Ryan, twenty-eight, considers himself an "urban homesteader." He raises chickens and quails in the backyard of his suburban Charlotte house, keeps bees, and grows a healthy fraction of his own vegetables. He also sews, cooks all his meals from scratch, and cans jam. To him, these old-fashioned domestic skills are about sustainable, low-on-the-food-chain living. He hopes to one day live off the grid and be completely self-sufficient.

In Charlotte, a Southern city anchored by the classically macho banking industry and surrounded by traditional-minded small farming towns, a man sewing and canning raises a few eyebrows. And Ryan's family is confused that Ryan, a straight young guy with a master's degree and plenty of job prospects, should want to live this way.

"These are extremely basic life skills that you need to live," Ryan says, scoffing. "Everybody has to eat—you should know how to cook, male or female."

Elizabeth and Sammy, a same-sex couple, are both highly educated (Brown, Sarah Lawrence) and had plenty of career opportunities. But what they really want is to be "stay-at-home, homeschooling, cooking, crafting mamas." Yes, both of them. So, rather than pursue conventional success, they've set themselves up with an at-home computer business that allows them to work from their suburban Durham home. They're now busy trying to get pregnant via sperm donor—Elizabeth, thirty-two, is going to go first, since she's slightly older.

Sammy's mother was a "very, very high-status" vice president of a Philadelphia bank who was "very insistent that women can rule the world," says Sammy, thirty-one, offering me a homemade chocolate cookie as we sit at their kitchen counter, a pot of homemade chai bubbling away on the stove. "But she was also depressed and had out-of-control diabetes and hated her life."

Sammy's take-home message was that "the corporate world doesn't care about home-life balance" and "women were sold the idea that they could do it all."

"Why let your company handbook dictate how much time you spend with your family?" she asks, turning her palms up in exasperation. "That's the trade-off my mom made."

Sammy and Elizabeth don't want that. They want to be hands-on attachment parents for their planned "three to six" children. They want to cook all their meals from scratch like they do now—homemade granola for breakfast, home-canned fruits and veggies, slow-simmered bone broths, homemade sauerkraut—and grow their own veggies ("When we eat out, we're letting somebody else choose the quality of our vegetables," Sammy says).

Elizabeth and Sammy truly seem to revel in their domestic bliss. They've even stopped posting pictures of their house to Facebook, for fear their friends would think they were bragging. "They don't understand how we have all this time to make smoked-turkey stock," says Sammy, laughing.

But they also think their lifestyle is spreading. People are sick of long work hours and crappy convenience foods, they say. They're ready to get back to basics. They're ready to return home.

## WHAT DOES THIS MEAN?

In my late twenties, fairly recently married, and thinking hard about questions of how best to live my life, I was fascinated to watch the rise of this New Domesticity. Was this incredibly modern or a total throwback? Was this sexist or liberating? Or somewhere in between? And where did it come from?

In this book, I'll try to answer these questions. I'll look at how crafts like knitting, sewing, and embroidery have staged a comeback. I'll examine the new DIY foodie culture that has so many of us baking our own bread and raising chickens in our backyards. I'll investigate today's hyperintensive parenting culture (think "attachment parenting," homemade baby food, homeschooling) and look at how parenting became the ultimate DIY project in a DIY-crazy culture. I'll hang out with some neo-homesteaders and see why "Return to home and hearth!" has become a radical rallying cry. I'll look at how Americans on the right and left sides of the political spectrum are increasingly meeting over their beliefs about the home— Christian homeschooling parents trading tips with crunchy liberal "unschoolers," Ron Paul–loving libertarians banding together with lefty locavores over the right to drink raw milk, Mormon stay-at-home moms bonding on Etsy with radical lesbian knitters. Throughout this, I'll look at how New Domesticity relates to our growing disenchantment with the mainstream workplace, which has failed young people, mothers, and families in so many ways.

And I'll ask questions about what this means, especially as it relates to gender and class. Do the picture-perfect homes portrayed on the ever-growing universe of "lifestyle" blogs raise the standards of homemaking for all of us? Has the rhetoric about the "soul-sucking" modern workplace gotten so negative it's discouraging young people, especially young women, from going all-out in their careers? Does the embrace of all things "natural," from organic gardening to breast-feeding, set us up for a new brand of gender essentialism ("But it's just natural for women to nurture," etc.) that harms both women and men? Does the DIY-mania of New Domesticity (homeschooling! Grow your own veggies!) mean a retreat from the public sphere, one that might harm the underprivileged who don't have the time or money to "do it themselves"?

While New Domesticity is largely a female-centric phenomenon at this point, it is certainly not all about women. Though this book focuses most intensely on the complex relationship women have always had with domesticity, I'm also extremely interested in showing how men's relationships with home and domestic life have been rapidly evolving.

Throughout the book, I'll connect the rise of New Domesticity and its do-it-yourself mentality to the decline in public, communal solutions for things like food and child care. When the national food system doesn't seem safe, people become more interested in knowing exactly where their food comes from. When there's little decent, affordable day care available, parents are more likely to invest in ideologies about babies "needing" Mom at home. When the government does a sorry job of fighting environmental destruction and climate change, people feel the need to take matters into their own hands. Hence the mania for eco-minded domesticity: making your own soap, hanging laundry on old-fashioned laundry lines, using cloth diapers instead of disposables.

So pour yourself a glass of home-brewed kombucha, and let's start to untangle this complex, fascinating subject that reveals so much about our culture and our era.

# CHAPTER 1

# The Pull of Domesticity
# in an Era of Anxiety

The draw of nostalgic domesticity is not surprising. We're living in scary times. The economy has been in the toilet for several years now, with little sign of rebound. Our neighbors are laid off, our friends have lost their health insurance, even the wealthy are no longer safe. The environment's a mess—greenhouse gas emissions are spiraling upward and upward, temperatures are spiking, drought billows across the country, politicians don't seem to care. The food system no longer seems safe, what with all the YouTube videos of bloated, antibiotic-pumped chickens stewing in salmonella-streaked filth, the recalls of E. coli–poisoned spinach, the stories of factory farms spewing sludge into our waterways.

People are on edge. The month I began working on this chapter, there was a freaky, once-a-century East Coast earthquake followed closely by a rare northeastern hurricane followed by disastrous flooding. In a sunnier era, people might have shrugged this off as a bizarre coincidence. Instead, even my most rational and even-tempered friends and acquaintances muttered darkly about apocalypse and global warming and the collapse of civilization. A week after the hurricane, tornadoes spun through central North Carolina, setting off sirens at the fire station down the street from my house. "Take shelter now. Take shelter now," intoned a recorded voice.

Well, we're taking shelter. We're learning to knit. We're embracing slow food. We're blogging about renovating our cozy, downsized cottages. We're fantasizing about ditching the corporate world to run a Vermont goat farm. We're reading books like *How to Sew a Button: And Other Nifty Things Your Grandmother Knew* and *The Prairie Girl's Guide to Life* and *Radical Homemakers: Reclaiming Domesticity from a Consumer Culture.*

This isn't, of course, the first time home and hearth have been put on such a pedestal—the 1950s brought us the Happy Housewife, while the 1980s served up a minor flurry of media stories about "nesting" and "cocooning" among professional women.

But this current domesticity-mania is unique in that it signals a profound social change among educated, progressive Americans. It's part of a shift away from corporate culture and toward a more eco-conscious, family-centric, DIY lifestyle, a shift that has potential to change the American cultural and political landscape. Part of this change is driven by economic necessity—the current recession, the worst since the Great Depression, has made high-flying consumerist lifestyles unfeasible. But it is also driven by a genuine feeling of disgust with the status quo, a sense that the American dream has turned out to be a big fat toxin-laden, environment-destroying nightmare. The government can't be trusted, corporations can't be trusted, even some of our most basic communal services like hospitals and public schools are under suspicion. Meaningful and lucrative careers, once the brass ring for ambitious young people, are preposterously hard to find these days. And, once found, they tend to come with a whole slew of thorny issues, many of them affecting women disproportionately—expectations of sixty-hour workweeks, lack of maternity leave, massive "mom penalties" on salary.

In this culture of anxiety, it's no wonder so many young people are looking to domesticity in search of a simpler, more sustainable, more meaningful way of life.

New Domesticity is the re-embrace of home and hearth by those who have the means to reject these things. It's the MBA who quits her corporate gig to downsize to a solar-powered renovated barn. It's the twentysomething New Yorker who spends her evenings blogging about her latest baking project rather than hitting the clubs. It's the young mom who, after her too-short maternity leave, decides to try to make extra money selling her knitting on Etsy rather than go back to work. It's the suburban dad turned neo-homesteader, raising chickens in his backyard and trying to grow all his family's veggies. New Domesticity is the embrace of the domestic in the service of environmentalism, DIY culture, personal fulfillment. Though it may resemble your grandmother's homemaking, it's not—this is something new, different, perhaps even revolutionary.

## THE STRANGE PULL OF DOMESTICITY

I first started thinking about this book when I wrote a newspaper story profiling several young, educated women who canned jam. Canning jam had always struck me as a fun, nostalgic hobby, but for these women it was part of something much larger. They spoke of self-sufficiency, of rescuing "lost" domestic arts, of sustainable lifestyles, of reclaiming the concept of "homemaker."

The idea resonated with me, rather unexpectedly. I was twenty-seven years old, recently engaged, and beginning to think hard about questions of work, family, and what constitutes a meaningful life. At the time, I was living in a shoe-box-sized Chapel Hill bungalow with a claustrophobic, dishwasher-less kitchen. I traveled several months out of the year for work, rarely bothering to unpack my toiletry kit. My diet consisted largely of Trader Joe's tortillas and melted cheddar, eaten by the glow of my laptop. I often worked until two or three A.M. and fell asleep with my fingers on the keyboard.

There was something undeniably appealing about the idea of a simpler, more home-centric life, a life made to look especially alluring on the thousands of food-, home-, and domesticity-related blogs multiplying rabbitlike across the Internet. And I was noticing that many of my friends and acquaintances suddenly had similar feelings. The cultural winds seemed to be shifting.

When I was in college in the early 2000s, there was a sense that we were the future masters of the universe, sprinting full tilt into a future of eighty-hour workweeks and corner offices. My peers paraded off to I-banking interviews dressed in pinstriped skirt suits, flew to Silicon Valley giddy with the prospect of hitching their wagon to a rocketing start-up, or went to law school, where they were lavishly feted by corporate firms hoping to snag them for associate positions after graduation.

But by a few years later, the entire landscape had shifted beneath us. The economy headed into the gutter, many of our industries (in my case, newspapers) were breathing their last gasps, people were thinking harder about what kinds of jobs were moral and fulfilling—suddenly, working at, say, an investment bank held about as much appeal as being a census taker for Satan. There was a rising sense, fueled by the media, that careerism was on the downslide. Economist Sylvia Ann Hewlett was on the airwaves talking about the infertility epidemic and the impossibility of combining work and family life, warning young women to reconsider their freewheeling nonmonogamous twenties. *New York Times* writer Lisa Belkin's infamous "The Opt-Out Revolution" story—in which she interviewed several thirtysomething Princeton grads who had shucked off high-powered careers to stay at home with their children—was spawning endless discussions about whether work was really all that meaningful after all.

At this point, women my age—the oldest end of Generation Y—were beginning to lead the way into marriage and parenthood, and were squinting hard at the road map our baby boomer mothers had left behind. We women had been weaned on "You can have it all," but, having watched our mothers struggle, we were wary. We'd grown up in a culture where careers defined who you were, but all of a sudden careers were harder to come by, and we were increasingly skeptical of their powers to fulfill us.

So New Domesticity seemed to fill a hole many of us were feeling. For some of my friends, New Domesticity was simply about knitting to relax after a long day in the office. For others, it was about growing their own vegetables in the name of sustainable living. For still others, it was about reevaluating long-held notions about what constituted success—maybe being with family was more important than earning that corner office. It wasn't just women feeling this way. Gen Y men, though acculturated to value money and power, were becoming increasingly interested in work-life balance, and increasingly disinterested in "working for the Man." The guys of my generation were suddenly talking about opening artisan food trucks, or starting a backyard farm, or moving into shared housing in order to afford to focus on what really mattered—their band, their relationship, their art, their cooking projects. Some called this slackerdom or Peter Pan syndrome, but I wondered if it wasn't about something more.

Given that most of us were raised by working baby boomer parents—lawyers, social workers, computer programmers—who had happily rejected traditional domestic work, this was an interesting turn of events.

And it got me thinking—where did this New Domesticity come from?

Why did it have such a pull for educated, ambitious young people like my friends and me? What were its potential implications?

As I started to research this New Domesticity—talking to ordinary women and men; looking at data; interviewing sociologists, historians, and economists; hanging out at urban homesteads; attending crafting conferences—I began to see that the phenomenon was deeply rooted in the sweeping social, environmental, and economic factors that have transformed America from the ego-drunk boomtown of the 1990s to the rather humbled, nervous nation of today.

Though these factors are complex and intertwined, several stood out dramatically:

1. A rising sense of distrust toward government, corporations, and the food system
2. Concern for the environment
3. The gloomy economy
4. Discontent with contemporary work culture
5. The draw of hands-on work in a technology-driven world
6. An increasingly intensive standard of parenting

By looking more closely at these factors, I began to realize that New Domesticity was about far more than hobbies or a love for retro fashion. It was really about the ways America had changed over the past decade. And its implications were broad—not just for women, but for men, families, society.

Let's look at these factors in a bit more depth, with an eye to how they might be affecting women in unique, distinct ways.

## A GROWING SENSE OF DISTRUST IS SPURRING DOMESTIC DIY-ISM

*The only way to know what's in your food is to make it yourself.*
—Cat, 26, Pennsylvania

*I really want to explore homeschooling. At public school, I'd worry about what my son was eating at lunch and the advertising at schools and the pop in vending machines and the cleaning solutions.*

—Courtney, 31, Iowa City

Widespread feelings of disgust and distrust toward government, business, and institutions are changing domestic life. As people lose faith in communal solutions for social, economic, and environmental problems, there's been a dramatic shift toward an ethos of family-based self-reliance, an ethos that's quickly moving from the fringes and into the mainstream.

A growing distrust of the industrial food system has led to a revolution of DIY food production. Across America, people are growing their own vegetables, raising the much-discussed backyard chickens, even grinding their own flour for bread. As Cat, the twenty-six-year-old quoted earlier, told me, "The only way to know what's in your food is to make it yourself," a sentiment that might as well be the motto of twenty-first-century food culture. The practice of going to painstaking lengths to know where your food comes from is known as "food vetting" among industry analysts, who consider it to be one of the decade's most important trends.

One female blogger in Austin, Texas, who has completely abandoned shopping at grocery stores in favor of DIY gardening and farmer's markets, succinctly describes the current atmosphere of food fear:

The last 21 months has seen many food recalls, a massive ground turkey recall, huge egg recalls, deadly listeria yielding melons, several beef recalls, a revelation that the apple juice in children's juice boxes contains unreasonable levels of arsenic, sourced from China and Argentina, and I don't even remember what else . . . I don't want to worry about those things. I don't want to wonder what's in my food, or where it came from.[1]

A growing skepticism toward conventional medicine has led to an increasing reliance on home or alternative remedies—nearly 40 percent of American adults now use what the National Institutes of Health describes as "complementary and alternative medicine," and numbers are significantly higher among women.[2] This skepticism leads to behaviors that range from benign (researching symptoms online, trying out different traditional diets) to dangerous—the mother-led vaccine-refusal movement has led to a resurgence of near-vanquished childhood diseases in affluent, liberal areas like Boulder, Colorado, and Northern California. In these parts of the country, an ethos of homespun, traditional wisdom reigns. This is never so evident as in the growing popularity of home birth—rates of home births rose 20 percent between 2004 and 2008, with a 94 percent increase among white women.[3]

In a similar vein, distrust in the school system has led a growing number of progressive-minded mothers (as many as 99 percent of homeschool instructors are women) to take their children's educations into their own hands. The number of homeschooled American children jumped from 850,000 in 1999 to 1.1 million in 2003 to 1.5 million in 2007,[4] and nonreligious "concern about the school environment" was the number one reason cited for choosing to homeschool,[5] revealing how the movement has leapt from the religious right to the mainstream. Among women I've interviewed, common reasons for choosing homeschooling ranged from "schools suppress kids' natural creativity" to "I worry about what they're feeding them in the cafeteria." These attitudes often go hand in hand with the increasingly popular theory of attachment parenting (which emphasizes co-sleeping, extended breast-feeding, and copious amounts of skin-to-skin contact) and the notion that day care is bad for children, an idea that holds increasing sway over American parents. Nearly three-quarters of Americans now disapprove of day care, a percentage that's higher than it was in the 1980s, famous as the era of bogus "day care Satanic sex cult" stories.

Though most of the phenomena I've just described are associated with a progressive, relatively affluent demographic, we're actually seeing similar things on the right side of the political spectrum as well. Conservative Americans' long-held suspicions of government are also beginning to manifest in a DIY culture that looks mighty similar to what you see in the liberal enclaves of Berkeley or Boulder. We're all familiar with the antigovernment rhetoric of the Tea Party, which took the 2010 midterm elections by storm with promises of church- and community-based solutions for large social ills. But we're also seeing a new breed of so-called crunchy cons—conservatives motivated by progressive notions of environmentalism and self-sufficiency, albeit with a religious or anti–Big Government gloss. Among religious Christian women, for example, there's a growing interest in the natural parenting movement, whose ideologies of motherly instinct, rejection of day care, and 24/7 mother-child attachment appeal to conservative notions of femininity.

Across the political spectrum, nostalgia reigns. Over and over again we hear that the world used to be a safer, more trustworthy place. *Schools used to really teach kids, rather than herd them like sheep. Doctors didn't used to shoot babies full of so many unknown chemicals—the number of vaccines has risen from three to thirty-six! Our great-grandmothers used to know exactly where all the food they put on the table came from; now you can't even pronounce the ingredients on the back of a soup can.*

While this rising sense of distrust is certainly not limited to women, the resulting DIY culture does rest heavily on female shoulders. From the liberal Brooklyn mom concerned over BPA in her canned black beans to Sarah Palin's "mama grizzlies" defending their families from government intrusion, women are still very much considered the gatekeepers of family health and safety. When the government, schools, and the medical system aren't trusted, the responsibility is handed back to Mom.

## ENVIRONMENTALISM HAS MOVED FROM THE PUBLIC SPHERE INTO THE HOME

*A lot of my homemaker-y stuff—growing vegetables and cloth diapering—stems from my desire to do my part for the earth as much as anything else.*

—Carla, 29, Northern California

Oil spills. Fracking. Contaminated groundwater. Rising seas. Global drought. From an environmental perspective, we're living in very frightening times indeed. But, despite years of activism, the possibility of the kind of legislation that might make a dent in the problem seems to recede further and further into the distance. Progressives elected Barack Obama with high hopes for increased energy standards and cleaner air and water policies. But his actual record has been tragically disappointing.

It's not surprising, then, that people are turning to their own homes to try to make a difference. In recent years, the environmentalist's mandate of "Be the change you want to see in the world" has expanded far beyond carrying a canvas tote bag to Whole Foods. A significant minority of Americans are dedicating themselves to locavore diets, giving up driving in favor of bikes, purging their homes of nonorganic cleaners. A smaller but highly influential minority is going even further, unplugging refrigerators, growing all their own vegetables, downsizing their houses, or dedicating themselves to eco-friendly philosophies like voluntary simplicity or frugal living or neo-homesteading.

This kind of self-abnegation in the face of nature is as old as Thoreau. But never before has it been quite so mainstream—laundry is once again flapping on the line in suburban backyards; major corporations sponsor "bike to work" days. And never has it been so female led. The locus of environmentalism has moved from the public sphere to the domestic, where women—for better and for worse—still do most of the decision-making, controlling 93 percent of food purchases and at least 73 percent of overall household spending.[6] The once-radical concept of "eco-feminism"—the idea that women are the natural protectors of Mother Earth—has gone mainstream, with "eco-chicks" and "green moms" using their "innate" nurturing capabilities to fight for the environment.

"Love your family, love the planet" is the tagline of EcoMom.com, one of many environmentalist "lifestyle activism" sites aimed at women. But it might as well be the motto of this new environmental movement as a whole: change happens at home, and it begins with our domestic choices.

## THE PROLONGED RECESSION IS DRIVING US HOMEWARD

*You know, maybe I don't need to be buying things from a store, maybe I can figure out how to make stuff without just being a consumer all the time.*

—Sara, 29, South Dakota

*People are realizing that they don't have to work to make money to buy certain things, they can just cut out the middle process. I can clean my own house, I can make a toy for my kid.*

—Jason, 30, Northern California

Few of us are living high on the hog these days. The iron-gray clouds of recession, which settled over the nation in 2008, show no signs of dissipating. Unless your name is Kim Kardashian, you've probably had to tighten your belt. We're all pinching pennies, downsizing, making do.

The resurgence of old-fashioned domestic arts—the knitting, the preserving, the sewing your own clothes—is partially rooted in a recession-based ethos of frugality. Though baking your own bread may only save a few dollars a month, the domestic DIY movement provides a sense of control over a very out-of-control situation: we may not be able to cover our mortgages or keep our jobs, but we can streamline the grocery bill by using white vinegar instead of pricey cleaning gels. We can't control what's outside the home, but we can control what's inside.

Some of today's more extreme domestic philosophies, like voluntary simplicity or urban homesteading, are heavily influenced by economic factors as well. Though many people cite environmentalism or a desire for self-sufficiency as the main reason for choosing downscaled, home-centric lifestyles, economists point out that these lifestyles are much more popular in times of economic woe. In other words, someone who jettisons go-go city life for a rural farmstead after a layoff in the name of "a simpler life" (like many of the memoirists I mentioned before) may simply be rationalizing their decision to make the best of a bad economic situation. In the flush 1990s, they may have simply looked for another job. In the recession-plagued 2010s, they're being forced to make more dramatic lifestyle changes. Domesticity has become an "out" for the casualties of an exploded economy.

Women still control most of the domestic purse strings and do most of the domestic work, regardless of whether they work outside the home. So when it comes time to cut back on household spending, they tend to be in charge. Former Miami University English professor and domesticity expert Sherrie Inness describes the idealized image of the money-saving homemaker thusly: "Growing her own vegetables, saving heels of bread to turn into breadcrumbs, serving inexpensive meatless meals, and using leftovers rather than discarding them—anything to stretch money a little further."[7]

This is, in fact, a description of the idealized Depression-era housewife. But it could easily have been ripped from the pages of last month's O, the Oprah Magazine or Real Simple. The image of the thrifty, resourceful, self-sufficient homemaker still carries a huge amount of cultural currency. And in our current recession economy, she's become a veritable heroine.

## DISSATISFACTION WITH THE WORKPLACE

*Second-wave feminism promised us that we'd be able to break through the glass ceiling. So then we all went to work and realized, "Oh, this sucks—I don't have enough parental leave, I can't have it all, there is no such thing as work-life balance."*

—Melanie, 38, Austin, Texas

The working world of the twenty-first century demands more and more from employees while promising less. For professionals, the forty-hour workweek is more like a sixty-hour workweek, and 24/7 smartphone contact is a given. But pay is stagnant, benefits have been cut, and the specter of layoffs haunts every office corridor.

Amid this unhappy landscape, there's a sense that the way our parents' generation did things is no longer going to work. There's a new feeling of unwillingness among the youngest generation of workers to give over their entire lives to a cruel and fickle workforce. For women, who continue to carry the lion's share of domestic and child-rearing responsibilities, the "juggle" mentality is especially unappealing. We saw our mothers struggle with it, and we've been weaned on a decade of media stories about how it's impossible to "have it all." Our baby boomer mothers busted down the boardroom doors, leaving us to wonder, "Do I really want to be a CEO anyway?"

Being a CEO or making partner is not only less obtainable than ever, thanks to the economy, but it's also less appealing to a generation weaned on a "follow your passion" ethos. There's a sense among everyone, male and female, that we can no longer rely on jobs and careers to give us a personal identity or a sense of security. This sense is greatest among mothers, who have long felt particularly disenfranchised by the corporate world's antifamily policies.

While men with children are no more or less likely to be hired than men without, women with children face a dramatic "motherhood penalty" of hiring discrimination and lowered salaries. While the recession has spawned a few family-friendly innovations, like job-sharing, these are few and far between. Corporations, looking to tighten their belts, rarely offer the kind of perks that seemed like the wave of the future in the boom-time 1990s—nap pods, on-site child care, company-sponsored yoga. And any hope we once had for federally funded child care is now laughable in the face of deficits and slash-and-burn spending cuts.

"If we had a boyfriend or a spouse who treated us this badly, most of us with healthy self-esteem would peg him as an abuser and dump him," writes Shannon Hayes, author of *Radical Homemakers,* a book whose rallying cry of "Back to home and hearth!" was cited as a major inspiration for many of the women I've interviewed. To Hayes, the way the workforce treats women is so irredeemably awful that continuing to fight for more family-friendly, gender-equitable workplaces is tantamount to "a therapist working with a wife-beater to at least stop smacking her around on Sundays"—an unacceptable act of appeasement.

This attitude represents a shift in thinking about the workplace that can only be described as extreme. A decade ago, progressive women who left the workforce often couched their decision in somewhat apologetic terms, citing "personal choice" and "it was just what was right for our family." Now an increasingly visible subculture of women sees quitting work as not just a personal choice but an explicitly political act.

"This is the new wave of feminism—women taking back the home," said one twentysomething Chicago mom who quit her job as a sommelier to stay at home with her young son and work part-time as a birth doula. "This is my domain."

I'll talk about this all much more in chapter 7, where I look at women, New Domesticity, and the workforce.

## THE RE-SKILLING MOVEMENT AND THE NOSTALGIA FOR HANDS-ON WORK

*It is really fulfilling and sort of empowering, the idea of "Here's dinner on the table—I grew it, I cooked it, I served it on napkins I sewed."*
—Carla, 29, Northern California

*Up until a few generations ago, most women knew how to cook, clean, and sew. I grew up my whole life pushing buttons and flicking switches. I grew up with microwaves and the Internet and Saturday-morning cartoons.*

—Jenna, 29, upstate New York

Our grandmothers saw convenience food as a liberation from kitchen drudgery and viewed cheap, mass-produced baby clothing as a relief for hands tired from sewing. Our mothers, busy working baby boomers, gave little thought to the traditional domestic arts—who had time?! Who wanted to be stuck in the kitchen? And, anyway, what was the point of making coq au vin when you had precooked rotisserie chicken and bags of spinach salad available at every suburban grocery store in America?

My generation increasingly sees things differently. We talk of "lost" crafts and "reclaiming" traditional women's work like crocheting and quilting and baking homemade bread. We value the handmade, the from-scratch, the rustic, the personal. In an increasingly tech-oriented society, we're hungry for hands-on work and hand-produced products.

For many of us, this interest in old-fashioned handwork is simply a hobby—doing needlepoint as a way to kick back after a hard week of dissertation writing, baking an elaborate cake for a friend's birthday party. But some see themselves as part of what historians and sociologists are calling the "re-skilling movement," which is aimed at restoring prestige to historically devalued traditional domestic arts and skills.

For modern young stay-at-home parents, the re-skilling movement is being embraced for its potential to make homemaking fulfilling in a way it never was for Betty Friedan's desperate housewives. The rise of labor-saving technologies has made homemaking progressively less skilled throughout the twentieth century. As a result, it became less satisfying—skilled work is, after all, more fulfilling than unskilled work. Going to the fishmonger, examining the fish for freshness, and haggling over price is a more stimulating experience than chucking a frozen tilapia fillet in your cart at Trader Joe's. Baking a cake from scratch and being praised for your skill gives you a sense of reward greater than mixing up a box of Funfetti cupcakes. We're all familiar with the narrative of the Valiumfogged 1950s housewife, adrift in her suburban home with nothing to do. Young women don't want that.

As one young, elitely educated California mom told me, if it weren't for her interest in what she calls "modern homemaking"—canning food, making handmade baby clothes—she "would probably end up pursuing a career, because [she] would be bored."

## STANDARDS OF IDEAL PARENTHOOD HAVE GROWN EVER HIGHER

*I'm very into natural parenting and that whole scene—it has sort of taken over my life!*

—Gina, 27, Chicago

*I was really obsessive about doing everything right. I put so much expectation on it . . . When you've approached your own life as a series of projects—school and work and so forth—parenting becomes one more.*

—JJ, 32, Los Angeles

As I'll examine at length in chapter 6, ideals of what constitutes "good" parenthood seem to rise higher and higher with each passing year. We've seen a recent growth in the kind of parenting philosophies that necessitate a deep commitment to domesticity, whether that commitment means spending leisure time making homemade baby food or dropping out of the workforce entirely. The premiere example, the oft-discussed "attachment parenting" method, introduced to the mainstream by William Sears's 2001 *The Attachment Parenting Book,* has been gaining in popularity over the past decade. The method, and others like it, emphasizes extreme responsiveness to babies' cues—nursing on demand, not allowing babies to "cry it out"—and near-constant skin-to-skin contact, such as "babywearing" (carrying children in cloth slings) and co-sleeping. Other time-consuming practices, from child-led weaning to cloth diapering to homeschooling, are also on the rise. Many of these philosophies and practices are, as I mentioned before, rooted in a distrust of current institutions (public schools, hospitals, day cares) combined with a twenty-first-century veneration for all things "natural" and a healthy dash of today's libertarian spirit.

There's an element of backlash against our baby boomer parents here too—I spoke with many young parents who lamented not having enough quality time with their own busy working parents. "I was kind of a latchkey kid, and that definitely influenced my decision to stay home," said one thirtysomething mother, in a common refrain. Young people today are measurably more family focused than their parents were. Surveys show that Gen X and Gen Y rate themselves as "family-centric" in significantly higher numbers than baby boomers, and that young people are more likely than older people to describe childlessness as "bad for society."

This new parenthood culture is deeply intertwined with some of the factors I've already discussed. Parents concerned about food safety are more likely to make their own baby food or grow their own vegetables. Parents worried about the environment are more likely to choose cloth diapering. And women who are unhappy in the workplace may feel more drawn to intensive parenting methods that give them a reason to stay home. The romanticization of family life is a natural response to a scary, unpredictable outside world.

## WHAT ARE THE IMPLICATIONS OF EMBRACING DOMESTICITY?

It's easy to be positive about New Domesticity. After all, who doesn't value a less money-obsessed, more sustainable, more family-centric culture? On the right side of the political spectrum, people see New Domesticity as a vindicating return to tradition, a sign that feminism has failed and young women are seeing the light. On the left side, it's viewed as a happy outcome of postfeminism—women can now choose to enjoy domesticity without shame or feeling like they've let the sisterhood down. Many progressives point out, quite rightly, that some aspects of domesticity are becoming increasingly popular with men as well.

But the rise of New Domesticity raises some difficult questions. What will happen as we abandon society-wide solutions for problems like climate change, food safety, and affordable child care in favor of a DIY approach? Does the burden of "do it yourself" fall harder on women than men? Does this new romanticization of family and motherhood put undue pressures on women, and does it disenfranchise men? Does our dismissal of the "women can have it all" notion bode ill for workplace equality?

These are questions I'll be looking at in greater depth in coming chapters. But to start off, let's look at some statistics on the state of women today, statistics that suggest that we're still living (in the words of writer Peggy Orenstein) in a "half-changed world" when it comes to gender and class equality.

Women still do the vast majority of the housework in America. "Despite the perception that 'Mr. Mom' is on the rise, our research shows that traditional gender roles still exist among married and cohabiting parents. Mothers in those relationships assume the bulk of household and child-care responsibilities regardless of whether they work or not," reports *Advertising Age,* summarizing a lengthy 2009 report on the new female consumer.

According to the National Survey of Families and Households, among heterosexual American couples, women do an average of thirty-one hours of housework a week, while men do fourteen.[8] Among families where the man is the sole breadwinner (only about 20 percent of all families), the ratio, unsurprisingly, skews even further. But even among dual-earner couples, women still work the infamous "second shift," doing an average of twenty-eight hours of housework a week compared with men's sixteen hours.[9] Working women spend eleven hours a week on child care, while working men spend three, a ratio that has surprisingly not shifted all that much since the 1930s.[10] In the kitchen, women cook some 78 percent of all home dinners, spend nearly three times as many hours on food-related tasks as men, and make 93 percent of the food purchases. Overall trends, however, suggest we're headed, slowly, toward a more egalitarian gender divide at home—young men tend to do far more housework and child care than their fathers did. While stay-at-home fathers are a tiny minority of stay-at-home parents (less than 3 percent of all stay-at-home parents are dads),[11] anecdotal evidence suggests their numbers may be rising, and hard evidence shows that young dads today spend much more time with their kids than a generation ago.

Despite huge amounts of progress over the decades, there are still major issues when it comes to women and the workplace. Statistics show that women's labor-force participation began to level off in the late 1990s and has remained stalled at 61 percent ever since. In many male-heavy fields like finance and computer science, women's once-burgeoning participation has taken a dramatic plunge. "Women are fading from the U.S. finance industry," reports *The Wall Street Journal*, noting that the number of women between the ages of twenty and thirty-five working in finance has dropped 16.5 percent over the past decade, while the number of men in that age range grew by 7.3 percent.[12] "I think in recent years the advances made by women in the 1990s have reversed," said Elaine La Roche, a former Morgan Stanley executive, in the *New York Times*.[13] The number of women in computing-related careers—one of the twenty-first century's biggest job-growth areas—has fallen steadily since the early 2000s; women leave computing at twice the rate of their male peers (even before they become mothers) and represent only 9 percent of IT management positions.[14] In politics, women hold 23.4 percent of available statewide elective executive positions, down from 27.6 percent twelve years ago. The situation's so distressing to many female politicians that New York senator Kirsten Gillibrand recently launched a campaign called Off the Sidelines to help motivate what she sees as young women's "stalled" political progress.

Human resources departments wring their hands over the "leaky pipeline"—women start strong at the beginning of their careers, but few make it to the highest levels of most industries. Women still represent fewer than 20 percent of law partners, 6 percent of CEOs and other high-level executives (and only 4.2 percent of Fortune 500 CEOs), 12 percent of state governors, and 17 percent of U.S. senators. More than 90 percent of corporate boards have two or fewer women, while in Silicon Valley, until 2012, none of the most buzzed-about new companies—Facebook, Twitter, Zynga, Groupon, Foursquare—had a single female board member.[15]

Women working full-time still earn less money than men—77 cents to every male dollar[16]—and are more likely than men to live in poverty, especially during their childbearing years (and again in old age). While women are participating in higher education at higher rates than men now, they need to—a woman needs a PhD to earn as much as a man with a BA. In heterosexual households where both partners work, working wives contributed only 29 percent of household income in 2008, a number that has changed little since the 1980s. And though the vast majority of young women say they value financial independence, women are still far less likely than men to view careers as "very important"—36 percent versus 57 percent.[17]

Despite these statistics, only about half of young women aged eighteen to twenty-nine see a need for social change to ensure gender equality (older women think differently—70 percent call for social change). Young women tend to feel that the work of feminism is largely done, leaving decisions about career and domesticity a depoliticized matter of "personal choice." As one woman, an educated stay-at-home homeschooling mom in Boulder, told me, "If I was living in the seventies, I would totally have been out burning my bra too—everything is about timing."

But this attitude has come under intense fire from some prominent middle-aged female thinkers lately, who warn darkly of the perils of ignoring the past, the dangers of thinking it's okay to take the mommy track or rely on your husband's income to launch your "fulfilling" craft business. Legal scholar Linda Hirshman blasted women for opting out or taking "soft," lower-earning paths in her 2006 manifesto, *Get to Work*. Erica Jong made headlines in 2010 and 2011 for her screeds on what she sees as a prudish, domesticity-obsessed generation of young women (a generation that includes Jong's own daughter, a thirty-two-year-old stay-at-home mother of three). Famed French intellectual Elisabeth Badinter recently made international waves by charging that the current ideals of "green," "natural" motherhood—the extended breast-feeding, the babywearing—are in fact a new form of oppression of women. Leslie Bennetts, former *Newsweek* writer and author of the anti-opt-out manifesto *The Feminine Mistake*, worries that young women are choosing domestic paths that may diminish their ability to earn an independent living: "There are aspects of the New Domesticity that are lovely, but it is no substitute for being able to support your family," she told me.

In the following chapters, I'll look at how the re-embrace of domesticity squares with long-held goals of gender equality, female economic independence, and the pursuit of work-life balance and meaningful happy lives, for women and men. Where does this New Domesticity lead us?

# CHAPTER 2

# From Angels in the House to Crunchy Domestic Goddesses: The History of "Women's Work"

Throughout this book, we'll hear from twenty-first-century people talking of "reclaiming women's work" and "returning to domesticity." Well, what exactly is women's work? What is domesticity? Who has done this work throughout history? How have they felt about it? And what are we reclaiming it from?

To better understand how domestic work has been constructed throughout the ages, here's a (very) brief look at the history of domesticity. Rather than talk about child care in ancient Rome or how people feel about cooking in Laos (interesting topics, no doubt), I'll start at a slightly more familiar place and time: America, the 1600s.

## EARLY AMERICA: THE NOBLE FRUGAL HOUSEWIFE

So you're a Colonial American woman and you'd like to cook chicken for dinner? Step one: get up at dawn and find yourself a chicken. Step two: slit the chicken's throat. Step three: spend an hour or more plucking thousands of feathers. Step four: gut and clean the chicken. Don't forget the oil glands behind the tail! Step five: cook the chicken over an open fire, in a cast-iron pot that weighs more than your six-year-old.

But wait—do you have firewood? And have you swept the flue? And what about the bread? Do you have corn? If you do, have you already ground it?

When you're done with the chicken catching/slaughtering/carcass preparing, you might like to wash the chicken guts off your hands. But you're out of soap, and it'll be months until the autumn livestock slaughter provides you enough animal fat to make more.

Damn.

In Colonial America, extreme domestic DIY—grinding flour, making soap from animal fat and wood ash, sewing blankets by candlelight—was simply a necessity for the largely rural population. Colonists did rely on some import goods from England, but they were on their own for most domestic needs. Most people lived on isolated homesteads, where men and women worked side by side, albeit doing separate tasks. It was hardly an egalitarian world—married women were essentially their husband's property[1]—but male and female labors were both valued, and there was no divide between "breadwinner" and "housewife."

Writer Laura Shapiro describes the jaw-dropping daily work of early American women:

> The wife, with her daughters and the other women of the house, took charge of spinning, weaving and sewing, making the family's clothing, linens and quilts. She gardened and perhaps did some back-yard butchering, made soaps and candles, preserved the fruits and vegetables, salted and pickled the meat, churned butter, and baked enormous quantities of bread, pie and cake. She was responsible for daily house-cleaning, weekly laundering and ironing, and major spring and fall cleaning; she was teacher, nurse, doctor, and midwife.[2]

It was an exhausting life (a French visitor noted, with a Gallic combination of snootiness and pity, that American women were "faded at twenty-three, old at thirty-five, decrepit at forty"),[3] but crucial for a family's very survival.

In the years leading up to the American Revolution, women's domestic labors took on serious political significance as well. The frugal housewife, who rejected British silks and teas in favor of rough linen and bitter, chicory-laced coffee, became an image of patriotic heroism (as she would again many, many times in the future). Women suddenly had a public role in supporting the fight for independence by weaving their own cloth and making soap for the troops to compensate for the boycott of British-made goods. Homespun clothing became a "badge of patriotism";[4] women's spinning and sewing circles were vibrant political events.

"Women whose previous job descriptions had included little outside the family circle must have been astonished at the new perimeters of their responsibility," writes historian Anne Macdonald.[5]

Many women, roused by this new sense of purpose, wanted to take their political efforts outside the home. Members of ladies' sewing circles tentatively took steps toward door-to-door fund-raising and other nondomestic efforts.

But when the war ended, women were pushed away from the political realm. Men of the era, even the most enlightened, saw public life as simply unbefitting for gentle ladies. On a visit to France, Thomas Jefferson was shocked—shocked!—to find Parisian women participating in political salons. America's "good ladies" are too wise to "wrinkle their foreheads with politics," he wrote in a 1788 letter. "They have the good sense to value domestic happiness above all others. There is no part of the earth where so much of this is enjoyed as in America."[6]

Many women disagreed. Eliza Wilkinson, a young Charleston woman who had managed her entire family plantation during the war, was incensed to be excluded from political discussions. "Surely we have sense enough to give our opinions," she wrote, "without being reminded of our Spinning and household affairs, as the only matters we are capable of thinking, or speaking of, with justness or propriety. I won't allow it, I positively won't."[7]

Unfortunately for Wilkinson and women like her, there wasn't much choice.

## THE 1800s: THE CULT OF DOMESTICITY

The Industrial Revolution of the 1800s dramatically changed the way people thought about home and work. In the Colonial era, men and women had worked side by side on their own family farms. Now, for the first time, men were leaving the homestead en masse to go work in offices and factories. Industrialization made it unnecessary for women to do everything themselves from scratch at home—homemakers of the burgeoning middle class could now buy the things they used to make, things like clothes and soap and tea cakes.

On a Colonial homestead, both men and women had clearly contributed to the bottom line by raising pigs and sowing wheat. But in the new, cash-reliant economy of the 1800s, labor was now valued by the amount of money it earned. Therefore, men did "work," while women did "homemaking." The world was split into separate spheres: home became "inside" and the domain of women, while the working world became "outside," the province of men. The separate-spheres ideology of "woman housewife, man breadwinner" was born.

The era was full of change, which, as always, made people anxious. Strange new technologies—textile mills, steam locomotives, telegraph wires—appeared, some belching smoke over the horizon. Westward expansion was starting, cutting families off from their roots and breaking apart the old order of the East Coast. The increasingly urbanized economy meant people were exposed to a much broader range of humanity than they were during the days of rural Colonial homesteading—"outside" began to be seen as dirty and frightening (and, in cities, it often was— streets were filthy, men spat tobacco everywhere, rape was rampant). The home, writes historian Glenna Matthews, "seemed to represent a haven of stability" and became "sentimentalized to an unprecedented degree."[8] Enter the Cult of Domesticity, as historians would later dub the era.

The Cult of Domesticity glorified women's domestic role as God-given and natural, the rough working world unfit for their delicate sensibilities. Writers, theologians, and politicians of the day waxed poetic about women's godly role as homemaker—"The household altar is her place of worship and service . . . A woman has a head almost too small for intellect but just big enough for love," said prominent physician Charles Meigs in 1847,[9] reflecting medical orthodoxy of the time. Women's supposedly unique virtues—piety, submissiveness, sexual purity, self-sacrifice—were placed on a pedestal, seen as a necessary corrective to the stressful, ugly outside world of men's work.

The home, which in the Colonial era was a center of economic production, was now meant to be a hideaway from the world of commerce, a refuge for work-weary men. Hence the light-blocking velvet draperies, the sound-muffling carpets, the living rooms shrouded in doilies hand-tatted by the missus herself, all common features of the middle-class Victorian home. Here, a proper lady was meant to read the Bible aloud until her eyes crossed and embroider handkerchiefs for her husband until her fingers bled.

This ideal Victorian wife was the "angel in the house," a title lifted from an immensely popular, immensely syrupy poem by English poet Coventry Patmore about his own saintly wife. The Angel was sweet, submissive, and wanted nothing more than to serve her husband and children through her domestic labors (Virginia Woolf would later roll her eyes at the Angel's brand of mommy martyrdom: "She excelled in the difficult arts of family life. She sacrificed herself daily. If there was chicken, she took the leg; if there was a draught she sat in it").[10] Though this ideal was only achievable for middle- and upper-class women, it nonetheless set the tone for how women were meant to behave.

New standards of motherhood also promoted feminine self-sacrifice. In the Colonial era, children were basically farmhands— loved, sure, but generally viewed as mini-adults. In the 1800s, a middle class began to arise that no longer needed children to tend livestock and comb wool, and middle-class children began to be seen as creatures in need of nurturing and affection. Americans and Europeans alike absorbed the ideals of Jean-Jacques Rousseau and other Romantic thinkers, who extolled the virtues of intensive motherhood (Rousseau scooped the La Leche League by some two centuries, promoting breast-feeding at a time when most women of means thought it was beneath their dignity). If children went astray, it was now seen as a mother's moral failure.

"This style [of motherhood] was much more intense and demanded more of the mother emotionally than was required in previous generations," writes Glenna Matthews.[11]

Young girls were taught the domestic arts in order to create a genteel, civilizing atmosphere in the home. Activities like embroidery, lace making, and serving tea were considered morally uplifting in and of themselves—doing domestic work helped women rein in their less-than-civilized urges (embroidery was considered a particularly good bulwark against teenage masturbation—"idle hands" and all that!).[12] The hardest work, tasks like cooking over sweltering woodstoves and beating the laundry with wooden paddles, was often done by immigrant servants. In the South, it was often done by slaves.

Novels about cheerful, resourceful homemakers began to flood the market, as did tomes on housekeeping, many of them written by some of the era's greatest female thinkers—feminist and abolitionist Lydia Maria Child's *The American Frugal Housewife,* educator (and sister of *Uncle Tom's Cabin* author Harriet Beecher Stowe) Catharine Beecher's *A Treatise on Domestic Economy,* and writer and editor Sarah Josepha Hale's *The Good Housekeeper.* These nineteenth-century Martha Stewarts, all smart and well educated but barred from most careers, attempted to make housework seem like the most noble pursuit possible. And it worked. Magazines like *Godey's Lady's Book* (founded in 1830) spread the homemaking ideals of the East Coast elite to housewives across the country—now a poor Nebraskan pioneer wife could covet the lace capes and crocheted sofa cushions of her wealthier coastal sisters.

Though the middle-class Victorian housewife wasn't working her hands bloody milking cows and spinning flax like her Colonial counterpart, the increased standards for homemaking meant that her domestic work was no less time-consuming. Victorian housewife Abby Diaz described her 1875 daily routine:

> Setting tables; clearing them off; keeping lamps or gas-fixtures in order; polishing stoves, knives, silverware, tinware, faucets, knobs, &c.; washing and wiping dishes; taking care of food left at meals; sweeping including the grand Friday sweep, the limited daily sweep, and the oft-recurring dust-pan sweep; cleaning paint; washing looking-glasses, windows, window-curtains; canning and preserving fruit; making sauces and jellies, and catchups and pickles; making and baking bread, cake, pies, puddings; cooking meats and vegetables; keeping in nice order beds, bedding, and bedchambers; arranging furniture, dusting, and "picking up"; setting forth, at their due times and in due order, the three meals; washing the clothes; ironing, including doing up shirts and other "starched things"; taking care of the baby, night and day; washing and dressing children, and regulating their behavior, and making or getting made, their clothing, and seeing that the same is in good repair, in good taste, spotless from dirt, and suited both to the weather and the occasion; doing for herself what her own personal needs require; arranging flowers; entertaining company; nursing the sick;

"letting down" and "letting out" to suit the growing ones; patching, darning, knitting, crocheting, braiding, quilting.[13]

When I'm feeling overworked, I like to reread that passage a couple of times.

## THE PROGRESSIVE ERA: UTOPIAN FEMINISTS AND HOME ECONOMISTS

Unsurprisingly, many women were getting sick of the high expectations for housewifery. By the later 1800s, early feminist thinkers began to talk about another, radical option: a techno-utopia where housework would be mechanized and professionalized.

Writer Charlotte Perkins Gilman was one of the most prominent of the so-called utopian feminists who advocated for professionalizing housework. Most of us know Gilman best for her famous 1892 short story "The Yellow Wallpaper," a common assignment in Feminism 101 classes. In the story, an intelligent woman is confined to the home because of a "nervous condition" and slowly descends into gibbering insanity. It's a pretty clear metaphor for the oppression of domesticity, so it's no surprise that its author was no fan of housework. In books like *The Home: Its Work and Its Influence* and *Women and Economics,* Gilman envisioned a world of communal kitchens and cooperative child care and elder care.

"What would shoes be like if every man made his own?" she wrote. "What every man does alone for himself, no man can ever do well—or woman either. That is the first limit of the 'housewife.'"[14]

In other words, why should a housewife bake her own bread and sew her own clothes and generally try to be a Jill-of-all-trades? Wouldn't it make more sense to buy great bread and clothes made by professionals, while spending the rest of her time doing whatever she's personally good at?

Gilman wasn't alone, either. Efficiency expert Martha Bensley Bruère called for cooperative apartment buildings with meals and maid service. Writer Edward Bellamy's smash-hit futuristic novel *Looking Backward* (1888) envisioned the year 2000 as a socialist utopia where housework was done by a cheerful "industrial army."

For a while, it seemed like technology might indeed be the answer to housewives' woes. In the late 1800s, a new academic discipline arose, one that attempted to apply the latest scientific principles and technologies to housework: home economics. Just as mid-1800s housewife writers like Catharine Beecher and Lydia Marie Child aimed to make homemaking a pursuit worthy of an intelligent woman, the home economists also wanted to elevate homemaking, this time through science. Many of the early home economists were bright women who'd been frustrated in their desires to have careers. Ellen Swallow Richards, considered the founder of the discipline, was the first female MIT grad but was forbidden to complete her PhD because of her gender. Poor Richards, ever hopeful, hung around cleaning labs on campus and darning professors' shirts in the hope that her earnestness would be rewarded with a degree.[15] It wasn't.

Barred from the male world, women like Richards sought to claim honor for housewifery by turning it into a career. "We need to exalt the profession of home making to see that it is as dignified and requires as much intelligence as other professions," urged an editorial in the *New England Kitchen Magazine*.[16]

To achieve this, Richards and other home economists applied the era's newly discovered (though often laughably wrong) scientific principles to housework. They set up academies to teach young ladies the science of homemaking, instructing them in subjects like domestic efficiency and the chemistry of soap. They started cooking schools, where they taught women how to cook the most nutritionally sound food. At the time "nutritionally sound" meant whatever had the most calories and took the least time to digest—pork was thought to take an unwholesome five hours to move through the gut. "The cook who can compute the calories of heat which a potato of given weight will yield, is no drudge," said Richards proudly.[17]

Home economics was clearly well intentioned. But it had some unintended consequences. It drowned America's vibrant regional and ethnic cuisines under layers of aspic and gooey white sauces, since a bland diet was considered by home economists to be the most healthful (plus, bland food was thought to keep those pesky carnal thoughts at bay). It tore down traditional women's crafts and pastimes in the name of "efficiency." Instead of elevating the housewife, home economics often served to denigrate her as an "amateur" whose traditional approaches that had been passed down to her from the generation before couldn't hold a candle to science.

Sociologists Robert and Helen Lynd wrote in the 1920s, "Daughters, fresh from domestic science in school, ridicule the mothers' inherited rule-of-thumb practices as 'old fashioned.'"

Traditional women's work, which had already become de-skilled during the Industrial Revolution, became even less skilled as women were taught not to trust the wisdom of their own mothers and grandmothers. And, disappointingly, increased efficiency and new technologies did not exactly translate to more free time for women—housekeeping standards simply rose higher and higher. A nineteenth-century housewife might have done a thorough sweeping once a week, while an early-twentieth-century owner of a Hoover Model O "electric suction sweeper" was now expected to vacuum daily. The fun stuff—the skilled crafts like needlework and lace making that had been the pride of Victorian ladies—had little place in the modern middle-class home other than as a quaint leisure-time hobby.

## FROM MRS. CONSUMER TO ROSIE THE RIVETER: THE 1920S THROUGH WORLD WAR II

At the dawn of the twentieth century, American homemaking became more and more about consuming rather than producing. By the 1920s, the burgeoning advertising industry had targeted women as the household spenders. The American housewife became, in the words of Thorstein Veblen, "the priestess of the temple of consumption . . . the limitless demander of things to use up."[18] This new "Mrs. Consumer" wasn't interested in *making* things, she was interested in *buying* things.

The 1920s were a shopaholic's heaven. The Roaring Twenties brought us many of the modern domestic innovations we enjoy today—synthetic stockings, sliced bread, swivel-tube lipstick, Gerber baby food, handheld hair dryers, home radios, frozen food—as post–World War I prosperity ushered in the era of consumer culture. People began to work fewer hours, and the middle class began to enjoy leisure time and spare cash for the first time in American history. Store-bought items were seen as marks of status, while handmade clothes or linens signaled poverty.

This new era of consumerism helped young women earn a new kind of freedom. Unshackled from the stove, women wore shorter skirts, drank alcohol in public, and drove cars. The giddy young flapper, with her bare knees and boyishly short hair, became a daring new feminine ideal. At least for a few years.

Then the stock market crashed.

The Great Depression returned women to the kitchen as back-to-basics skills became once again necessary. "Forced to rely once more on their grandmothers' producer skills, housewives accepted the challenge valiantly and took a renewed pride in their work at home, since their efforts were obviously keeping their families alive," writes Annegret Ogden in *The Great American Housewife*. "Women no longer viewed canning, cooking, and sewing as creative hobbies but as sheer necessities."[19]

The media and the government promoted the idea of the perfect frugal housewife with great vigor. Posters and magazine articles of the day showed women cooking with bread heels and beet greens, saving tinfoil, and happily darning socks.

The increased respect for frugal homemaking may have been one of the reasons women's morale remained higher than men's during the Great Depression. As two 1930s sociologists noted, "the men, cut adrift from their usual routine, lost much of their sense of time and dawdled helplessly and dully about the streets; while in the homes the women's world remained largely intact and the round of cooking, housecleaning, and mending became if anything more absorbing."[20]

During World War II, though, women went to work in record numbers, taking over the manufacturing jobs their soldier husbands and brothers had left behind. At the same time, however, they were also meant to be perfect frugal housewives. The "home front" was considered a critical factor in winning the war, and women were mobilized to do their bit. Just as spinning homespun cloth had been a patriotic duty for Revolutionary War–era homemakers, World War II homemakers helped their country by saving tin cans and leftover cooking fat to be turned into war materials. Government posters urged women to grow victory gardens to ease wartime food shortages and to can their own vegetables for winter provisions. "Food is a weapon—Don't waste it!" barked a World War II food poster, reminding women that their private domestic choices had vast public consequences.

A wartime wife and mother might have spent her days in a munitions factory, her evenings straining leftover bacon grease through a fine mesh sieve and baking mock apple pie out of Ritz crackers (apples were in short supply because of the war). She was exhausted and sorely in need of a domestic shortcut. And, just as soon as the war was over, corporations would be ready to provide her with shortcuts aplenty.

## THE HAPPY HOMEMAKER

By the late 1940s, the purposeful, patriotic homemaker of the Great Depression and World War II had given way to the consumption-minded suburban housewife. The middle-class American woman was comfortably ensconced in front of her turquoise Magic Chef stove in her postwar ranch house, stirring "just add water" Betty Crocker cake mixes and ordering new draperies from the Sears catalog. Marriage ages had fallen to record lows—half of all American women were married by their twentieth birthdays—and birth rates were at highs not seen in decades.

Though many women had enjoyed the challenge and camaraderie of working during World War II, they were now forcefully urged to cede their jobs to returning soldiers. In retrospect, many historians now see this cult of the Happy Housewife as a backlash against feminist gains in the first half of the twentieth century—the liberated flapper of the 1920s, the Amelia Earhart girl pilots of the 1930s, the Rosie the Riveter of the wartime 1940s. The powers that be felt Americans needed a return to stability and old-fashioned values, which meant a return of women to traditional homemaker roles.

But the de-skilling of the American homemaker, in process since the Industrial Revolution, was now complete. Suburban supermarkets meant women no longer needed to know how to spot the freshest fish at the fishmonger or the best chicken at the butcher. Frozen foods and boxed casseroles took all the skill out of cooking. Dryers meant women no longer spent Monday afternoons hanging laundry in the backyard and chatting with neighbors. Homemaking had become . . . boring.

But woe to the middle-class woman who admitted she was less than satisfied with her domestic life. Sociologists and psychoanalysts of the era taught that unhappy housewives were psychologically maladjusted, unfeminine, perhaps even suffering from penis envy! Psychiatry and psychoanalysis had become vastly more popular in the postwar years; admitting to taking the "talking cure" was even trendy among a certain demographic of educated Americans, so seeing a psychiatrist had become increasingly common. But many women who sought mental-health help were simply prescribed tranquilizers—within a year after Miltown (a tranquilizer, a.k.a. "mother's little helper") was introduced to the market, as many as one in twenty Americans had tried it. Many of them were middle-class homemakers who were told that the pills would help them feel happier with their duties as wives and mothers.[21]

The Happy Homemaker was, in fact, often miserable. So when the feminist movement started talking, she was ready to listen.

## "ACTING THE LADY": AFRICAN-AMERICAN WOMEN AND HOMEMAKING

It's important to point out here—and throughout this book—that the cultural norms around homemaking have always varied for women of different racial, ethnic, and socioeconomic backgrounds. This is especially obvious when looking at the experience of African-American women.

The 1950s-era pressure to stay home was not as dramatic for black women, who had a long tradition of working out of economic necessity. By midcentury, even wealthy black women were more likely to work outside the home than wealthy white women. Therefore, black women were given more latitude to pursue careers without being accused by their communities of unfemininity, though obviously this didn't negate the immense challenge of navigating the workforce as a black woman in racist midcentury America. African-American-directed magazines like *Ebony* from the postwar period were far more likely to portray glamorous working women than were their white counterparts, which focused nearly exclusively on women as mothers and homemakers. A January 1963 issue of *Ebony*, for example, features singer Eartha Kitt on the cover, proudly proclaiming that she takes her baby daughter on worldwide tours with her. Inside, features include a profile of a "top woman Civil Rights lawyer," a profile of a Cornell-trained female ethnomusicologist who specializes in Javanese music, and a profile of Germany's first black fashion model, which features the West Indies—born Gill Lator strolling the streets of Hamburg after work, drinking a beer with her feet kicked up on the table.

Ironically, black women who did choose to be homemakers received negative judgment for *that,* often accused by the white community of laziness. In fact, black women have long faced prejudice for being homemakers rather than workers—in the post–Civil War period, Southerners accused black housewives of getting above their station and "acting the lady"; today poor black stay-at-home moms are accused of being "welfare queens" while their white counterparts are praised for their dedication to their children.

## FIXING THE PROBLEM THAT HAS NO NAME: THE ERA OF WOMEN'S LIBERATION

Betty Friedan's earth-shattering 1963 book *The Feminine Mystique* famously begins by describing "the Problem That Has No Name":

> Each suburban wife struggled with it alone. As she made the beds, shopped for groceries, matched slipcover material, ate peanut butter sandwiches with her children, chauffeured Cub Scouts and Brownies, lay beside her husband at night—she was afraid to ask even of herself the silent question—"Is this all?"

Thousands upon thousands of unhappy suburban homemakers recognized themselves in this description. Mainstream American women began to question, en masse, the idea that a woman's place was in the home.

Over the next decade, the second-wave feminist movement (the term "first wave" is used to describe early suffragettes, while "third wave" denotes the feminist movements of the late twentieth and early twenty-first centuries) fought battles that would change the face of American domesticity. Women demanded access to careers and higher education. They questioned why homemaking should be "women's work" and tried to get their male partners to participate in cooking and cleaning and child care. This was not an easy task, and feminists often took radical measures in their attempts to achieve domestic equality. Alix Kates Shulman, a second-wave feminist activist, famously wrote up a marriage contract formalizing the division of labor—"Wife does most home laundry. Husband does all dry cleaning delivery and pick-up," etc. The 1969 contract was reprinted everywhere from *Life* to *Ms.* to *Redbook,* proving that Shulman had hit close to home for millions of American couples.

By the end of the 1970s, things looked very different than they had a decade and a half before. Women had the right to have their own credit cards, to rent or buy their own homes without a husband or father's signature, and to start a business in their own name, to list just a few of the achievements of the feminist movement. They could no longer be kicked out of court for wearing pants, fired from a job for being too old, or jailed for using birth control (yes, contraception was illegal in some states until 1965). Title IX meant they had equal access to any federally funded education program. *Roe v. Wade* in 1973 gave them the right to safe, legal abortion.

But did feminism also kill homemaking?

Throughout the subsequent chapters, we'll hear intelligent, educated people repeatedly claim that feminism went "too far" and "ruined" domestic life. We'll hear Michael Pollan claim that feminism killed home cooking. We'll hear *Mothering* magazine editor Peggy O'Mara say feminism denigrated motherhood. We'll hear dozens and dozens of smart, liberal-minded women say feminism "pushed" women into the workforce. This idea—that feminism, while well-intentioned and important in many ways, went "too far"—has become conventional wisdom. In the 1980s and 1990s, this was a right-wing theory. But today it's become accepted without pause among many liberals as well, people who have become disenchanted with the workplace and look nostalgically toward a "simpler era" of fresh-baked pies and home-canned green beans.

I'd argue that this is the wrong way to look at things.

Indeed, many feminists rallied against 1950s-style consumerist domesticity. Some scorned housework completely, finding ironing and vacuuming dull and repetitive, aprons a symbol of oppression. Some ultra-radicals like Shulamith Firestone even argued that biological motherhood and nuclear families were inherently oppressive and that we should seek to reproduce via artificial wombs. Needless to say, that was a minority opinion (though, when I recently told a very pregnant friend about this, she said, "Great idea!"). Most feminists—Betty Friedan included—simply thought that housework and child rearing should be shared with men and that women had the right to seek stimulating careers just like men did.

Contrary to popular belief, feminism was not responsible for women's entry into the workforce. Feminists certainly believed in women's rights to have careers and financial independence, but they did not, as many today suppose, invent the two-career family. The economy did that.

In the 1970s, inflation got so bad that it was impossible for a family to survive on one income. Wages stagnated while housing and energy prices climbed.[22] Women continued to pour into the workforce, but most of them were not seeking "fulfillment" or trying to prove they could "act like men"—in fact, most were entering low-paid, understimulating pink-collar jobs.[23] They were trying to make a living.

For those who say feminism turned women against full-time homemaking, well, it's clear that women were already unhappy with it. In fact, by the 1950s, many middle-class mothers were encouraging their daughters to have careers because they themselves were unhappy with their own limited options.[24] The feminist movement simply made it okay to say you weren't content as a full-time housewife, or that you wanted to continue your education or find a job. Betty Friedan didn't invent the Problem That Has No Name. She just chronicled it.

## RIOT GRRRLS TO RADICAL HOMEMAKERS: THE "RECLAIM DOMESTICITY" MOVEMENT OF THE EARLY 2000S

As homemaking fell by the wayside in the 1970s, '80s, and '90s, it became unfashionable and uncool. And as women tried to be taken seriously in the workforce, they often felt the need to shun traditionally feminine activities or risk male scorn ("If I stopped knitting it was partly because you couldn't knit at a faculty meeting the way you could knit at a consciousness-raising group," says Susan Strasser, a historian).

But in the late 1990s, attitudes began to shift. A few thing contributed to this makeover. First, starting in the 1990s, third-wave feminists like the Riot Grrrls, a punk subculture in the Pacific Northwest, began earnestly "reclaiming" traditional women's work like knitting and embroidery, reappropriating these old-fashioned activities as a form of cool, anticorporate rebellion. This reappropriation helped spark a growing trend for handcrafts and handmade goods—knitted scarves, embroidered tote bags, hand-sewn 1950s-style aprons. The then-new Internet spread this retro, handcrafted aesthetic to all corners of the country, far outstripping its punk rock beginnings. Domestic DIY became cool again.

This DIY-mania began to dovetail with the burgeoning foodie movement. Inspired by eco-minded books like Michael Pollan's *The Omnivore's Dilemma* (2006) and Barbara Kingsolver's *Animal, Vegetable, Miracle* (2007), people were becoming increasingly interested in where their food came from. The term "locavore," coined by four San Francisco women in 2005, was on the tip of everyone's tongue by 2007, when it was named word of the year by the *New Oxford American Dictionary*. This new interest in food sparked an intense fascination with back-to-basics kitchen skills, and activities like yogurt making and bread baking became newly chic.

This foodie movement was part of a larger environmental movement, which also affected the domestic sphere. The mantra "All change begins at home" was taken literally by many. Now making your own cleaning supplies from white vinegar, hanging your laundry on the line rather than using the dryer, and growing your own organic veggies took on a sense of environmentalist purpose. Parenting styles, which had become increasingly intense throughout the late twentieth century, reached their apotheosis in the popularity of methods like "attachment parenting." Educated women became deeply invested in extended breast-feeding, and parents spent ever more time worrying about their child's environment. Everything from the content of jarred baby food to the floor-cleaning chemicals used in kindergarten became an area of parental scrutiny.

The recession added fuel to the fire. The domestic DIY zeitgeist was already rising when the economy hit the skids in 2008. But the recession gave these activities a much greater sense of purpose. Just as the Great Depression restored prestige to women's work, the Great Recession has created the Heroic New Homemaker. And this Heroic New Homemaker was increasingly disenchanted with the contemporary workplace, due to lessened job opportunities, longer and longer workdays, and the continued difficulty of balancing work with child care. Domesticity began to look ever rosier. The symbolism around homemade items began to shift—if a jar of home-canned tomatoes was once a sign of poverty, it now became a sign of an enlightened attitude toward food and the environment. If an apron was once a symbol of oppression, it was now a kitschy-cool reminder of the joys of cooking.

The New Domesticity was born.

# CHAPTER 3

# June Cleaver 2.0:
# Bloggers and the
# Rise of Domestic Chic

Women in aprons. Blueberry muffins. Teakettles in hand-knitted cozies. Babies in hand-knitted caps. Laundry flapping on the line.

I'm sitting here browsing my Google Reader, but it feels more like peering into a time machine beaming images from 1959.

These peachy domestic tableaus are not, of course, from the 1950s. They're from today, from the vast and ever-growing region of the blogosphere called "lifestyle blogs."

Unless you actually *have* been beamed from 1959, chances are you've seen some examples of these blogs. There are mommy blogs full of breast-feeding tips and funny stories about potty-training disasters. Craft blogs with sewing patterns and pictures of gorgeous handmade tablecloths. Neo-homesteader blogs about making butter and raising chickens. Cooking blogs bursting with drool-inducing imagery of fresh-baked scones and paeans to the joys of family dinner and local eating. Home-decorating blogs—vintage-inspired love notes to the aesthetics of a cozy, romantic past of overstuffed couches and chipped china and cabbage-rose wallpaper.

Dozens of my own friends and acquaintances—ambitious, educated women who might have turned up their noses at anything domestic had they been born a generation earlier—have blogs dedicated to cupcakes or knitting or vintage home decor. One former college classmate blogs about what she calls "housewivery"—ironing tutorials, beauty product endorsements, tips on picking out the best peaches.

This is the face of New Domesticity. And the general public's beginning to take note.

"The next generation of domestic goddesses—brimming with creativity, bound by recessionary budgets—is taking the blogosphere by storm," writes the *San Francisco Chronicle* in a 2010 story.

"A new generation of female bloggers is championing the importance of being a good wife and partner," reads a 2010 *Los Angeles Times* headline on a story about the popularity of housewife-themed blogs.

"Women's blogging: the new home front" announces a headline in a 2009 London *Times* story, which goes on to say that "the most dramatic difference the Internet has made to women is in terms of what we must slightly patronisingly call 'the domestic sphere,' particularly parenting and family life."

Domestic blogs are not just a trend; they're big business. Some lifestyle blogs are so wildly popular they've actually earned their authors hundreds of thousands of dollars in ad revenue and sponsorship deals.

Blogs are also the best way into the booming memoir and cookbook market. You hardly have to swing a (free-range) chicken to hit another person who's earned a book deal from blogging about cooking or crafts or stay-at-home motherhood.

Some of these women have even become household names. There's Ree Drummond, the Oklahoma rancher's wife behind the widely beloved (and equally widely hated) *The Pioneer Woman,* who has now published both a best-selling memoir and a best-selling cookbook, and has a Hollywood biopic in the works. There's Rebecca Woolf, the tattooed L.A. hipster mom of four who blogs about child rearing on *Girl's Gone Child,* who has published a popular memoir and earned a paid blogging spot on numerous high-profile websites. There's Amanda Blake Soule of *Soule Mama,* a young mother of five who blogs about crafting, jam making, and other joys of simple living from her rural Maine farmhouse. Each of Soule's posts earns hundreds, sometimes thousands of comments; she's already published three books on homemaking and rustic, hands-on family life.

"This is a real social movement," says Marcie Cohen Ferris, an American Studies professor at the University of North Carolina who has recently become interested in the homemaker blog phenomenon. "These incredibly beautiful domestic blogs are so seductive. They're really a new kind of creative empowerment for women."

There's nothing new about women writing about homemaking, of course—*Ladies' Home Journal*'s been going strong since 1883, after all. But this new generation of Homemaker 2.0 bloggers has a unique and crucial role in the current revival of domesticity: they're actively trying to make traditional women's work *cool*.

## STRANGELY COMPELLING

I grew up in the progressive, left-leaning college town of Chapel Hill, North Carolina. My mom was a newspaper editor. My friends' moms were psychologists, doctors, computer programmers, social workers. Sure, some women I knew stayed home when their kids were young. But none of them treated homemaking as any great art form. Frankly, I don't know if anyone ever even used the *word* "homemaking."

Except for one. Patty Johnston. Mrs. Johnston was our neighbor, the mother of my friend Elizabeth-Anne. A doctor's wife, Mrs. Johnston had a puffy corona of short permed hair and favored peach-colored cardigans and pleated khakis, which she called "slacks." She always seemed to be at home—baking popovers after school, dusting the living room, sewing pouf-sleeved dresses for Elizabeth-Anne on a well-worn Singer. My strongest memory of Mrs. Johnston is watching her sit quietly on the couch, cross-stitching a pillow. My mom never cross-stitched. My mom never sat quietly.

For years, Mrs. Johnston has been burned into my brain as the über-homemaker. Sweet but dull. Terminally uncool. Voiceless. Even as an undergrad, when I began to surreptitiously watch reruns of *Martha Stewart Living* in bed at two A.M., I never considered that doing things like sewing pot holders or baking petits fours was anything more than a kitschy time-waster for bored middle-aged women.

After college, I moved to a new apartment and, for the first time in my life, got interested in making my living space look like something more than a dorm room. So I went online to look up decorating tips and found myself falling down a rabbit hole into the world of stylish homemaker blogs.

These bloggers were in their twenties or early thirties. They blogged about doing fun craft projects (owl throw pillows! homemade marmalade!) and reupholstering their ottomans with vintage fabric they'd picked up at a funky little fabric shop in the Garment District. Their photos showed adorable toddlers, all chubby cheeks and hand-knitted hats, and houses that looked like Anthropologie catalogs. Clicking the "links" page on one blog would lead to another just like it. Then another. Then another. Then another.

These women were nothing like Mrs. Johnston. They were like me. Better-dressed, more cheerful-looking versions of me with much nicer houses, anyway. I found their blogs utterly mesmerizing, as did many of my friends.

It seems as though everyone was suddenly interested in food and cooking, inspired by the locavore movement and the vogue for vegetable gardening. Knitting and other kinds of old-fashioned crafting were chic again, as evidenced by the dizzying rise of Etsy and, later, Pinterest. With the recession, everyone was talking about frugal housekeeping and reclaiming the self-sufficiency skills of our grandmothers.

These blogs tapped into all that, giving faces to the gathering phenomenon of New Domesticity. Even for a childless, fairly nondomestic twentysomething like me, they were strangely compelling. I found myself sucked in, spending hours perusing pictures of rhubarb pies and wildflowers in Mason jars. I was not alone.

## AN INCREASINGLY FEMALE PASTIME

Though it seems like ancient history now, just a few years ago blogs were pretty much a joke, considered the navel-gazing pastime of pimply, tech-obsessed geeks living in their parents' basements. Today studies suggest that the typical blogger is more likely to be a thirty-two-year-old stay-at-home mom than an eighteen-year-old male video gamer.

American women spend significantly more time online than men, and more of their time is engaged in social networking, including blogging and blog reading. About 40 percent of American women read blogs, a percentage that's much higher in the Millennial and Gen X demographics.[1]

About 18.9 million American women write blogs, a number that has been steadily rising.[2] Women have "driven much of the blogging and photo-sharing activity" online, reports Internet marketing agency comScore.[3]

A 2009 study showed that the five most-read blog topics were, in order of popularity: life/family, entertainment, food, health/wellness, and recipes/cooking.

"Food and Parenting are our top two categories, reflecting more than half our unique visitors," says Elisa Camahort Page, a founder of the influential BlogHer network for female bloggers, which culls blog posts from around the Web and sponsors several yearly conferences on women's blogging.

It's no wonder. One in three bloggers is a mom, often a stay-at-home mom.[4] Only 27 percent of female bloggers work full-time, compared with about 50 percent of adult women in the general population.[5]

Technorati, a blog-index site that's considered the authority on blog analytics, specifically called out women bloggers and mom bloggers as a major trend in 2010. To quote its most recent "State of the Blogosphere" report: "the influence of women and mom bloggers on the blogosphere, mainstream media, and especially brands has never been higher."[6]

It's clear that women are online, women are blogging, women are online blogging about family, homemaking, and domesticity. The blog, an entirely new medium of self-expression, is being used to express something so . . . old-fashioned.

## AN ONLINE KNITTING CIRCLE: BLOGS CREATE AN OLD-FASHIONED SENSE OF COMMUNITY

Spending a lot of time in the home, whether you're raising kids, homesteading, or running an at-home business, can be isolating. As midcentury housewives discovered, loneliness was no minor malady. Cut off from urban life and the camaraderie of school or the workplace, many homemakers of the 1950s and '60s grew exhausted and weepy, developed psychosomatic rashes, were dispatched to psychiatrists for Nembutal prescriptions. Think *Mad Men*'s Betty Draper, wandering wraithlike around the silent halls of her suburban Colonial, cigarette in hand.

"I used to put the kids in the car and just drive because I couldn't bear to be alone in the house," one midcentury American housewife told Betty Friedan.

Yikes.

Women of my generation aren't going to put up with that kind of isolation, even as they embrace traditional domestic roles. Older than the average midcentury housewife when we marry and have children, we've had years to run wild with tribes of friends, to joke and drink with coworkers, to share apartments with groups of peers, to meet new people on trains and in coffee shops. So even when contemporary young women choose a more domestic path—staying home with children, moving to the country—they're not going to settle for a life of solitary pie-making.

And with the Internet, they don't have to. In an era of near-universal Web access, even the most traditionally isolated of women—homebound mothers of newborns, farm dwellers, work-at-home-ers living far from family—can be connected.

Homemaker 2.0 blogs have become online versions of the knitting circles and quilting bees of preindustrial America, which were themselves created to stave off the loneliness and isolation of pioneer life. Online, women swap skills, tips, and recipes; give advice; offer emotional support. Women whom Technorati defines as "mom bloggers" are significantly more likely than other bloggers to post comments, to link to other blogs, and to say they enjoy interacting with readers and other bloggers. In our supposedly isolated *Bowling Alone* culture, blogs have created a frankly old-fashioned sense of community.

"Blogs kind of take the place of that strong, matriarchal society in which women share the same lore," says Rebecca, thirty-seven, an Ohio-based part-time professor and hobby farmer who is an avid blog reader. "If I'm canning salsa and I want to get the right level of acidity, I go to a blog. It's real-life experience, so much better than books."

For young mothers, blogs provide a particularly needed sense of community. When Lynn was on maternity leave with her first child, the then-thirtysomething Portland Web designer decided to start a blog to share her love of traditional domestic skills—knitting, frugal grocery shopping, the many and various uses of baking soda. But one of her biggest motivations was simply to connect with other women.

"I was in need of some community," she said. "I think that's the reason so many women bloggers start blogging, just to find someone out there who knows what they're going through."

Within a few years, she had so many readers—95 percent of them women, by her estimation—she was making as much money off ad revenue as her telecom-worker husband made in a year, and was spending much of her day responding to readers' comments.

JJ, a thirty-two-year-old writer and mother of two in Los Angeles, was a "desperate consumer of mom blogs" when she was pregnant with her first baby. Living far from her own parents and, at twenty-eight, having few friends who'd had kids yet, she had no idea what motherhood would look like. So she'd look to blogs.

"'Who am I?'" she remembers asking herself as she scrolled through blog after blog. "'Am I more like *Girl's Gone Child*? More like *Dooce*?' I was looking for these blogs to tell me, how should I feel?"

Later, when her daughter was born, she would look to blogs to reassure herself that her feelings were normal.

"Are other people bored to tears at the playground?" she'd wonder. "Is it so awful that I don't always want to be doing this?"

In fact, studies suggest that blogging actually makes new moms happier.[7] According to one Penn State study, new mothers spend an average of three hours a day online, and frequent blogging predicated "maternal well-being, as measured by marital satisfaction, couple conflict, parenting stress, and depression."

Courtney, a thirty-one-year-old stay-at-home mother of one in Iowa City, thinks she would have found motherhood "much more lonely" without her blog.

"I probably would have struggled more . . . not having that sort of an outlet or a way to connect with people. I live in a suburban area; it is a really poorly planned suburban subdivision where there's no sidewalk, so I can't even go outside and take the baby for a walk. I don't know my neighbors. It would be really hard to connect with people [without my blog]."

Fifty years ago, Courtney might have joined the Junior League, chatted with neighbors over a flapping laundry line, played bridge with her friends. But in a world where membership in civic organizations is down, fewer than half of Americans know their neighbors,[8] and Americans have fewer close friends than they did just two decades ago,[9] these may no longer be viable options. Instead, Courtney—and women like her—are increasingly turning to the Internet for geography-defying camaraderie.

Intense personal bonding with readers is a hallmark of domestic blogs. Even bloggers with readerships in the millions interact with readers in a way unimaginable to, say, novelists or traditional journalists. When Ree Drummond of *The Pioneer Woman* cleans her closet, she actually donates her old shirts and jackets to her readers, a sort of online hand-me-down system. A recent post about closet cleaning generated more than six thousand comments from readers hopeful to snag a castaway fuchsia blouse. When Stephanie Nielson, author of the widely read homemaking and motherhood blog *NieNie Dialogues,* was badly burned in a small plane crash, hundreds of readers immediately started donation funds for her hospital bills. They eventually raised more than $100,000. When Molly Wizenberg, a food blogger who often shared the intimacies of her daily life with her readers, opened a Seattle pizzeria with her husband, readers made pilgrimages cross-country to eat there. When she announced her first pregnancy, more than five hundred readers wrote to congratulate her.

"I'm verklempt and I don't even know you!" wrote one reader. "Except that I feel like I do through your book and your blog."[10]

"Once you have read someone's personal blog for a while you no longer consider them someone you 'don't know,'" says BlogHer founder Elisa Camahort Page. "Research shows that women consider such online friendships to be as 'real' as their offline friendships."

Many blogs also connect to readers through communal projects. Amanda Blake Soule of *Soule Mama* invites readers to post a weekly Friday picture of a "simple, special, extraordinary moment"—a cup of tea, an infant's hand, a skein of yarn, a bowl of clementines. Other popular bloggers encourage readers to share gratitude lists, birth stories, or rundowns of their favorite memories of the month, or to bake different variations on the same recipe each week.

Through this type of sharing, blogs transcend the digital world and become genuine communities. They serve many of the same purposes communities always have—for shared information ("Ooooh, you have to try this mango salsa recipe I found—I'll DM you the recipe"), for inspiration ("Your blog has inspired me to start training for my own half-marathon!"), for practical advice ("Do you think $16,000 is a fair price for a 2009 Honda CRV with 60K miles?"). And, perhaps most importantly, the blog community serves as a digital shoulder to cry on in hard times. Despite—or because of—the fact that Americans have fewer close confidants than in the past, we've learned to pour out our hearts online. Fifty years ago, a woman with depression or breast cancer or a disabled child would likely try to put on a shiny lipstick smile and assure the world that everything was okay. Today women use blogs not only to talk about life's ordinary miseries—layoffs, weight problems, tantrum-prone toddlers—but also to admit the kind of deep, dark secrets women of a generation past might have told only their priests. Not feeling instant love for their newborn. Wondering if they might be gay. Having an unfaithful spouse. Suffering bipolar disorder.

In this sense, the Internet offers a one-up over real-life communities. While your best friend may be sympathetic to your repeated miscarriages, she doesn't really understand. Online, thousands upon thousands of other women who have had similar experiences can offer not just sympathy but genuine empathy.

## I'M NOT JUST A HOUSEWIFE, I'M A BLOGGER: BLOGGING GIVES VALUE TO UNAPPRECIATED DOMESTIC WORK

In the post–World War II era, women's magazines devoted a lot of ink to the problem of the educated young woman who felt insecure or ashamed of being "just a housewife." These magazines encouraged women to get over their "self-pity" by realizing that they were far, far more.

"You are an expert in a dozen careers simultaneously . . . business manager, cook, nurse, chauffeur, dressmaker, interior decorator . . . ," wrote a *Ladies' Home Journal* columnist in 1949.[11]

More than half a century later, women—many still experiencing the same ambivalence about staying home with children or otherwise pursuing less-than-full-bore careers—are adding "blogger" to that résumé.

Domestic work and motherhood have long suffered from a lack of respect. Now many women are discovering that blogging can fundamentally change that equation. By blogging, women are creating value for undervalued, unsung "women's work."

"I cook a lot, and I often feel that my cooking is not as appreciated at home as it could be," says Sofya Hundt, a thirty-one-year-old Wisconsinite who blogs about from-scratch homemaking at *The Girls' Guide to Guns and Butter*. "But when you put a recipe on the Internet, people appreciate it, they admire the photos, they discuss it."

Sara, a twenty-nine-year-old stay-at-home mother in South Dakota who blogs about sewing projects and her adventures in sustainable eating, says blogging helps earn homemakers the kind of external validation they've grown used to as students and employees.

"We grow up going to school, where you get the gold star, you get the A-plus," she says. "At work you're constantly being evaluated. Then you become a homemaker and suddenly nobody is giving you any feedback. Suddenly nobody's paying attention to what you're doing. Blogging is a way to get this validation from other people. You put up a recipe and people go, 'Hey, that's a great photograph.'" Clearly blogs can give emotional value to housework. But if a blogger is actually making money from a blog, even a little bit of money, it can make the blog even more validating.

Marcie Cohen Ferris, the American Studies professor, thinks the New Domesticity phenomenon wouldn't even exist without blogs, because educated women crave the kind of external validation they're used to getting from careers. Until the Internet, no one got much attention for cooking dinner. "This lifestyle wouldn't work if women were raising their perfect, happy locavore children in the middle of the woods with no Internet connection," Ferris says.

## "NOTHING SHORT OF REVOLUTIONARY": DOMESTIC BLOGGING AS A FEMINIST ACT

While some Homemaker 2.0 bloggers are socially conservative, with a genuine nostalgia for a time of traditional gender roles, many others view "reclaiming" domesticity as a progressive, even rebellious act, an attitude that's in line with the New Domesticity philosophy.

A quick look at the names on some of the blogs is revealing: *The New*

*Homemaker. Evolving Homemaker. The Hip Girl's Guide to Homemaking. The Happy Housewife. Hollywood Housewife. The Accidental Housewife. A Charmed Wife.* These women often use words like "homemaker" and "housewife" in cheeky good spirits, reminding me of the way nineties Riot Grrrls and other third-wave feminists reclaimed the words "bitch" and "cunt."

"When I was a girl, there was nothing more reviled than a homemaker," says Lynn, the Portland blogger. "There was an outright, in-your-face assumption that homemaking was worthless. It's time to step forward and say, 'Women's work has value.' I see my blog as doing that."

"Home is not the enemy, so why do we continue to treat all things home with aversion and disdain?" writes Kate Payne of *The Hip Girl's Guide to Homemaking,* in a post called "Keep the apron, pitch the bra."[12] As the title of her blog suggests, Austin, Texas–based Payne has made it her mission to teach her peers about the joys of the domestic sphere. Its popularity earned Payne a book deal—the book version of *The Hip Girl's Guide to Homemaking* was published in 2011.

"I often find myself doing matronly, homemaking-esque tasks on the sly, for fear my 21st century liberators and peers might deem me regressing to an inappropriate era," Payne writes. "I don't take women's lib lightly, though."

Women like Lynn and Payne see themselves as part of an entirely new wave of feminism, one that reclaims traditional domestic work from the scrap heap and connects like-minded women in a new electronic sisterhood. For them, blogging is not just personal, it's political.

Sofya Hundt, the Wisconsin blogger, could be New Domesticity's poster girl—she sews, she bakes, she gardens, she makes rustic venison casseroles from deer she shoots herself. For Hundt, her blog is a tool to promote her philosophy about the importance of stay-at-home motherhood and homeschooling and self-sustainability, a philosophy she says is informed by her feminism and college education.

"It seems like such a natural thing for a woman to do, to care for children and the home and so forth," she says. "I guess, as a result of the feminist movement—which was good in so many ways—it came to be viewed negatively. But in my town, there are tons of people my age who have consciously made the choice to transition back to a more traditional life. They view this as a rebellious act."

When Hundt decided, at the age of twenty-five, to settle down in rural Wisconsin to bake bread and raise kids, it was a very conscious choice. She certainly wasn't forced or pressured. She was a modern, educated woman, one who spoke six languages and had traveled the world. She had options. But this is what she chose, deliberately, and she feels her choice was a feminist one: she did exactly what she wanted, even though it was unconventional.

This attitude is certainly a 180-degree turnaround from our mothers' brand of feminism. In the 1970s, women struggled against what they saw as the male-dominated media's glorification of traditional housewifedom, at one point even staging a sit-in at the office of *Ladies' Home Journal* editor John Mack Carter. Among their demands: an end to the "Poor Woman's Almanac" column of tips for frugal housewives, and an end to "romantic stories glorifying women's traditional role." (*Ladies' Home Journal* was famous for stories about women who tried to get above their station by working outside the home but got taken down a peg and realized that being a housewife was truly the ultimate fulfillment.)

Now, if anyone's glorifying housewifedom, it's young female bloggers. Who would have thought that forty years after the *Ladies' Home Journal* sit-in, writing about homemaking might be considered an act of feminist rebellion? "This seems to me nothing short of revolutionary," writes British author India Knight. "I'd go as far as to say that the writing of the 'mummy bloggers' is as epoch-defining as anything that Marilyn French or Betty Friedan ever came up with."

## BLOGGING FOR CASH: THE SWAG-FILLED WORLD OF SUCCESSFUL LIFESTYLE BLOGGERS

The 2010 BlogHer conference for female bloggers drew some twenty-four hundred women to the New York Hilton for a weekend of workshops and networking. Hot on their heels were nearly one hundred corporate sponsors, companies who all but tap-danced to attract the bloggers' attention. Sara Lee built a pop-up kitchen on the expo floor to showcase its Jimmy Dean–brand breakfast sausages. Hershey and Kraft turned a hotel suite into a faux suburban home where attendees could toast s'mores in the living room "fireplace." Procter and Gamble set up a "Home Away from Home" area with "bathroom," "bedroom," and "laundry room" areas filled with P & G home products—Bounty, Tide, Swiffer. According to reports, BlogHer attendees, many of them stay-at-home moms from distinctly nonglamorous parts of the country, were loaded with more swag than Beyoncé backstage at the Grammys—Sony Cyber-shot cameras,[13] tote bags, iPod charging docks, Victoria's Secret shower gels, Mr. Potato Head toys.[14] Though the wider world may not take homemaker bloggers seriously yet, advertisers most certainly do. As well they should. Popular bloggers have incredible power over their readers' purchasing decisions. Women are increasingly turning to blogs, not magazines, for product recommendations on everything from cleaning agents to vitamins to concealer. A recent study commissioned by BlogHer showed that women are more than twice as likely to have bought a beauty product recommended by a trusted blogger (63 percent) in the past six months than a product recommended by a magazine (26 percent).

This new power of influence has helped elevate a number of homemaker bloggers to a level of clout rarely seen outside the boardroom.

Take Heather Armstrong of Dooce.com, one of the original and most widely read mom blogs. Armstrong, who writes with crotchety, direct-from-the-foxhole humor about the struggles and banalities of stay-at-home motherhood, gets one hundred thousand readers a day and is said to make a million dollars a year on advertising. Recently, *Forbes* named her as number 26 on their "Most Influential Women in the Media" list, right after *Newsweek* editor Tina Brown.

A few years ago, Armstrong's Maytag washing machine broke down and the repairman failed to come, leaving now-thirty-six-year-old Armstrong hip-deep in dirty baby clothes. After calling the repair service numerous times, Armstrong did what anyone with a million Twitter followers would do: she tweeted about Maytag's incompetence. "So that you may not have to suffer like we have: DO NOT EVER BUY A MAYTAG. I repeat: OUR MAYTAG EXPERIENCE HAS BEEN A NIGHTMARE." The Twitter community exploded with responses, and Maytag found itself with a PR nightmare on its hands. By the next morning, a Maytag executive from corporate HQ called Armstrong to offer his sincerest apologies and to personally arrange a repair. Armstrong's machine was fixed, and in the ensuing hoopla, a rival company donated a new machine to a nearby women's shelter.

Imagine the same scenario, minus the blog. A stay-at-home mom with a newborn, a preschooler, and a history of severe postpartum depression. A broken washing machine. A pile of unwashed baby clothes beginning to stink in the August heat. An indifferent customer service rep, ignoring pleas for help. It's a vision of homemaker-dom at its most powerless, a vision Armstrong has turned on its head with the strength of her pen (well, her keyboard).

Being a homemaker has traditionally meant giving up a certain level of economic power and independence. But today blogging offers a tantalizing vision—not just making money *while* being a stay-at-home mother, but making money *from* being a stay-at-home mother.

There's something amazing, almost magical, about turning dirty diapers and broken washing machines into cash. Feminists have long said that women should be paid for domestic work. Now, at least sometimes, they can be.

Thousands of women would love to follow in the *Dooce/Pioneer Woman/Soule Mama* model, as evidenced by hundreds of sites like www.profitablemommyblogging.com and www.mommybloggersguide.com, offering information on how to monetize your recipes, cleaning tips, and cute kid stories.

"Women who blog are the new Oprahs, Marthas and Ermas," says BlogHer's Elisa Camahort Page.[15] ("Erma" refers to the inimitable—yet much imitated—humorist Erma Bombeck, whose best-selling books and syndicated columns on motherhood and homemaking were beloved in the 1960s and '70s.)

At a recent BlogHer conference (BlogHer puts on a half dozen per year), I spent three days listening to panelists tell an eager audience how to make money from blogging. We learned about how to gain Twitter followers, how to use Google ads, how to attract corporate sponsorship. (One woman suggested tweeting about how much you love a certain company until that company's PR rep takes notice.)

In a panel on working with corporate sponsors, Loralee Choate, a successful homemaker blogger from Utah with three sons and a wild mane of red hair, talked proudly of being invited to McDonald's headquarters in 2010 for an insider's tour, part of McDonald's effort to reach out to mom bloggers. "I love the team, and I consider them friends," said Choate of her McDonald's experience.

McDonald's partnership with mom bloggers has been a major part of its recent, highly successful campaign to rebrand its food as healthier and more natural. Paying bloggers to write reviews is a way for a company to connect with an audience suspicious of corporate ad campaigns. Nobody trusts McDonald's claims that its own food is both delicious and healthy. But when a trusted mom blogger says so . . .

"Blogs' influence and trust level drive purchase intent," concludes a 2012 BlogHer report on women and blogs, adding that 81 percent of U.S. women trust what they read on blogs.[16] (Curiously, only 67 percent of women trust what they read on Facebook, a place where they presumably actually know the people who are providing the info.)

"Bloggers are trusted peers," advises Technorati's 2011 "State of the Blogosphere" report. "Work with them to create or curate unfiltered, credible content and reviews, in order to create a conversation around your brand. Focus on building long-term relationships."[17]

True to her position as "brand ambassador" for McDonald's, Choate mentions several times throughout the panel how much she adores the company's new oatmeal. This love seems to be heartfelt. To those reading her blog, Choate seems like a pretty heartfelt person—she writes about kitchen disasters, the difficulties of homeschooling, and her grief over the SIDS death of a baby son several years ago. This sense of authenticity is exactly what corporations are looking for. Choate has done compensated reviews for everyone from MasterCard to Welch's to Estée Lauder, received an eighteen-month supply of free Tide, and been put up for free in the "Palace Suite" at a fancy Salt Lake City hotel.

Though paid reviews must, by law, be clearly marked, there's no law that says a blogger must give her honest opinion of a product. Another blogger on the BlogHer panel talked about receiving a "crappy camera" from Sony, which she was expected to review for a sponsored post. Uncomfortable about writing a negative review, she tried to be honest while putting a "positive spin" on the camera. After all, Sony was paying the bills.

"It's not biased to have sponsorship—you're a journalist and deserve to be paid," said Jenny Lauck, a BlogHer representative, speaking to the audience.

Of course, journalists *aren't* actually allowed to be compensated by the companies they write about. On the contrary, accepting paid corporate compensation and freebies is considered the height of unethical behavior.

But are lifestyle bloggers journalists? Many don't claim to be. In fact, for many, the idea is less "journalist" and more "work-at-home entrepreneur"—an at-home moneymaking opportunity that can be seamlessly integrated into a busy family life. The idea of making money while doing something that one would be doing anyway is, as we've seen, powerfully appealing.

But the million-dollar question is this: how many lifestyle bloggers are really making money?

The answer, it turns out, is "very few." While *Dooce* may make enough moolah to boss Maytag around, only 18 percent of bloggers make *any* nonsalary money off their blogs. And of those, the average yearly earnings are less than $10,000. Enough money to buy a new Maytag (or ten), but not enough to actually live on. So if women are looking for so-called pin money, blogging may be a viable option. But if they're hoping for financial self-sufficiency, they'll probably do better looking for a nine-to-five.

Mitra Parineh, a research fellow at King's College London who studies women and blogging, worries that all the talk about "monetizing your blog" lures people into thinking blogging for cash is feasible.

"Women say, 'Oh, I'll go do that—lots of people have had a lucrative career blogging from home.' But a lot of these big, impressive blogs take ten years to get off the ground," she says.

## AUTHENTICITY AND SELF-COMPARISON

Some of the most popular bloggers trade on their "just folks" identities while actually making lots of money and receiving celebrity-like levels of external validation. It's a fine line to walk. A blogger with a vested interest in being seen as an expert by her readers might not always be sharing a 100 percent accurate picture of what home life is like every day. A woman like Ree Drummond may make homeschooling four children on an isolated Oklahoma cattle ranch look fun and fulfilling, but you have to wonder whether it would be as much fun if she weren't making hundreds of thousands of dollars in ad revenue and book sales, and interacting with thousands of appreciative readers. Not exactly "just a housewife."

"She offers forth this idealized throwback vision of domestic femininity without acknowledging that it's all a fantasy, it's all a construct," says Melanie Haupt, a thirty-eight-year-old writer and college instructor in Austin, Texas, who has written about women's blogging culture. "She's making money off women who buy this narrative hook, line, and sinker."

Blogs give us a historically unprecedented peek into strangers' domestic lives. And, even though we know better, we expect blogs to portray life realistically. We all know that Martha Stewart's a pro, but bloggers are supposed to be our friends, our sisters, our neighbors. So when we see what looks like an organized, stylish picture of domestic bliss portrayed on their blogs, there's a natural tendency to hold ourselves up against that; if our lives don't measure up, well, we feel like crap. This is one of the more insidious effects of lifestyle-blog culture.

Jennifer Reese, the author of a book about DIY food mania called *Make the Bread, Buy the Butter,* calls Soule Mama her "bête noire." Soule Mama, a.k.a. Amanda Blake Soule, makes life in rural Maine look like living inside an impressionist painting—sun-dappled picnics in the woods with her five cherubic children, home-cooked dinners on mixmatched vintage plates, chubby babies toddling through dewy grass dressed in homemade smocks. The way she writes, you can just *tell* she's a nicer person than you: she talks of "gratitude" and "inspiration," quotes her grandmother saying things like "There's nothing that a little bit of imagination, elbow grease, and a can of paint can't fix," and lovingly describes her husband as "Soule Papa."

"I admire her so much and I could never be anything like her," Reese says, laughing. "She's always so peaceful and grateful. And her husband will never leave her! . . . She makes me feel bad, not just because I'm not doing all these things as well and as beautifully—I don't knit—but also because I'm not as happy as she is."

Of course, Reese knows she has no idea whether Amanda Blake Soule is truly happy or not. But her half-joking admission speaks to a profound truth: people will never stop "comparing their insides to other people's outsides." It's just human nature, and if you think you're exempt, ask yourself how much time you've spent stalking your ex-boyfriend's current girlfriend's Facebook page! *Damn, they look so disgustingly happy in their Italian vacation photos. Why can't I make my stupid hair look cute in a "messy ballerina bun"?!*

"Our moms had Martha to make them feel inadequate. But we have a whole new generation of perfection which is rapidly proliferating online," writes the feminist website Jezebel, in a 2010 post about the rise of homemaking and home-design blogs.

"I keep having to remind myself that these women have design degrees and tons of free time," says my friend Gigi, who often has fits of shame over the state of her own home after reading too many blogs. Looking around at my own (tiny, rather dusty) house, I know the feeling.

In *The Feminine Mystique*, Betty Friedan criticized female magazine writers who wrote shiny, upbeat stories about their love of housewifedom, when, in reality, they were actually accomplished professional journalists. Ironically, Friedan herself has been called out for the same thing. Soft-pedaling herself as, in the words of Stephanie Coontz, "just another unhappy housewife who stumbled upon her subject almost by accident,"[18] she rarely mentioned that she was something else too: a hardworking, successful, well-paid writer.

Negative self-comparison is enough of a widespread problem in the blogosphere that some lifestyle bloggers have lately taken to doing special weekly "reality posts." A blogger who generally posts lovely backlit shots of fresh-made pies will post a picture of a kitchen disaster—a fallen cake, a sink full of scummy dishes. A blogger who writes about her idyllic days homeschooling her angelic blond children will post a picture of her toddler throwing a temper tantrum.

Still, these reality posts do little to quell the overall sense that lifestyle blogs are raising the bar on domesticity for all of us. Ten or fifteen years ago, a woman could only compare her house and cooking abilities and child-rearing techniques to those of people she actually knew. And, since she actually knew them, she knew perfectly well that their living rooms smelled like kitty litter and their kids needed a dram of Ritalin to stay still for pictures.

Now we're able to see the insides of strangers' houses in far more intimate detail than those of our actual friends. (Seriously—how often have you seen the inside of your best friend's bedroom closet? Well, I've seen the inside of the Pioneer Woman's, complete with jealousy-inducing sliding barn door and built-in hardwood shelves.) But many of these lifestyle bloggers are showcasing their domestic lives as a subtle promotion for their photography or craft or interior-decorating businesses. Pictures of the blogger's winsome kitchen and flea-market finds showcase an interior designer's good taste, while photos of a blogger's baby in an embroidered onesie help sell a line of hand-sewn baby clothes. While there's certainly nothing wrong with that, the way that it's presented as the blogger's natural state of living blurs the line between reality and fiction for many readers. And when we compare ourselves to semiprofessional bloggers, we inevitably come up short.

## ENVY AND INSPIRATION:
## THE APPEAL OF HOMEMAKER 2.0 BLOGS

It's pretty clear why these Homemaker 2.0 blogs are popular among women whose lives resemble the bloggers'—stay-at-home moms, crafters, passionate home cooks. They offer a sense of community. They provide a space where traditionally devalued "women's work" has value. They're a potential moneymaker.

But these blogs are also fascinating to women who don't have the time, money, or inclination to craft or bake or reupholster their ottomans in vintage chevron-print fabric. Women like my friends and me.

"I'm just jealous," sighs my friend Gigi, a thirty-year-old PhD candidate who is about as overscheduled as a human being can be without blowing an aneurysm. In her (little) spare time, she pores over Homemaker 2.0 blogs written by strangers, looking at baby pictures and knitting patterns and recipes. "I want to stay home and arrange flowers all day too," she says.

She doesn't, really. At least I don't think she does. But I understand the sentiment. After a long day of work, of rejection e-mails, of eating takeout out of the plastic carton in front of Netflix, it's frankly relaxing to read about other women's gorgeous, fun-looking domestic lives.

"I'm not crafty, I don't cook, I'm not into home design," says my friend Francesca, a twenty-nine-year-old college instructor. "But these blogs sort of provide an outlet for me to imagine these things, to think about what it means to be a wife, what it will mean to be a mother."

Many Homemaker 2.0 bloggers are quite open about the fact that they blog in order to show the happy, appealing side of domestic life. Sarah Gilbert, a thirty-eight-year-old stay-at-home mom in Portland, Oregon, gets some ten thousand unique visitors a week to her homemaking blog, *Cafe Mama*. An ex-stockbroker, she writes about cooking, knitting, yoga, and the joys and trials of raising three rambunctious boys. Even when she's alone—her army reservist husband is currently deployed in Kuwait—the blog gives her a window into the larger world.

"I feel like I really do have an impact on the world, even though I'm spending a lot of my time each day washing dishes," she says. "The things I'm writing, people read it."

An ardent environmentalist, Gilbert hopes to use her blog to promote her eco-conscious, frugal lifestyle—she often posts pictures of herself biking with her kids, since she doesn't have a car, and writes frequently about her organic garden and her penchant for handmade and recycled housewares.

"People say all the time that I've inspired them," Gilbert says.

Readers have told Gilbert they've given up driving and bought bikes similar to the one she writes about riding. They've told her they've changed their eating habits or started buying meat from different sources.

Gilbert is quite open about the fact that she uses her blog to promote a certain lifestyle. In fact, she views herself as somewhat of an evangelist. Her "raw authenticity" is key to her influence, she says. By writing about her marriage struggles and her children's issues and her family's money problems, she invites readers—even those who live thousands of miles away—into her circle of trust.

Natalie Holbrook, who writes about babies and married life on her popular blog *Nat the Fat Rat* and at Babble.com, enjoys a similar type of influence. Many of her readers are twenty- and thirtysomething women with graduate degrees but no husbands or children, and Holbrook, a married Mormon mother of one, thinks they read her blog to enjoy an upbeat perspective on marriage and motherhood.

"A comment I often get is 'You are making me want kids, and I've never wanted kids!'" she says. "I'm happy to show an alternative side of parenting and marriage than what we get from traditional media, because this side is just as real, only way more fun."

This is a portrayal women seem to be hungry for. Young people are ready to push aside the 1980s- and '90s-style notion that domestic life is inherently uncool, the purview of the unintellectual, unambitious woman. We want to see images of women knitting or baking or raising kids *not* to please a husband or to live up to some societal notion of proper femininity, but because they find it personally fulfilling.

## FROM "CHAIN-SMOKING PARTY GIRL TO WIFE AND MOTHER"

Despite all this pro-feminist talk, Homemaker 2.0 blogs can feel distinctly retrograde.

There's a certain narrative that emerges from many Homemaker 2.0 blogs, one that makes some of us squirm. It goes something like this: "I had a swingin' life as a single career girl, but then I met a man and had a few kids and—whoa—here I am, knee-deep in dirty dishes. I'm much happier now." Or "I was riding high in my fast-paced job, but then I had an epiphany about the importance of the simple life and quit to raise goats in rural Vermont. I'm much happier now."

These narratives are both modern and distinctly old-fashioned. Their embrace of fulfillment over achievement, relationships over things, quality time over money is appealing, but it's hard not to wonder if they're glossing over some of the harder realities of women, work, and equality.

The prototype of the genre is undoubtedly *The Pioneer Woman,* a blog with so much cultural traction it's been featured everywhere from the *New York Times* to the Food Network. Its author is the irrepressible Ree Drummond, a self-described "spoiled city girl" who was living in Los Angeles when she met-cute with a rugged Oklahoma farmer and became a "domestic country wife." Some two million readers a month now visit her blog to read about her adventures and misadventures on an isolated cattle ranch. Her cookbook, *The Pioneer Woman Cooks,* hit number one on the *New York Times* best-seller list with retro favorites like chicken-fried steak and pineapple upside-down cake. *Black Heels to Tractor Wheels,* her memoir of her unexpected courtship with the Marlboro Man (as she calls her husband), came out last month. A movie, said to be starring Reese Witherspoon, is in the works.

Then there's *Girl's Gone Child,* which chronicles the transformation of twentysomething Los Angeleno Rebecca Woolf from "commitment-phobic chain-smoking party girl to wife and mother." After unexpectedly becoming pregnant at the age of twenty-three, the tattooed, be-pierced Woolf married her husband in an ironic Vegas ceremony and now spends her days cooking quinoa and visiting museums with her four whimsically named children. And blogging about it. The blog has spawned a memoir, *Rockabye,* and a prominent spot for Woolf on the mom-blogging circuit— gigs writing for parenting magazines like Babble, an HGTV web show about nursery decor.

The words "[transforming a] commitment-phobic chain-smoking party girl to wife and mother" are awfully revealing. *I've slowed down, reprioritized, gotten in touch with my roots, learned what's really important. Home is better than work. Married is better than single. Simple things are better than big, complex ambitions.*

*I've become domesticated, and I'm happier now.*

Many bloggers write their opt-out stories into the narrative fabric of their blogs in a way that suggests careers are overrated.

"I used to be an attorney, but it made me grumpy. Now I write about life, sweet and savory, as a wife and mother to two small boys," writes one popular blogger in the "About Me" on her blog's home page.[19]

"I have to remind myself sometimes of what life was like then," writes one "Simple Living" blogger. "I got up at 6:30 every day to be at work and was home at 5 to see our daughter for a few short hours before bedtime. . . .[Now, since leaving her job] I live in a small house, one that oozes love and charm and character because I have the time, energy and desire to make it that way. I have learned from this home to appreciate so much, and that living simply is living beautifully."[20]

I even stumbled upon the blog of a dominatrix turned stay-at-home mom!: "I traded in my clients for a toddler, my whip for a hand trowel, a dungeon for a garden and my vinyl catsuit for a pair of food stained yoga pants."[21]

There was a time (remember the nineties?) when being a commitment-phobic, chain-smoking party girl was *cool.* This was the era of angsty female alterna-rockers screaming about men and sex and pain—Liz Phair, Alanis Morissette, Bikini Kill, Courtney Love. It was a pro-urban era, a time of career over home, of friends over family—think *Friends, Sex and the City,* "urban tribes." Think of Carrie Bradshaw (I know, I know).

Indeed, some old-guard feminists have openly criticized the glossy spin that homemaker bloggers put on domestic work.

"They [bloggers] want to live in this perfectly art-directed world," says Michele Kort, senior editor at *Ms.* magazine, in an interview with the *Los Angeles Times* about the rise of homemaking blogs. "It's an illusion that if you have all the right clothes and right accessories that your life will be perfect. This is a throwback to stuff like *The Total Woman* [Marabel Morgan's infamous 1970s Christian self-help book for wives, which suggested women greet their husbands at the door in nothing but Saran Wrap] . . . that a wife should be subservient and be all about making a man comfortable and having the perfect household . . . for the women of the '50s, it wasn't so happy-making."

While I disagree with Kort that Homemaker 2.0 blogs are about subservience or making a man happy—even the more conservative bloggers tend to speak about personal fulfillment rather than Stepford-esque man-pleasing—I do take her point. These blogs *are* intensely art-directed. It's easy to be lulled by glossy photos of apple pies and hand-sewn curtains. All the rest of the work that went into it—the sink full of dishes, the stench of dirty diapers, the tedious hours spent sewing those gorgeous curtains—well, that's not really blog fodder, is it?

To read lifestyle blogs is to inhale a curious combination of unvarnished honesty and high-gloss fantasy. One minute, you're nodding along with a blogger's heartfelt rant about her nosy mother-in-law, the next minute you're reading a half-veiled promotion for Swiffer dusters. For bloggers, blogs are not necessarily just an outlet to vent or a source of community. Frequently, bloggers are deliberately painting a highly controlled picture of their lives in order to make money, sell products, or promote certain lifestyles or political agendas. Readers, who look to these blogs for community, are often getting an unintended dose of marketing and commercialism as well. But more worrisome than the semi-hidden advertising is the fact that, by painting idealized pictures of their "real lives" in order to make a living, bloggers are selling fantasy but calling it reality.

# CHAPTER 4

# Knit Your Own Job: Etsy and the New Handmade Culture

It's lunchtime at the Brooklyn headquarters of Etsy, the online craft marketplace. I'm sitting at a blond wood table in a brightly lit, vaguely Scandinavian dining room eating heirloom radish salad, roasted sweet potatoes, chicken with creamy mustard sauce, and cupcakes with bits of Dutch *stroopwafel* cookies on top. A jar of turquoise crochet hooks decorates the tabletop in lieu of flowers.

It's Tuesday, and Etsy serves free lunch to its employees every Tuesday and Thursday. They also have free yoga classes, the dates of which are marked on a whiteboard calendar by the reception desk, along with employee birthdays. Next week, though, free yoga has been canceled—this is noted by a frowny face.

Etsy's loftlike office space, just next to the Manhattan Bridge in the industrial-chic Dumbo neighborhood, is the Temple of Twee, the mother ship of today's omnipresent culture of cute. The exposed ductwork has been covered in crocheted "sweaters." A twelve-foot-tall cardboard monster sculpture stands sentry in the corridor. In the high-ceilinged open work area, dozens of young programmers and customer service reps and marketers sit at wooden desks adorned with little owl sculptures or stuffed whales or knitted finger puppets—each new Etsy hire receives a handmade desk, along with one hundred Etsy dollars to decorate it, explains PR director Adam Brown as he shows me around the offices.

The whole place feels like a 1990s-era dot-com (albeit with more crochet), the kind of hip, perk-loaded workplace I thought had crumbled along with the rest of the economy. If someone skateboarded down the hall, I wouldn't be the least bit surprised.

Etsy is considered one of the great business success stories of the gloomy twenty-first century, its concepts analyzed everywhere from *Businessweek* to the business pages of the *New York Times* to the cover of *Inc.* magazine to *Wired*. When it was launched in 2005 by a trio of young, male New York University buddies, Etsy pulled in $170,000. In 2006, it made $3.8 million. In 2007, $26 million. In 2008, $87.5 million. In 2009, $180.6 million. In 2010, $314.3 million. In 2011, $525.6 million, and investors are drooling over rumors of an initial public offering. (TechCrunch named Etsy a "Top 10 IPO candidate" in 2010, and in 2011 *Businessweek* named it to its "Next Wave of Tech IPOs" list. As of now, it has yet to go public but is valued at more than $600 million.)[1] The company has mushroomed from the original three employees to some 275, with offices in Brooklyn, San Francisco, Berlin, and upstate New York. It now has more than 800,000 active shops, 20 million "members" (both buyers and sellers), 1.4 billion monthly page views, and about 1.7 million Twitter followers (in Twitter terms, this puts it just above *Newsweek* and ABC News,[2] though slightly below Kim Kardashian's mother). It is now one of the top 50 most-visited websites in America.[3]

The concept is straightforward: anyone can set up their own free virtual Etsy "shop" to sell their handmade or vintage items—anything from felted baby booties to artisan goat-milk soaps to coffee tables made from antique suitcases to crocheted vibrator cozies (yup). Etsy makes money by charging a $0.20 listing fee per item, plus a 3.5 percent commission on all items sold. The site savvily fosters a sense of community through user message boards and "quit your day job" profiles of successful sellers. It's a simple yet stunningly effective business model.

I've been a fan of Etsy ever since an early-adopter friend turned me on to the site in late 2006. Things I have bought or received from Etsy over the years include: a vintage etching of a pig reprinted on an old dictionary page; a hand-sewn plush squid; A Beanie Baby monkey stitched together with another Beanie Baby monkey to look like Siamese twins; a hand-tooled leather Kindle case; a salad bowl made from a tree stump. When I was planning my wedding, I spent a truly embarrassing amount of time on Etsy, poring over images of hand-cut Mexican paper banners, sewn-to-order 1940s-style birdcage veils, and quirky letterpress invitations. Etsying, as any Etsian (as Etsy sellers call themselves) will tell you, is a highly addictive pastime. Like many other professional women I know, I've also occasionally fostered fantasies about quitting my job and opening my own Etsy shop, though these fantasies are quickly curtailed when I remember I don't really know how to, well . . . make anything.

Etsy—as all the Etsy employees I talk to are very quick to tell me—aims to be about more than just buying and selling stuff. Like the growing "buy handmade" movement of which it is a part, Etsy purports to turn what might look like pure consumerism into an assault on the status quo. The company's mission statement speaks to its grand goals: "Our mission is to empower people to change the way the global economy works. We see a world in which very-very small businesses have much-much more sway in shaping the economy, local living economies are thriving everywhere, and people value authorship and provenance as much as price and convenience. We are bringing heart to commerce and making the world more fair, more sustainable, and more fun."

When I ask Brown about the, well, *hugeness* of the mission statement ("change the way the global economy works"!), he shrugs and says, "I don't see why not. Aim high."

The rise of Etsy (and its many, many online imitators) is interesting for several reasons. One, it shows just how huge the once-radical "indie crafting" movement has become. Two, it's part of a new type of "artisan economy" that has emerged on the back of the crafting movement. Three, it's a symbol of people's—especially women's—dissatisfaction with the current job market.

Because here's the interesting thing: the people who are being "empowered" to change the global economy via craft culture's "very-very small business" model are women. Etsy is vastly, overwhelmingly female—as many as 97 percent of Etsy sellers are women.

The craft revival, which began as a rebellious feminist "reclaiming" of old-fashioned domestic arts in the 1990s, has become part of something much larger and much more complicated.

## THE PUNK ROCK FEMINIST ROOTS
## OF THE CRAFTING MOVEMENT

Traditional women's crafts—knitting, embroidery, sewing, etc.—have always been around to one extent or another. But by the latter part of the twentieth century crafting was most definitely out of fashion, pigeonholed as the TV-hour hobby of grannies and Midwestern moms in bad Christmas sweaters. Seen as embarrassingly old-fashioned, and feminine, it was the kind of thing modern, ambitious young women didn't necessarily identify with—certainly bringing your knitting needles to the office would have been a career faux pas in an era where women were still trying hard to be taken seriously in the workplace. Today, though, young book editors happily crochet on the train on their way to midtown, lawyers brag about their Etsy sideline selling homemade aromatherapy soaps, and quilting circles are a hip way to pass time among high-flying urban working women.

To understand how crafting went from "Christmas sweater" to cool, I called up Jean Railla, who might be called the godmother of indie crafting. Railla, a forty-one-year-old New Yorker, launched one of the earliest craft websites, Get Crafty, in 1997; wrote a popular 2004 book of the same title; and helped consult on the launch of Etsy in 2005.

Railla's mom never taught her to knit or sew. A 1970s homemaker, she was transformed by second-wave feminism ("She read Betty Friedan's book on the beach one day, and it changed her life," Railla says). She gave up full-time homemaking to go back to school, get a master's degree, get a job. She never passed on any of her domestic skills to Railla—she assumed her daughter would never need or want them.

For a long time, Railla didn't. As a women's studies major at UCLA in the early 1990s, like her peers she had total distaste for anything even vaguely domestic. Says Railla, "I decided I was never going to be domestic and I never wanted to get married. I never kept house—I lived on a futon on the floor until I was twenty-eight."

Instead, Railla worked as a filmmaker and bounced around from L.A. to Washington State doing "the whole Riot Grrrl thing." Riot Grrrl was a feminist punk subculture that arose in the Pacific Northwest in the 1990s, partly in reaction to the macho "no girls allowed" attitude of the punk scene at the time. The movement was epitomized by politically oriented female-led bands like Bikini Kill and L7 (the latter made infamous when its lead singer removed her tampon onstage and tossed it at a heckling male audience member) and an outspoken embrace of taboo topics like rape, body image, and sexual harassment. Riot Grrrl embraced the long-standing punk tradition of DIY, making zines (homemade magazines), mix tapes, and screen-printed concert posters as a way of carving out a space for itself outside the mainstream music scene.

Somewhere along the line, Railla had the proverbial lightbulb moment: "I kind of said, 'Hey, crafting is DIY,'" she recalls. She learned to cook, taught herself to knit, and started sewing up a storm, all in the name of independence and antimainstream feeling.

Turns out, Railla wasn't the only 1990s punk rock woman with that idea. Across the Pacific Northwest and other hotbeds of antiestablishment culture, women began to reclaim the old-fashioned domestic arts with a sense of feminist purpose. As University of Tennessee geographer Benjamin Shultz, who has studied the rise of the indie craft movement, explains: "[These women] transferred the spirit of rebellion and independence from Riot Grrrl to the domestic realm, where they could give new meaning to devalued 'feminine' skills like sewing and knitting. Just as the Riot Grrrl phenomenon had challenged the status quo by making a place for women in punk music, indie crafting challenged the perception that traditional skills were boring, uncreative, and old-fashioned."[4]

Jenny Hart, who was one of the biggest names in the early crafting movement, remembers how edgy and political the early indie crafts were—throw pillows embroidered with daggers, images of topless retro pinup girls or politicians—as women attempted to give crafting a new, modern identity distinct from the "geese in bonnets" of their grandmothers' needlepoint projects. The very concept of "make it yourself" felt radical, she says, and there was a huge sense of excitement among crafters that they were part of something revolutionary.

*Bust,* the influential alternative women's magazine, began covering the burgeoning crafting and women's-work revival in the late 1990s and early 2000s, back when it was still fairly misunderstood. By running stories about things like "one woman's journey from Betty Friedan to Betty Crocker" and finding "your inner Martha,"[5] *Bust* helped challenge the notion that traditional handiwork was unfeminist and unfun. (Skeptically, the *New York Times* asked, "Wait a minute . . . Is this feminism or Cosmo?").

"There was very little interest in that stuff when we first started publishing it," says *Bust* editor in chief Debbie Stoller. "It was so devalued and looked down upon."

By the late 1990s and early 2000s, the Internet had brought indie crafting and handmade culture out of the punk rock fringe and into mainstream America's consciousness. Sites like Railla's Get Crafty let crafters across the country bond over their love for quilting or embroidery and helped spread the new, hipified craft aesthetic nationwide. It was soon joined by new sites, then magazines like *Craft* and *ReadyMade,* then indie crafting TV shows on cable channels like the DIY Network. The number of young knitters increased by more than 150 percent from the early to mid-2000s,[6] sales of yarn shot through the roof, and publishers began to pump out youth-oriented "how to" craft books at record speed. By the mid-2000s, female-dominated indie craft fairs were popping up across the country in nearly all major and midsized (and many minor) cities. The best-known is Chicago's massive, edgy Renegade Craft Fair, bursting with everything from fishing-lure jewelry to vintage criminal mug shots to coffee cups emblazoned with woodblock prints of monster trucks. Founded in 2003, it later spread to L.A., San Francisco, New York, Austin, and London. But you can find major indie craft shows everywhere, from Washington, DC's Crafty Bastards to Pittsburgh's Handmade Arcade to Oklahoma City's Deluxe Indie Craft Bazaar.

In the past few years, the new craft culture has dovetailed with the rising DIY foodie culture (cure your own bacon/bake your own bread/can your own jam, etc.) and the eco-conscious locavore movement. It's also become increasingly affiliated with ideas of sustainability and localism, part of the "artisan economy" seen by progressives as an alternative to big business. Buoyed by these sentiments, "buy handmade/buy local" initiatives and pledges have sprung up around the country. People have also recently begun to talk about "re-skilling"—relearning the forgotten self-sufficiency skills of our ancestors. Men and women alike are making all kinds of things, from clothes to chairs to sauerkraut, all in the name of sustainability, frugality, and a decreased reliance on big corporations.

In 2009's best-selling *Shop Class as Soulcraft,* philosopher-slash-motorcycle-mechanic Matthew Crawford looks at the increasingly dumbed-down nature of white-collar work and suggests, provocatively, that working with your hands is in fact more fulfilling than going to an office job. Crawford thinks the current mania for "the home economics of our grandmothers"—the knitting, the gardening, the sewing your own clothes—is really about the search for purpose in an increasingly impersonal high-tech culture, a struggle he sees as being "at the very center of modern life."[7]

Many would agree. Even as I type these words in a Chapel Hill coffee shop, there's a young woman knitting a nubbly oatmeal-colored scarf in the armchair across from me; these days, it's hard to find a coffee shop where someone is *not* knitting. For most young knitters, embroiderers, and jewelry makers, crafting is just a fun hobby. But for others, crafting has become a culture, a community, and—increasingly—a business opportunity.

## CRAFT HITS THE MAINSTREAM: THE EVOLUTION OF CUTE CULTURE

Early indie crafters were often very vocal about the sweeping political motivations of their work: "With globalism, factory labor, and sweatshops as growing concerns, and giant chains like Starbucks, McDonald's and Old Navy turning America into one big mini-mall, crafting becomes a protest," wrote Railla in *Craft* magazine.[8] Some took the idea of protest more literally, participating in forms of "craftivism" by "yarn-bombing" public infrastructure like lampposts and parking meters in knitted sweaters (in 2010, a yarn bomber covered the iconic Wall Street bull statue in pink-and-purple yarn) or staging "knit-ins" to protest things like the G8 summit.

These days, many have embraced crafting as a hobby or a potential source of income without any particular thought to globalism or factory labor or feminism. In fact, sites like Ravelry and Etsy are the rare kinds of places where people with all sorts of political affiliations (or lack thereof) can meet. One of America's highest concentrations of Etsy sellers is in Mormon-dominated Provo, Utah (ranked as America's most conservative city),[9] followed directly by crunchy-as-can-be Olympia, Washington (Riot Grrrl's spiritual home and the birthplace of the Homo A Gogo "queercore" arts and music festival).

Across America, the handcrafted look has become so trendy it's actually beginning to be co-opted by big-box stores—you can buy faux hand-knitted hats at Target and "vintage" quilts at Walmart these days, stuff indistinguishable (at a distance, at least) from what you might find on Etsy. In 2011, Walmart even brought back the fabric and sewing section it had abandoned a few years prior.[10]

For the Riot Grrrls, rocking a frilly apron or covering throw pillows with appliquéd eggbeaters was a way of reappropriating feminine imagery in an ironic way. It was kitsch, deliberately retro, delivered with the playful wink of a drag queen.

Today's hyperfeminine culture of cute often seems to veer more toward nostalgia than irony. The vintage cardigans, the Pinterest pages filled with aprons and cupcakes, the faux-primitive clothespin dolls currently in vogue as wedding-cake toppers (guilty), the grannyish maximalism that fills the pages of design blogs (cabbage-rose wallpaper! Vintage teapots! Needlepoint!)—all this can read like sincere longing for Ye Olde Days Gone By. This rubs plenty of critics the wrong way. They connect the vintage dresses with vintage ideas about femininity, the girly hair ribbons with an infantilization of women.

"The cupcake obsession, the clothes—all of it makes me realise I am living in the most conservative time I can remember," writes the *Guardian* columnist Suzanne Moore. "So it is now fitting we have women back in unthreatening frocks, baking away while abstinence and fidelity is being touted, if not adhered to."[11]

"This weird retro world of cooking, heirloom tomatoes and Jane Austen is starting to feel a bit smug and smothering," writes Peg Aloi in the *Huffington Post*.[12]

I generally find comments like these irritating and unproductive. The enjoyment of baking has nothing to do with abstinence or sexual repression (if it did, Texas would hand out cupcake recipes in sex ed class). And wearing an "unthreatening frock" hardly makes one an exemplar of conservative values. Yet sometimes, when I'm up to my ears in pink teapots and peonies and adult-sized rompers, I find myself wondering if they've got a bit of a point.

Now, I highly doubt that the average hipster decorating her bedroom with sparrow prints is trying to instantiate the value of frailty, or that the wearer of a vintage cocktail gown is trying to say she wants to live in a pre–*Roe v. Wade* era. But the dominance of the cute aesthetic does speak to a culture-wide nostalgia for a romanticized past. When we're constantly faced with media-generated panics about commitment-phobic men with "Peter Pan syndrome," we look rosily upon a past when men were men and women were women. When the economy is crappy, we fantasize about a *Little House on the Prairie* era when a resourceful lady could sell her quilts or eggs for a little extra cash. When our workplace is a mind-numbing blur of white walls, computer screens, and Skype conferences, we might dream about the spicier, scotch-and-smoke-filled offices of *Mad Men,* with men in fedoras and women in figure-hugging sheaths.

## "WE **HAVE** TO BE CREATIVE": THE GEN Y URGE TO "MAKE STUFF"

The rise of interest in crafting is connected to a broader urge, one that seems to especially define Gen Y: the desire to work creatively with your hands. At one level, this desire is an obvious response to a tech-saturated culture: if you spend all day in front of a computer, of course you'll crave some hands-on hobbies. In a recession economy, crafty pastimes are a cheap source of fun for the young and broke—forming a knitting circle with friends is a nifty alternative to swilling overpriced drinks at a nightclub. Not only that, but crafts are a natural hobby for young people looking at everything as potential income—selling soap on Etsy, hawking scarves at a neighborhood craft fair.

But on a deeper level, the urge to make things can be seen as a reaction to the gloomy job market and the perceived dearth of engaging career opportunities for recent college grads—in the absence of satisfying jobs, educated young people are looking for a way to express their creativity and individuality. For middle-class Gen Y-ers, encouraged in their creative pursuits since preschool, this outlet has become a lifeline in an era of un- or underemployment. This is true for both men and women, of course, and it's true even for people with "good" jobs—some of the best jobs of the information economy can still be alienating and soul-squeezingly dull.

In a 2011 *New York* magazine cover story on Gen Y, twentysomething writer Noreen Malone observes:

> And since we are, as a generation, more addicted to positive reinforcement than any before us, and because we have learned firsthand the futility of finding that affirmation through our employers, we have returned to our stuff-making ways, via pursuits easily mocked: the modern-day pickling, the obsessive Etsying, the flower-arranging classes, the knitting resurgence, the Kickstarter funds for art projects of no potential commercial value . . . this is a golden age for creativity and knowledge for their own sakes. Our pastimes have become our expressions of mastery, a substitute for the all-consuming career.

I can certainly relate. When I was just out of college, I worked in the epidemiology department at the University of North Carolina. It was a good job: decent pay; nice coworkers; clean, pleasant office environment; interesting subject matter. My parents were thrilled. I knew I should have felt lucky—even then, pre–Great Recession, stable jobs for recent grads were not easy to find, and many of my expensively educated friends were waiting tables at the Cheesecake Factory or carrying trays in nursing homes. Mentally, though, the job was numbingly boring—hour after hour of inputting data about Guatemalan cancer sufferers into an Excel spreadsheet, turning people into numbered codes. To kill the time, I would measure out the baby carrots from my lunch bag in five-minute intervals. Every five minutes, another carrot. Sometimes I'd stab my palm with a pencil to stay awake. *Is this what adult life is supposed to be like?* I wondered. I knew it was important work, but . . .

Nothing in my education had prepared me for this kind of tedium. Like many people of my generation, I'd spent my nearly two decades of schooling immersed in creative activities. In seventh grade, a math project had involved wading into a local creek to measure water-flow rates. In freshman English at Chapel Hill High, we'd created decorative A's to represent *The Scarlet Letter,* cutting Hester Prynne silhouettes out of Styrofoam board, drawing demons. In college, my urban planning professor sent us wandering around the city with sketch pads to capture the "visual rhythms of city life."

Sitting in an office all day working with intangible data? It felt alien and alienating, like being a lab monkey in somebody's weird science experiment. I had all this creative energy and nowhere to put it. It was during this period that I got somewhat obsessively interested in doing "projects" around my apartment—stencil-painting my microwave, making candies in weird flavors until the bottoms of all my pans were blackened with burned sugar.

Now, just a few years later, an early twentysomething in my position might try selling those candies at the farmer's market or turning her stencil designs into an Etsy shop. Maybe she'd even quit the office job to try it full-time; maybe she's turned to these projects with such vigor because she couldn't get an office job to begin with.

Making and selling one's own creations is increasingly viewed as a viable career option for young workers. As economists and business experts note, Gen Y is a generation of "born entrepreneurs"[13] who expect to have a "personal career" with autonomy and creative self-fulfillment: a third of Gen Y-ers have started their own side business in addition to their regular jobs, and one in five eighteen-to-twenty-nine-year-olds plan to quit their job to start their own business this year.[14] Some critics sourly pin this on Gen Y's narcissistic inability to take orders and accept their spot in a hierarchy—"Wah, you all think you're such special snowflakes!" But for a generation who grew up idolizing renegade entrepreneurs like Steve Jobs and Mark Zuckerberg, and disdaining the corrupt big business of companies like Enron and BP, it's hardly surprising that today's young workers don't want to be the (wo)man in the gray flannel suit. And much of Gen Y's interest in creative self-employment stems from lack of other options: unemployment rates are upwards of 25 percent for those ages twenty to twenty-four, and more than 13 percent for those twenty-five to thirty-four.[15] Desperation is the mother of innovation, and the handmade economy seems like a possible boon for young workers.

As *New York Times* "Consumed" columnist Rob Walker noted in his look at the indie craft phenomenon:

> The women who have led the craft movement don't want to work for the Man. But many are also motivated by having reached adulthood at a time when the Man is slashing benefits, reneging on pensions, laying people off and, if hiring, is looking for customer-service reps and baristas.[16]

"My parents keep asking when I'm going to get a real job," says Ali, twenty-three, a recent William and Mary graduate who, along with her boyfriend, has been trying to launch an artisan jam business here in Chapel Hill. "Nobody my age can find a real job. We *have* to be creative. I have a friend with dual master's degrees who's been unemployed forever; now she's making and selling donuts."

## THE NEW CRAFT ECONOMY

Ali's jam business may not be quite as silly as her parents think. Lately, some economists have begun taking the idea of a new "artisan economy" quite seriously. A 2008 study by the Institute for the Future confidently predicted that "the next ten years will see a re-emergence of artisans as an economic force,"[17] and the past few years have seemed to bear that out as artisan businesses have exploded in every sector—from microbreweries to urban farms, home bakeries to handmade bikes.

Economist Juliet Schor thinks a more small-scale, handmade economy is the wave of the future. She writes about "self-provisioning"—making your own clothes, growing your own food—as part of a significant economic shift away from working long hours and toward a smaller-scale, more sustainable economy. This new economy will be a "synthesis of the pre- and postmodern," she writes, which includes "skilled artisans producing for their own use as well as for the market."[18] Lawrence Katz, the Harvard economist and former chief economist for the U.S. Department of Labor, also talks of the comeback of artisans as an important job class. The artisan, Katz argues, may have more stability in the twenty-first-century economy than the corporate employee, since they can work either inside or outside the system.[19]

Crafting is a big part of this new artisan economy. The Institute for the Future study called out Internet-based craft sellers like Etsy as the kind of "personal businesses" that will "threaten mass production's stronghold of industry." Writing a year after the 2008 financial collapse, *Entrepreneur* magazine noted that "crafting is bucking the economic meltdown" and that selling crafts was an increasingly popular way to "step outside the system"[20] and make some extra cash. Progressive, educated areas like Brooklyn and Portland have lately become strongholds of small-scale production, with weaving and artisan salsa making outstripping painting and poetry writing as the new ambitions of the creative class. Brooklyn, a historically industrial borough whose industry fled decades ago, has reinvented itself as ground zero for the new artisan economy, offering everything from custom-made quilts to locally made jam produced with local fruit to locally made chocolate bars that sell like gangbusters at $12 a pop. (The chocolatiers responsible for the $12 bars, the lushly bearded Mast brothers, are exemplars of the nostalgic rhetoric of New Domesticity, once quoting Pete Seeger on their website: "I want to turn the clock back to when people lived in small villages and took care of each other.")[21] "Everybody would like to work for themselves—it's the dream," says Sue Daly, the thirty-three-year-old director and founder of the Renegade Craft Fair. "And the Internet has made that more of a possibility for people. That's playing a part in why this movement's taken off."

Those looking for craft business advice can also turn to *Etsy Success: How to Make a Full-Time Income Selling Jewelry, Crafts, and Other Handmade Products Online* (2010), *Starting an Etsy Business for Dummies* (2011), *How to Make Money Using Etsy* (2011), *The Complete Idiot's Guide to Selling Your Crafts* (2010), *The Handmade Marketplace: How to Sell Your Crafts Locally, Globally, and On-Line* (2010), *Etsy-preneurship: Everything You Need to Know to Turn Your Handmade Hobby into a Thriving Business* (2012), *How to Sell Your Crafts Online: A Step-by-Step Guide to Successful Sales on Etsy and Beyond* (2011), and many other books, all published within the last few years.

Charles Heying, a professor of urban studies at Portland State University who studies the artisan economy, says the new work-at-home artisan culture is actually part of what's enabling our general mania for all things home and hearth—cooking, decorating, gardening. All those entrepreneurial twenty- and thirtysomethings who are abandoning—or have been abandoned by—traditional jobs are hanging around the house, making stuff: websites, jewelry, bikes, homemade marmalade. And since they're at home all day, the domestic sphere naturally becomes more important.

"I think the work-at-home thing has allowed for a return to domesticity," he says. "People are at home more, they're in the neighborhood . . . it's sort of changing the meaning of 'home.'"

Liz, a thirty-two-year-old crafter in Asheville, North Carolina, is a success story of the new artisan economy. A self-taught seamstress, she'd long harbored secret fantasies of working from home. But she never considered it a realistic option until, on a whim while on maternity leave from her nursing job, she set up an Etsy shop. The shop, which sells Liz's punky cross-stitch samplers and vintage fabric necklaces, was a quick success. Merchandise began flying off the (virtual) shelves as fast as Liz could make it. In fairly short order, the business became so successful that Liz was able to quit her nursing job. Soon after, she taught her husband, a drummer, to sew, so he could help with production. Her Etsy income now supports her family. Liz, her husband, and their two children have never been happier, she says, pushing her light brown hair back from her delicate-featured face as she curls one hand around her cup of coffee in an Asheville café.

"We are all very much involved in each other's lives in a way that would not be possible if we worked traditional nine-to-five jobs," she says. "We have the freedom to make our own schedules and set—and rearrange— our own priorities. We are able to volunteer in our kids' schools and make time for all the things that really matter—family time. Another huge plus is that we are happy! Being full-time creatives just makes us happy, and happy parents equal happy family."

One of Liz's more popular items is a framed screen print of a house with the words "If you lived here, you'd be at work already," a shout-out to other work-at-homers living the dream.

If you're not at least a tiny bit jealous at this point, you might want to check for your own pulse.

## FOR WOMEN, A DREAM OF FAMILY-FRIENDLY ENTREPRENEURSHIP

On a recent trip to Asheville, I wandered into a very cool fabric store in the very, very cool West Asheville neighborhood, the kind of neighborhood where the hipster hair salon offers free PBR with your haircut and the city's best restaurant is hidden inside a cinder-block shed with no sign. Opened just over a year ago, Kitsch Fabrics caters to the new generation of crafters, with spools of mod-print cottons arranged by color and a gleaming rack of Frida Kahlo-esque oilcloth. As I browsed, a woman in her early twenties with pink-dyed hair, her pants cuffed around one calf and a bike helmet in hand, popped in to inquire about the weekly sewing classes.

A few minutes later, I asked the owner, a fortysomething Lucille Ball look-alike in cat's-eye glasses and a chambray housedress, about these classes. Who took them? The classes, she told me, were full of twenty- and thirtysomething women hoping to make something they could then sell for a little extra cash.

"Women used to call it 'egg money,'" she said, referring to the extra cash farmwives used to earn selling the leftover products of their henhouses, though it later came to refer to any money made from the odd bit of domestic entrepreneurship—selling jam, darning uniforms for the local school.

For women with children, the new handmade economy offers the tantalizing possibility of flexible, part-time, at-home work—the "egg money" of the twenty-first century. Like blogging, it offers a unique way to combine personal interests, family, and extra cash in a satisfying package. A few years ago, it would have been considered quixotic and hopelessly arty for a grown adult to even consider, say, selling homemade soap for a living. But the Internet has made it possible for anyone with a computer and a digital camera to (at least in theory) become an artisan entrepreneur without leaving the house. This, more than anything, seems to be the crux of why almost all Etsy sellers are women.

While lots of men *make* crafts, notes Benjamin Shultz, the geographer, he estimates that those who *sell* indie crafts—on Etsy and elsewhere— are 80 to 85 percent female. There have always been economic niches specifically designed for women to work part-time from home while raising kids—peddling Avon and throwing Tupperware parties are classic midcentury examples, while transcription and data entry are more modern ones. But crafting—well, that's a lot more fun. It's a way of monetizing a hobby that a woman was probably already doing, and it has the added benefit of plugging women into supportive online communities like the Etsy message boards, which can be a boon for women who feel isolated at home with young children.

"The facts are that women work in the home more, and they have fewer possibilities for corporate advancement," says Shultz, who researched the new crafting culture by poring through more than half a million Etsy accounts, attending numerous craft fairs, and conducting lengthy face-to-face interviews. "A lot of these women I talk to, selling crafts is their second job, and maybe their first job is taking care of a family."

The appeal of at-home work is particularly strong for women who feel like they've hit a glass ceiling or are being squeezed by family-unfriendly policies like lack of maternity leave.

"Women might feel like they have fewer opportunities in the workplace," says Jenny Hart, the embroidery company owner. Hart, thirty-eight, launched Sublime Stitching from her Austin home after being laid off from a dissatisfying museum job and now gets daily e-mails from women seeking business tips. In fact, she says, she gets as many questions about starting a craft business as she does about embroidery itself. "Maybe they deal with sexism in the workplace and they don't feel like they have as many opportunities for advancement," she says of the women who e-mail her. "Maybe they feel like they have more opportunity for control if they work for themselves."

Jean Railla puts it even more bluntly: "Workplaces are still very sexist—it's hard to be a woman in the workplace."

Craft-as-career increasingly overlaps with the much-buzzed-about concept of the "mompreneur." A combination of "mom" and "entrepreneur," the mompreneur is an old model (think Mary Kay or Avon) that has gained new legs through the rise of e-commerce. Unlike the boring ol' "working mother" or "female entrepreneur who happens to have kids," the mompreneur is a woman whose business venture is specifically designed around her lifestyle and child care needs. It's a term some embrace, while others find it demeaning and downright offensive (as a word, it's certainly annoying). Like it or not, it's being used a lot: "New success story: 'mompreneurs,'" a 2011 MSNBC headline announces, while the *Washington Post* profiles several mompreneurs who "do circles around the mommy track," and the popular parenting site Babble lists its "top 50 mompreneurs."

"[Women] are refusing to buy into the effort to have it all—at least, not all at once," write political strategists Kellyanne Conway and Celinda Lake in their book *What Women Really Want*. "The Mommy Entrepreneur or

Mommy Telecommuter tracks are increasingly common examples of women redefining their place in the world and at home."[22]

But "mompreneurism" is often code for low-wage, pink-collar microenterprise. And it has an unpleasant side, as *American Prospect* writer Sharon Lerner points out. "[A] vast, ugly free-for-all has sprung up to exploit mothers searching for flexibility and income,"[23] Lerner writes, pointing to the millions of online scams hawking fake "stay-at-home mother earning opportunities" to vulnerable, cash-strapped moms.

A current Google search for "mompreneur" leads directly to craft-related suggestions. On *Entrepreneur* magazine's "Mompreneur Center," several of the "20 business ideas for moms" are craft related, including "sewing" and "soap-making."

But is that dream realistic? How many people can make egg money, let alone a full income like Liz's, from the new artisan economy?

As it turns out, not many.

## THE REALITY OF THE ETSY DREAM

More than a thousand miles from Etsy headquarters, the inheritors of Etsy's "very-very small business" model are gathered in the ballroom of St. Paul, Minnesota's Crowne Plaza hotel, eating a breakfast sponsored by McDonald's. There are cardboard tubs of Fruit & Maple Oatmeal, plastic-wrapped apple slices, and disposable cups of McDonald's coffee. Decorating each plate is a coupon for a free McDonald's item redeemable at all qualifying McDonald's locations.

This is the "VIP Women's Entrepreneurial Breakfast" at the Creative Connection, a weekend-long conference on women and handmade businesses cosponsored by BlogHer, the women's blogging platform. It's one of several such conferences that have sprung up in the past few years to teach an overwhelmingly female audience the tools of the new handmade economy—using Etsy, monetizing your crafting blog, attracting customers via Twitter.

The Creative Connection is in its second year and is "much bigger" than before, as a second-time attendee tells me, whispering across the breakfast table. There are some five hundred women in attendance, from twentysomethings in vintage frocks to gray-haired Midwestern grandmas

with hand-beaded reading glasses. But the biggest demographic is clearly
young moms. Women pass around iPhones to show off baby pictures
during lunch and duck out of sessions to call their babysitters; a handful
trail husbands and children who've come along for the ride. While a few
are from Chicago or San Francisco or other progressive urban centers,
most are from Sarah Palin's "Real America"—Iowa and Texas and
Kentucky and Wisconsin. According to a conference survey, about half
already have craft businesses, while the rest are here to investigate their
options.

McDonald's is the conference's "platinum sponsor," while Starbucks—
which is giving away free "create-your-own" plastic tumblers on the
ground floor—is the gold sponsor. The "very-very small business"
economy seems to be, well, big business, with large corporations milking
the artisan economy for all it's worth. There are panels called "Creating
Community Through e-Commerce" and "Distinguishing Your Personal
Style as Your Professional Identity," in which a young, very pregnant
accessories designer offers to evaluate our body types (I'm an apple,
apparently). There's the Handmade Market, set up in the Minnesota
Ballroom, with attendees selling hand-sewn stuffed animals and earrings
made from vintage buttons. There's a "pitch slam" on the mezzanine, where
attendees bring their craft business ideas before a panel of experts for
professional criticism and—they hope—possible business connections.
("I don't think MaryJane liked my idea," whispers one woman after her
turn at the slam—"MaryJane" is MaryJane Butters, the beatific organic
farmer/rustic-chic lifestyle guru described by the *New Yorker* as "a farmer
in the same way Martha Stewart is a housewife").

The women here probably would not be offended to be called
"mompreneurs." Conference speakers begin and end their slide shows
with pictures of husbands and children; one flashes a quote from former
Mormon church president David O. McKay—"No other success can
compensate for failure at home"—as a reminder to attendees that "your
family is first."

Though family might be first, the need for money seems to follow
closely behind. The weekend is full of camaraderie and laughter, but
there's also a palpable undercurrent of frustration—desperation, even—
that's hard to ignore. I meet a Chicago-area mother of two who's just
been laid off from her health care job and is trying to launch a handmade

greeting-card business. I meet a young, laid-off lawyer from small-town Minnesota who's hoping to start some kind of at-home craft company with more family-friendly hours rather than try to return to the legal grind. I listen to a mom talk about her special-needs child and how important it is for her to work from home. She begins to cry, and several other women rush to comfort her.

Beneath all the talk of "creativity" and "empowerment" and "transitioning" there's another message throbbing like a drumbeat: "Today's workplace sucks, especially for moms." BlogHer cofounder Elisa Camahort Page sighs about how her own mother "doesn't understand what's so hard for moms today." The phrase "You can't have it all" is repeated, over and over, to approving nods and laughter. And here at the Creative Connection, not trying to "have it all" is admirable. A panelist named Becky Jorgensen, who runs an online sewing community while staying home to homeschool her four children, applauds the attendees as "women who would rather work for themselves than work for the Man."

Some of these women attending the conference will no doubt one day be as successful as the conference speakers, many of whom are very, very successful indeed. And some of the attendees are not particularly interested in money—they're starting craft businesses purely for personal fulfillment, a way to kick their personal hobbies up a notch while earning a few bonus bucks in addition to full-time jobs or child care duties. But those who are hoping to carve a self-sustaining career out of the new craft economy will likely be disappointed. Just being at the conference, with five-hundred-plus fellow wannabe craft entrepreneurs, must make an attendee pause and wonder just how much competition their dreamed-about greeting card company or homemade-sticker business will face.

## THE CRAFTY BUBBLE

Despite the optimism surrounding the new artisan economy, a very fundamental thing remains true: selling handmade goods is still an incredibly difficult way to make money. Though interest in crafting and handmade items has certainly grown, this very growth may have created a "bubble" around the craft economy.

Many veteran crafters have grown skeptical of the idea that an artisan economy is a viable thing.

Diane Gilleland, a former *Craft* magazine editor who runs CraftyPod, a popular Portland-based podcast on craft culture, says her attitude toward craft-as-business has shifted dramatically over the past five years.

"I see a real double-edged sword at work," Gilleland says. "On the one hand, yes, it's wonderful that so many crafters have easy access to starting businesses. On the other hand, this ease perhaps conceals a huge culture of unsustainable businesses . . . I think we're basically looking at a bubble, and a lot of the businesses out there, a large percentage of whom are Etsy sellers, will eventually die out."

Grace Dobush, though she has written a book on how to succeed in the crafting business, also has some deep skepticism about what she calls the "rah rah" culture of Etsy. "The thing about Etsy is that they've really propagated the concept of 'quitting your day job' and becoming a crazy-rich person on crafting," she says. "But I feel Etsy is a really horrible place for a business to grow," she adds, explaining that the site has become so glutted with low-priced "crap" that it's nearly impossible for a real artist to stand out.

While it might seem obvious that most people who try to make it in a creative field will not succeed, there's a mounting criticism leveled at Etsy and co. for selling the idea of microenterprise as the solution to women's woes. In fact, some have suggested that Etsy is selling women a "false feminist fantasy"[24] of self-employment but in reality is little better than those "Work from Home!" posters you see plastered on telephone poles. While it strikes me as unreasonable to blame Etsy—it's a for-profit company, after all—it's clear that crafty microenterprise is not the boon many hoped it would be.

Jenny, forty, an American jewelry maker living in England, used to work as a medical transcriptionist. But at thirty-one, she was diagnosed with fibromyalgia; she got so sick that she lost her job and eventually her home. Sitting around at home with no way to make money, she heard about Etsy from a friend. An artist since childhood, she decided to give it a shot.

Her jewelry is beautiful and romantic—earrings of dangling seed pearls and silver filigree, wrist cuffs of hand-dyed lace. But it doesn't sell.

"I couldn't give it away," Jenny says bluntly.

She's still trying, to little success.

"I would love to be able to contribute to the household income," she says. "But I don't know if that's going to happen."

Kae, a thirty-two-year-old mom from northern Utah, had been unemployed for two years when her sister-in-law suggested she try Etsy to sell her handmade jewelry. After all, Etsy was always promoting itself as a perfect at-home work opportunity.

"My hope was that it would get me enough in sales that I would eventually be able to support my family and myself," Kae says. Setting up her shop was easy, she said, and she was "thrilled" to have people looking at her jewelry. "I felt that before long, those people who were looking were going to want to buy. But . . . here I am, six or seven months later, and still no sales. To say that I was disappointed is an understatement," she says.

Self-employment is appealing in the face of recession and unemployment, says economist Nancy Folbre. But it's precisely during times like this that self-employment is most dangerous.

"It's a strategy that works a lot better for women when the economy is booming," Folbre says. "The idea that it's a good solution to a recession is really misplaced. I would be worried about people who say, 'Oh, I can't find a job, now's a good time for me to earn a little bit of money being self-employed.'"

Megan Auman, who runs a site called Designing an MBA, thinks the crafty culture presents an unrealistic picture.

"It creates this idea that you can have it all, you can run a business and you can make money and you can stay at home with the kids and cook dinner every night too," she says. "People get trapped in this weird hobby-business limbo. They start out, they're home based, and they . . . can't quite figure out how to get from side project to legitimate business."

At the end of the day, crafting is simply not very amenable to the kind of scaling up necessary for making significant money. Though Etsy has done more than any other entity to promote the artisan economy, it has also inadvertently driven down the prices on handmade goods. This is primarily because the site combines professional crafters looking to make a living with amateur hobbyists content to earn a bit of "egg money" by selling the odd scarf. The hobbyist may happily sell her scarf for little more than the cost of materials, while the professional knows she needs to price it at $60 to turn a reasonable profit. When buyers peruse Etsy sites, which scarf are they more likely to buy: the $20 one or the $60 one? People who do make a living selling crafts often wind up becoming mini-sweatshops in an effort to single-handedly meet customer demand. As Jenny Hart says, making a living off crafting is an "eye-watering amount of work." The most successful Etsians turn into employees of their own self-run sweatshops: an ex-lawyer who now sits in her living room and knits for thirteen hours a day, a Texas ceramicist whose round-the-clock production schedule became untenable once she had a baby, a laid-off Minnesota architect who turned her apartment into a mini assembly line to produce one-hundred-plus iPod cases in forty-eight hours.[25]

Additionally, the global nature of Etsy puts sellers in places like New York and San Francisco in direct competition with sellers in cheaper-to-live places like rural North Carolina (or, increasingly, developing-world countries like India). This downward pressure on prices affects even people who don't use Etsy, like those who sell handmade goods on their own websites or at craft fairs.

"From the moment Etsy put their first owl mug in their kitchen, they began brainwashing crafters into believing that handmade was important to everyone," writes April Winchell, the owner of the wildly popular Etsy-mocking site Regretsy. "And you know what? It's just not. Most customers don't want to pay three hundred percent more for something because someone made it, especially when we're talking about something that isn't particularly special. And by encouraging marginally talented people to crank out unremarkable work, Etsy is now flooded with shit. Some of it is expensive shit, and some of it is cheap shit. Most people want cheap shit, and Etsy wants their money."[26]

Etsy and Co's idea of empowerment through a "very-very small business" model is actually nothing new—microenterprise has long been promoted as an answer to women's work-life dilemmas. It's a tempting idea, especially in a country like America where mothers face an incredibly shoddy support system—lack of affordable day care, lack of maternity leave. Nearly fifteen years ago, anthropologist Tracy Bachrach Ehlers wrote:

> The promise of microenterprise has been communicated to the public through a deluge of uplifting Horatio Alger–like success stories about women-owned, largely home-based, businesses. In what could be deemed a microenterprise

crusade, the public landscape has been saturated with a vast array of self-help articles, books, videos, and television programs promoting microenterprise. The message is that microenterprise holds the key to satisfying work, higher income, and a more balanced intersection between work and home.

The study concludes bluntly:

> We found that despite the potential complementarity between a woman's life and her pink-collar business, most businesses fail to produce the financial and psychological transformations women were anticipating.[27]

The new culture of craft and artisanship is exciting and worthwhile. At the same time, it's hard not to worry that the "very-very small business" model is helping repackage old, failed ideas about microenterprise and women.

Ironically, what started as a movement to empower women seems to have inadvertently morphed into another low-margin pink-collar industry—enjoyable for many, lucrative for a few, but ultimately falling far short of its promises. The indie craft movement that began with the punk rock Riot Grrrls has traveled from radical political statement to creative-class hobby to corporate-sponsored big business, but wannabe craftpreneurs would be well advised to keep their day jobs.

But as we'll see in the next few chapters, the DIY ideal of the craft culture goes far beyond the desire to make money. For many, the skills of crafting—sewing, knitting, making children's toys—are part of a much larger ethos of self-sufficiency. Like the thrifty housewives of the Great Depression, these crafty women and men are turning the lost domestic arts into the tools necessary for frugal, simple living.

# CHAPTER 5

# Cupcake Feminists, Hipster Jam Canners, and "Femivores": The Rise of the DIY Food Culture

My grandmother, a 1960s housewife of the cigarette-in-one-hand-cocktail-in-the-other variety, thought a slab of frozen Sara Lee pound cake was a totally appropriate breakfast for her children. My mother, a busy working baby boomer, was a serviceable cook who mostly just wanted to get something healthy into her three kids' bellies before bath time. This meant lots of cheese quesadillas, rotisserie chickens from the Kroger, and "face plates"—slices of banana, mini chicken sausages, olives, and the like, arranged like smiley faces. We loved those. Now divorced and in her fifties, she says she's "done" cooking and happily subsists on granola bars and apples and hard-boiled eggs.

As for me, I've been learning to can jam, bake bread from scratch in my Dutch oven (though my husband is better at it), and make my own tomato sauce from a bushel of ugly tomatoes I bought at the farmer's market.

My grandmother, were she not dead (the cigarettes), would no doubt look at me like I'm crazy.

"Don't you know that you can *buy* that stuff?" she'd ask.

But it's not about buying stuff these days, it's about making it (if you're middle-class, liberal, and white, that is). Homemade, from scratch, DIY, straight from the backyard, fresh baked, artisan.

On a recent fall evening in Saratoga Springs, New York, I attended a "food swap" held after-hours in a knitting shop (owned, appropriately enough, by a young ex–urban planner looking for a more satisfying line of work). Homemade food, brought by the participants to trade with one another, lined several long tables squeezed in among the racks of colorful yarn. There were loaves of fresh egg bread, Ball jars of zucchini relish and carrot-ginger soup, Baggies of hand-cured beef jerky and fruit leather, take-home portions of vegan cookie dough.

The attendees, mostly twenty- and thirtysomething women, were members of the From Scratch Club, a group of women in the Albany area who get together to share their love of handmade and locally sourced foods. The From Scratch Club also runs a "DIY School" with courses on topics like making homemade baby food, curing bacon, and baking homemade bread.

Listening to the From Scratch-ers chat was a borderline-comical sampler of the received wisdom of the twenty-first-century middle class regarding food:

"The meat industry in our country is completely screwed up."

"People have become very disillusioned with where their food is coming from, especially once they have kids."

"My mom said I should be a farmwife."

"I always make my own English muffins."

"I want to teach inner-city kids about where veggies come from."

Though it's easy to mock this kind of thing as the twee preoccupation of the privileged classes, it's much deeper than that. These women are part of our country's burgeoning new food culture, a culture that places an immense amount of faith in the idea of food as a solution for a variety of social ills, from childhood obesity to global warming to broken families to corporate greed. In this culture, canning your own jam is the height of hipness, the origin of your pork chop is a matter of common concern, and no less a person than the president's wife has made healthy eating the core issue of her tenure as First Lady.

Welcome to the world of hard-core foodism, New Domesticity–style. In this culture, I'm a mere chipper, a dilettante hobbyist who bakes bread on the odd weekend and eats Skippy peanut butter off the spoon the rest of the week.

## FOOD IS MORE IMPORTANT THAN EVER

In progressive, middle-class circles these days, there's the overwhelming sense that procuring and cooking the freshest, healthiest, most sustainably sourced food should be a top priority for any thinking person.

Food choices have become important political acts, with deep moral and environmental consequences. As self-righteous and irritating as this attitude can sometimes feel, it's still speaking to a very real and scary truth. With rising obesity rates, a destructive system of factory farming, and terror-inducing 24/7 news stories about antibiotics in chicken and E. coli in spinach, many people have come to feel that their own food choices are among the most meaningful life decisions they can make. I recently saw a video of a speech by celebrated food writer Mark Bittman, in which he alternated a picture of a cow and a picture of an atomic mushroom cloud to illustrate his point: poor food choices equal environmental destruction, pesticide poisoning, global warming, death. This is not a subtle message, and people—specifically the educated middle class—are receiving it loud and clear.

People are cooking more, for health, economic, and environmental reasons. At the start of the recession, in 2008, 60 percent of Americans said they were cooking more than they had previously; by 2012, 37 percent of Americans said they were cooking more than the previous year.[1] And people who can afford it are willing to spend more money to buy organic, sustainable food—despite the recession, profits at Whole Foods, that palace of organic tomatoes and free-range chicken, jumped 31 percent in the first quarter of 2012, the best quarter in the company's thirty-two-year history.[2] Intensive, old-fashioned, from-scratch cooking—the kind of stuff not much seen since the 1930s—has exploded. Home canning, once the dying art of rural grannies, has gone viral as foodies have come to see home preserving as a way to control the food they eat. Sales of canning supplies have risen 35 percent in the past three years; sales of the classic *Ball Blue Book Guide to Preserving* have doubled over the past year. And these new canners are not grannies, either—43 percent are between eighteen and thirty-four.[3] Chicken keeping, scoffed at by Slate in 2009 as a media-invented "bogus trend of the week," is, in fact, very real. When the magazine *Backyard Poultry* came out with its first issue six years ago, it printed 15,000 copies. Today it prints 113,000. In response to the popularity of urban chickens, cities across America (including mine, Chapel Hill) have passed ordinances in the past year or two to legalize urban chicken keeping. In 2011, food industry analysts proclaimed "food vetting"—the act of finding out where your food came from, whether you're buying it directly from a farmer or growing it yourself—the top food trend of the year. Shelves at bookstores overflow with books on DIY cheese-making and rooftop beekeeping, most with hip graphic covers aimed at a young, educated demographic.

Best-selling books like Barbara Kingsolver's homesteading memoir *Animal, Vegetable, Miracle* (2007), Michael Pollan's *The Omnivore's Dilemma* (2006), and Eric Schlosser's *Fast Food Nation* (2002) have raised awareness of how food impacts our health and the environment, as have films like *Food, Inc.* (2008). Locavorism—eating only or mostly local foods—has become such a buzzword even massive supermarket chains now proudly label their locally grown produce with mini state flags. Slow food, a philosophy of regional, sustainable, from-scratch eating, has become massively popular—there are now 225 Slow Food USA chapters, and 2008's inaugural Slow Food Nation festival in San Francisco was the largest American food festival in history. People are increasingly aware of and concerned about specific ingredients—high-fructose corn syrup, genetically modified soybeans, "pink slime" beef by-products, high-arsenic-level chicken, all of which have been the subject of grassroots campaigns. Nearly 60 percent of Americans now say they're worried about the safety of their food.[4]

Many smart, educated, progressive-minded people, people who in other eras would have been marching for abortion rights or against apartheid, are now immersed in grassroots food organizing, planting community gardens and turning their own homes into minifarms complete with chicken coops. Others are food blogging, lovingly photographing and describing their gluten-free muffins or home-grown tomato salads to an appreciative community of other (mostly female) food bloggers and readers. Some are simply spending more time and thought shopping for and feeding their families.

Though restaurant kitchens are still heavily male (93 percent of executive chefs are men), women are disproportionately represented in the unique-to-the-twenty-first-century worlds of artisan food businesses, urban homesteading, food activism, and food blogging. Women also continue to cook the vast majority of home meals, as they've done since time immemorial—American women cook 78 percent of dinners, make 93 percent of the food purchases, and spend three times as many hours in the kitchen as men. And among those attempting to adhere to the slow food or locavore ethos, these meals have the potential to be much more complex and time-consuming than the rotisserie-chicken-and-frozen-veggie meals our own mothers served for us.

"The return to domesticity by young, intelligent, educated women like you see around here is a reaction against a broken food system in America," says Marcie Cohen Ferris, a professor of American studies at the University of North Carolina at Chapel Hill and an expert on food culture. "We've lost our connection to traditional handmade cuisine, kids could have shorter life spans than their parents [because of obesity and poor diet], there's global warming. This new food culture is a response to an industrial model that's not working."

Hank Shaw, a former newspaper reporter turned "urban foraging" expert who hunts, fishes, and searches for wild greens near his Sacramento-area home, has watched with interest as the DIY food culture has exploded over the past few years.

"There's a large-scale rejection of the industrial food complex, and everybody's going at it in a different way," he says. "Some people are raising chickens, some people are expanding their gardens, some people are planting fruit trees, some people are gleaning in urban areas, some people are hunting."

"My generation is just embracing this wholeheartedly," says Kate Payne, the thirty-year-old author of *The Hip Girl's Guide to Homemaking*, who teaches canning and preserving classes to eager crowds of wannabe DIYers in Austin, Texas. "Like me, a lot of these people didn't learn any of this stuff growing up—we had home-cooked meals, but it was grocery-store food, packaged meat, not sustainable . . . It's really kind of sexy to think, 'Wow, I can have more control.'"

Our country is clearly in a dire state when it comes to obesity and the environmental impact of factory farming, so the fact that more people care about food is terrific. But the kitchen's always been a fraught place when it comes to gender and class, and the twenty-first century is shaping up to be no different. For some, the new cooking culture is incredibly empowering. Others are finding themselves tied up in apron strings all over again.

## FROM DRUDGE WORK TO THE HEIGHT OF HIP: COOKING'S CULTURAL MAKEOVER

Cooking, once considered drudge work by women and "women's work" by men, has been subject to a total makeover in the past few decades. Food blogging is a valid path to celebrity, chefs have replaced rock stars as objects of cultural idol-worship, and few people make wisecracks about latte drinkers and arugula eaters now that there's a Starbucks on every corner and organic lettuce in every Walmart.

The mania for cooking is almost certainly connected to a feeling of disconnection with our high-tech work lives. For many of us, old-fashioned kitchen work, like crafting, is a way of indulging in the kind of tangible, hands-on work we rarely experience at the office.

"In the 1960s, women were being told that they could be free of the drudgery of kitchen work, and why would you spend time canning when you could get canned peaches from the grocery store and be free from the steam and the heat and the sticky syrup?" says Marisa, a thirty-three-year-old canning blogger and teacher in Philadelphia. "At a certain point, you become so disconnected from your food you need to find your way back."

"It's really satisfying for me to look at all these jars of canned peaches," says Erin, a twenty-nine-year-old acquaintance of mine who recently landed a coveted academic job after sweating through a PhD in English. She loves her job, but it's cerebral, hands-off. Though Erin works hard, the fruits of her labor—academic publications, invitations to conferences—are intangible.

"Canning is a confirmation that our generation hasn't forgotten how to do things," she says. "There's a reality to that stuff that I don't feel about my academic life."

For modern women, old-fashioned symbols of household drudgery have become playful expressions of modern femininity.

Take the cupcake. With its dainty size and beehive-hairdo-like whorl of frosting, the cupcake has long been used as a symbol of repressive feminine expectations: 1950s housewives holding forth trays of perfectly frosted pink cupcakes, or guilty working mothers up at two A.M. baking cupcakes for a school bake sale. Now the cupcake has been turned on its little frosted head to become a playful symbol of reclaiming women's work. At this moment, there are no fewer than forty-five novels on the market with cupcakes on the cover, and "opening a bakery" has become pop culture shorthand for "creative woman seeking personal transformation."[5]

The apron, that other symbol of domestic servitude, has been rehabbed as well. A search for "apron" on Etsy reveals nearly forty-five thousand results: vintage gingham aprons, saucy polka-dot aprons, aprons adorned with—of course—cupcakes. Anthropologie, always on the cutting edge of domestic chic, sells no fewer than twenty-one different aprons on its website, each described in breathless catalog copy ("Such a peppy, feminine cover-up nearly begs for a new cupcake [again!] recipe or a batch of fizzy pink cocktails," reads the description below the retro polka-dotted "Lady's Apron"). There is even—I kid you not—a magazine devoted entirely to aprons (*Apron-ology: Aprons with Attitude*).

In this new cultural climate, the sex-kittenish British celebrity food writer Nigella Lawson can describe her baking cookbook, *How to Be a Domestic Goddess,* as "a feminist tract," and nobody blinks an eye.

This rehabbing of cooking's image has made it possible for a new generation of women to embrace cookery with few qualms about being labeled a Suzy Homemaker.

"Nobody sees me as training to be a housewife," says Christine, a twenty-six-year-old member of the From Scratch Club who blogs about her cooking projects—homemade stock, water kefir (a fermented grain drink), from-scratch cheese. The director of development for Habitat for Humanity in Albany, Christine shares a downtown Albany apartment with her boyfriend, a music-store employee who also loves to cook. As a young professional woman, Christine says she feels free to indulge her love of vintage Pyrex and cupcakes without worrying she won't be taken seriously by her male coworkers.

For men, the rising tide of foodie-ism has helped validate cooking as a valuable, not to mention fun, activity. The popularity of male-hosted food and cooking shows on the Food Network and TLC has almost certainly had something to do with this, as has the visibility of celebrity chefs and celebrated male food writers like Michael Pollan, Anthony Bourdain, Gordan Ramsay, and Mario Batali.

Though women still cook 78 percent of home meals, men under forty-five are twice as likely to say they cook "sometimes" as men over forty-five,[6] and men are slightly more likely than women to say they like cooking.[7] My grandfather so thoroughly considered cooking to be "women's work" that he wouldn't even enter the kitchen to get his own glass of water. My husband, born sixty-one years after my grandfather, shows his love by bringing me coffee every morning and whipping up chocolate-chip cookies for friends' birthday parties. I think it's fair to say that few young men these days feel less masculine for knowing their way around a kitchen.

"To me, making homemade pasta is just as manly as building a cabinet," says twenty-nine-year-old Nick, an IT worker and food blogger in Colorado who regularly packs his lawyer wife off to work with homemade couscous salads for lunch. "They're both things that not a lot of people know how to do, and it's really empowering to be able to do them."

The power of food to create community in our fast-paced, high-tech world is a major draw of foodie culture as well. Chatting with the woman selling goat cheese at the farmer's market creates a human connection in a way that saying "excuse me" when you accidentally hit someone with your shopping cart at the supermarket doesn't. The food-blogging community is especially robust. Food blogging is an overwhelmingly female enterprise—a recent Washington, DC–area survey showed that 93 percent of local food bloggers were women, most of them young and educated. This community is like a vast, virtual church potluck, with nonstop recipe sharing, mild cook-on-cook rivalries, and endless rivers of support. For some food bloggers, especially those with young children, blogging about their recipes is a way of gaining validation for that most underappreciated of domestic chores, cooking the nightly dinner. As Sofya, the Wisconsin blogger from chapter 3, said: "I cook a lot, and I often feel that my cooking is not as appreciated at home as it could be. But when you put a recipe on the Internet, people appreciate it, they admire the photos, they discuss it."

## THE FEMIVORE PHENOMENON:
## COOKING AS CREATIVE HOMEMAKING

For young stay-at-home parents, a deep involvement in cooking and sustainable food culture can be a very twenty-first-century way of avoiding the notorious "just a housewife" trap. In 2010, writer Peggy Orenstein coined the term "femivore" to describe a certain breed of stay-at-home mom whose commitment to providing the purest, most sustainable foods has become a full-fledged raison d'être. These are the women who raise backyard chickens, grow their own vegetables for their children's salads, join raw-milk clubs to get illegal-but-allegedly-wholesome unpasteurized milk.

"Femivore" is an infelicitous-sounding term (do they eat *women*?!) but an on-target concept. Femivores, Orenstein says, use food as "an unexpected out from the feminist predicament, a way for women to embrace homemaking without becoming Betty Draper."

As Orenstein describes it, femivorism helps give social legitimacy to stay-at-home motherhood, which is something we see in many facets of New Domesticity. She writes:

> Femivorism is grounded in the very principles of self-sufficiency, autonomy and personal fulfillment that drove women into the work force in the first place. Given how conscious (not to say obsessive) everyone has become about the source of their food—who these days can't wax poetic about compost?—it also confers instant legitimacy. Rather than embodying the limits of one movement, femivores expand those of another: feeding their families clean, flavorful food; reducing their carbon footprints; producing sustainably instead of consuming rampantly. What could be more vital, more gratifying, more morally defensible?

Many of the women at the From Scratch Club fit this description.

Erika, thirty, couldn't look less like Betty Draper. With her magenta hair, dramatic makeup, and star tattoo on her wrist, she looks like she'd be at home behind the bar of a hip nightspot.

Raised in Phoenix, Erika was always an intellectual and a bit of a rebel. She was an English major at Fordham University in New York and interned at *Bust,* the punky third-wave feminist magazine. In her twenties, she had a "hard-core corporate life" managing a Calvin Klein store in Washington. Though she worked crazy-long hours, she loved her job. When she got pregnant with her son, now seven, she wanted to go back to work as soon as possible.

But when she and her husband, a navy mechanic, moved from Washington to upstate New York, she couldn't find a job that would pay enough to cover day care costs for her son. So she ended up nannying to make ends meet.

Bored, she decided to try her hand at cooking from scratch and found it "really, really easy." Slowly she got more and more involved in DIY—growing a massive garden, making her own laundry detergent, learning to can. She began volunteering on a local farm and started blogging about her adventures in DIY cookery. Later, she decided to begin homeschooling her son—regular school "wasn't jibing with his personality," she says.

"I never in a million years would have thought I'd be a homeschooler or a stay-at-home mom," Erika says, widening her eyes.

But she realized that modern homemaking could be creatively fulfilling in a way she'd never imagined. Unlike previous generations of housewives, who Erika imagines were bored and dissatisfied, Erika says women her age treat the duties of the home as outlets for their creativity.

"The fact that I'm not career driven makes some people say, 'You're crazy, you're a lazy sellout,'" she says. "But they don't realize how much work her DIY lifestyle is.

"Now to be a stay-at-home mom doesn't just mean you're playing with your kids all day and not fulfilling your passions," she says.

Plus, she reports, her husband is plenty domestic too, which makes her feel less like a traditional hausfrau. When he's home, he cures his own bacon. He taught himself to crochet on board a navy ship while deployed.

Liz, thirty, has round honey-colored eyes and a disarmingly sweet and open face. Raised in a working-class family in nearby Troy, New York, she got a degree in food science and worked at Kraft Foods before having her two kids. Now she stays home, working part-time doing research online for a law firm. But food is her grand passion, and working in the industrial-food sector convinced her that from-scratch is best. She makes all of her own butter from local cream, picks local fruit, cultures her own buttermilk and yogurt, cans tomatoes and peppers, bakes bread every other day, and raises turkey and chickens ("I haven't consumed factory-farmed meat in several years," she says proudly). Recently, she's bought a small flock of merino sheep, which she keeps at a local farm. They're for wool though, not for eating—Liz has recently learned to spin her own yarn, which she plans to use for her knitting.

"Not working full-time, I seek out little challenges like that," she says. "I need more than just my kids' schedules. Who I am is about more than just being a mother."

Liz thinks her from-scratch life is the best thing for her kids. "I want to do best by them," she says, "which means giving them wholesome food that I know where it comes from."

Liz's sister, a stay-at-home mom who's gone the more traditional playgroups-and-walks-in-the-park route, thinks Liz is nuts for doing so much from-scratch work. Liz thinks her sister is equally nuts, staying home all day without an outlet like baking or sewing or sheep. Liz would go crazy doing that.

"I'm like, 'Do you want to shoot yourself?'" Liz says. She sighs and smiles. "Sometimes I wish I was more content."

## BE YOUR OWN FDA: FOOD SAFETY FEARS HAVE DRIVEN THE RISE OF DIY FOOD CULTURE

Cat, twenty-six, grew up in a working-class Philadelphia family eating your Standard American Diet of canned this and processed that. As a young mom raising two sons in the Pocono Mountains of northeastern Pennsylvania, she continued cooking the same kinds of stuff she'd eaten as a kid. Then she saw *Food, Inc.*

For those of you who haven't seen it, *Food, Inc.* is the 2008 documentary that gives a Dantean tour of the fuming bowels of the food industry, complete with hidden-camera footage of fetid commercial chicken coops and testimony from parents whose children died of food-borne diseases. It put many of us off Chicken McNuggets for weeks. For Cat, it was life-altering.

"I saw *Food, Inc.* and that was just traumatizing," Cat says. "I think it was the beef and the story of the little boy who died from E. coli. And when the mother said he wasn't—" Cat's voice breaks. "I just thought about my own two kids, and I couldn't imagine that."

Ever since, Cat has been obsessed with cooking from scratch and knowing exactly where her food comes from. As a result, she's become a home-cooking dynamo. She bakes bread, she cans beets, she can whip up a "nose to tail" meal of a pig, complete with crispy fried ears. This is the only way she now feels comfortable feeding her children. She doesn't even like to eat at restaurants anymore, because she doesn't know what's in the food.

"Food's not what it used to be—all the chemicals and all the additives and all that stuff," Cat says.

You don't need to be a parent to be worried about your food these days.

"The processed food in the grocery store has gotten so insane," says Rebecca, the thirty-three-year-old director of development for a domestic violence agency in Northampton, Massachusetts, a crunchy college town where signs reading "Be a local hero, buy local grown" dot the grass in front of the grocery co-op. "I'm very afraid of it."

Rebecca, a tall honey-blonde who shares a modest cottage with her boyfriend, has become increasingly committed to local food and from-scratch cooking in the past five years. "I basically spend all my disposable money on food," she says. "I pretty firmly believe that cancer and heart disease, it's all because of food."

Cat and Rebecca are not alone in their feelings. A major part of today's food-ism is driven by the idea that our food supply is not safe. Our mothers' generation worried about whether or not we were eating our veggies; today we worry about whether those veggies are organic, whether they're genetically modified, whether they're contaminated with E. coli, whether they come in a plastic bag containing bisphenol-A (BPA), known to be an endocrine disrupter.

The result of these fears is a new kind of hypervigilance around food. Today, many people are trying to become their very own EPAs and FDAs, regulating their own foods with the zeal they feel these agencies lack.

"The only way to know what's in your food is to make it yourself," says Cat.

This intense focus on what control the individual can have on their food is a mark of today's DIY culture in general. Progressive food politics lauds individual action, having largely written off government regulatory agencies as hopelessly ineffectual, even corrupt.

As one mother, a lawyer and women's health advocate, quoted in a *New York Times* story, puts it: "Professional experience showed me that neither corporations nor the government could be counted on to care for my family."

Sean Timberlake, who runs the popular Bay Area–based canning blog *Punk Domestics,* says he and his husband, as well as many of his friends, are so skeptical of the American food system that they hope to opt out entirely one day. He'd like to eventually move to a place where he can grow his own food, and he says this desire is becoming increasingly common.

"This trend really blossomed around 2008," he says. "It was a perfect storm. People were more concerned with food scares, food coming out of China, E. coli in spinach, and things like that. People suddenly started to go, 'If I don't know where my food comes from, there may be risks involved that we were never taught to pay attention to.'"

The insistence on knowing where your food comes from is known as "food vetting" among industry analysts, and it's considered one of the biggest food-related trends of the twenty-first century.[8] According to a 2011 study by the International Food Information Council, Americans are more worried than ever about food safety.[9] Only half are confident about the safety of the U.S. food supply chain.

These worries are not without legitimacy. Government agencies *are* startlingly lax in regulating chemicals. Unlike in Europe, where companies must prove the safety of the chemicals used in household goods, in the United States chemicals are "safe until proven harmful." Banning chemicals is almost impossible—even asbestos is still on the market because of legal loopholes. There have been a number of high-profile incidents of food contamination—a cantaloupe-borne listeria outbreak of 2011 that killed thirty people (the worst such incident since the CDC began tracking outbreaks in 1970);[10] a 2009 outbreak of salmonella that sickened thousands and killed at least eight people, which was traced back to a filthy Georgia peanut butter factory.

But faith in the idea that one can control their family's health just with food can be near-mystical, in a way that speaks to romantic American ideals of self-sufficiency and personal agency.

Take the story of Sarah. Sarah, thirty-eight, has an MBA from Wharton. She spent years working as a stockbroker in New York before moving to Portland and getting a job in IT. Her career was fast paced, stimulating, and highly paid.

Then, one by one, her three sons were diagnosed with behavioral and developmental problems. Her oldest son, nine, has anxiety problems and oppositional defiant disorder, which leaves him prone to out-of-control rages. Her middle son, seven, has Asperger's syndrome. The youngest, four, has just been diagnosed with ADHD. Sarah and her husband were exhausted and bewildered, and desperate for an answer.

"It's as if there was something in the soil," she says. "Which there probably is . . . My family was kind of broken, and I needed to fix it somehow." Her first thought: rid her household of any potential environmental toxins. She started with food.

"Immediately I started really going after chemicals and processed ingredients in food," she said. "Then I really started thinking a lot more about how the stuff was grown and where it came from . . . So I started making everything from scratch."

She baked her own tortillas to avoid preservatives, canned her own tomatoes to avoid the BPA contained in commercial food cans ("There's so many studies about BPA and its effects on the brain"), got flour from a local farm to make her own sourdough bread (though she didn't grind her own flour, she knows people who do), tore up her lawn to build a garden ("I have enough raspberries back here to feed the whole block—and it's a big block!"). She belongs to a food "buying club" launched by a local woman who wanted to buy her food straight from the farmer; Sarah orders what she wants online and picks it up later at the store. Most of the other buying club members are fellow mothers, Sarah says, smart, educated women with major concerns about commercial food.

Sarah thinks that each of her children has different food sensitivities—her oldest, for example, gets "really weird" when he eats red food coloring, so Sarah occasionally yells at her husband for feeding him commercial strawberry shortcake ice cream bars. Sarah's husband, an army reservist currently deployed in Kuwait, is far less concerned about food than Sarah is—in fact, he keeps a separate fridge in the basement for his own nonorganic, nonlocal foods. This has caused some major tension in their marriage. But, Sarah believes, her focus on diet has wrought visible results in her children. No, they're not cured. But they're less hyperactive, more focused, she says.

Once a high-earning careerist, Sarah now only works a few hours a week as a freelance writer. The rest of her time is consumed with caring for her boys, gardening, and cooking. The family lives off her husband's army salary, which leaves them so broke they can't afford a car. Not that Sarah wants one anyway—she bikes everywhere instead. For her, the food has sparked a radical lifestyle change. What's important to her now is "just focusing on our home, our food, our personal space—just me engaging in the domestic part of life."

Sarah is now working on a memoir about what she calls "inconvenient eating," which she hopes to sell to a publisher. Her book description reads, in part: "We are hurting. Our children are hurting . . . Something deep within us, an ancient wisdom from very near the dawn of familial ties, rooted in the earliest flush of prolactin—the mothering hormone—tells us that food is the answer."

## THE WAY FOOD USED TO BE: THE MYTHS OF FOODIE NOSTALGIA (OR, IS MICHAEL POLLAN A SEXIST PIG?)

It's clear that the Standard American Diet of the twenty-first century isn't doing us any favors, health-wise. So it's not surprising that people are turning to the past for tips on how to live better. Food writers like Barbara Kingsolver and Michael Pollan entrance readers with their rhapsodies on the Way Food Used to Be, memoirists enthuse about trading their busy urban lives for a more "authentic" existence on a farm, while the official manifesto of the Slow Food movement cries for us to return to our preindustrial roots:

> Born and nurtured under the sign of Industrialization, this century first invented the machine and then modelled its lifestyle after it. Speed became our shackles. We fell prey to the same virus: "the fast life" that fractures our customs and assails us even in our own homes, forcing us to ingest "fast-food."

Homo sapiens must regain wisdom and liberate itself from the "velocity" that is propelling it on the road to extinction. Let us defend ourselves against the universal madness of "the fast life" with tranquil material pleasure.[11]

These narratives appeal to our collective sense of nostalgia: pink-cheeked farmwomen kneading homemade bread, mothers and daughters shelling sun-warmed peas on country porches, and multigenerational families gathered happily around the dinner table to tuck into Grandma's hand-plucked roasted chicken. As the oft-quoted Michael Pollan saying goes, "Don't eat anything your great-great-grandmother wouldn't recognize as food" (in my case, that would mean a steady diet of pierogies and cabbage).

Unfortunately, this cozy vision obscures the often-grimy truths about what cooking was really like for our foremothers and -fathers in the preindustrial, preconvenience era.

Contrary to the myth of the happy, apple-cheeked great-great-grandmother, cooking has rarely been seen as a source of fulfillment, historically speaking. In Colonial America, kitchen work was viewed as a lowly chore, often farmed out to servants (who, needless to say, did not spend a lot of time exulting in the visceral pleasures of pea shucking). In the 1800s, middle-class women supervised immigrant kitchen maids (or slaves), while pioneer women and rural housewives sweated over wood fires and heavy iron pots. (Fun fact: until the mid-1800s, many large households employed a small dog called a "turnspit dog" for the unpleasant task of turning the roast over the fire.)[12]

"People were happy to work in factories and get off the farm!" groans Chris Bobel, a women's studies professor at the University of Massachusetts, Boston. "The factory girls from Lowell [Massachusetts, one of the earliest textile mill towns], it was esteemed work, to be able to put on shoes and go sit at a sewing machine all day."

And while there are genuine problems with today's industrialized food system, the idea that food was purer and more wholesome in the past is also pure fiction.

"The media has done a good job of convincing people that their food isn't safe, when almost certainly the opposite is true," says Rachel Laudan, a food historian. Laudan points out that eating has always been an inherently dangerous enterprise, but one that has gotten progressively safer over the years with the rise of better sanitation and government standards.

Prepasteurization, children frequently died from cholera, listeria, or bovine tuberculosis after drinking tainted milk. Butter was often rancid or adulterated with anything from gypsum to gelatin fat to mashed potatoes.[13] Until the Pure Food and Drug Act of 1906, penny candy might be colored with lead or arsenic, pickles with copper compounds. Malnutrition was endemic well into the twentieth century, especially in the parts of rural America we like to imagine as pastoral paradises.

Yet, due to the pervasive romanticization of the preindustrial family farm, today only 60 percent of Americans say they believe they've benefited from modern food technologies (including pasteurizing, fermenting, drying, freezing, fortification, and canning). Of the 60 percent who believe there are benefits to modern food technology, only 30 percent say modern technologies have increased food safety.[14] In reality, we've all benefited vastly from these technologies, and many of us would actually be dead without them.

Perhaps the most troubling part of the narrative of the Way Food Used to Be is where the blame is placed for the downfall of the family dinner: squarely on the shoulders of Betty Friedan and co.

Right-wing *The Atlantic* writer Caitlin Flanagan describes feminist-run 1970s households thus: "There would be squalor beyond reckoning in the kitchen . . . Cooking nourishing dinners was an oppressive act."[15]

Okay, that's an extreme thing to say, but Caitlin Flanagan is a notorious conservative rabble-rouser who adores baiting feminists and other liberals. Of course she'd say that.

Here's another quote: "[The appreciation of cooking was] a bit of wisdom that some American feminists thoughtlessly trampled in their rush to get women out of the kitchen."[16]

Flanagan again?

Nope, that's Michael Pollan. Yes, *that* Michael Pollan, the demigod food writer and activist at whose feet so much of progressive America worships. *The Omnivore's Dilemma,* Pollan's pro-local, pro-organic manifesto, spent years on the *New York Times* bestseller list, and Pollan's motto of "eat food/not too much/mostly plants" can be heard murmured like a mantra in the aisles of local grocery co-ops nationwide.

Yet there he is again, in the *New York Times Magazine,* dismissing *The*

*Feminine Mystique* as "the book that taught millions of American women to regard housework, cooking included, as drudgery, indeed as a form of oppression." In the same magazine story, Pollan scolds that "American women now allow corporations to cook for them" and rues the fact that women have lost the "moral obligation to cook" they felt during his 1960s childhood.

Pollan is not alone in his assessment. Mireille Guiliano, author of the megabestselling diet book *French Women Don't Get Fat,* ratchets up the guilt by blaming feminism both for ruining cooking *and* for making women fat: "[Women] don't know how to deal with stress, and they eat when they're not hungry and get fat. They don't know how to cook, because feminism taught us that cooking was pooh-pooh," she says.[17]

As sustainability advocate Marguerite Manteau-Rao writes:

[During the era of] feminism, we, women made a bargain with the devil. Tired of being kept in the kitchen, we welcomed with open arms, promises from the food industry to make life more convenient for us . . . Of course there were compromises to be made, such as paying more for our food, and jeopardizing our health and that of our family.[18]

"Yes, it's feminism we have to thank for the spread of fast-food chains and an epidemic of childhood obesity," sniffs British celebrity cookbook author Rose Prince,[19] who later defends herself by telling me the feminists didn't *intend to* ruin cooking.

Comments like this make me—owner of not one but *two* copies of *The Omnivore's Dilemma*—want to smack Pollan and the rest upside the head with a spatula. Claiming that feminism killed home cooking is not just shaming, it's wildly inaccurate from a historical standpoint.

As should be obvious to anyone who's peeked at a cookbook from the late 1940s or early 1950s that promotes ingredients like sliced hot dogs and canned tomato soup, we've been eating processed crap since long before feminism. Yet the idea of the feminist abandoning her children to TV dinners while she rushes off to a consciousness-raising group is unshakable.

The rise of convenience food has to do with market forces, not feminism. After World War II, food companies began unloading packaged food products developed for wartime use on the domestic market: frozen fish fillets, powdered coffee, tinned spinach. These foods were aggressively marketed as wholesome and modern, since housewives were initially suspicious of products like ham that came in a can. But lots of women, it turns out, were simply not so fond of cooking. The twentieth century's two most popular pro-convenience-foods cookbooks, Peg Bracken's cheeky 1960 *The I Hate to Cook Book,* with its recipes like Skid Road Stroganoff ("Add the flour, salt, paprika, and mushrooms, stir, and let it cook five minutes while you light a cigarette and stare sullenly at the sink"), and Poppy Cannon's 1951 *The Can-Opener Cookbook* were hits long before second-wave feminism was so much as a gleam in Betty Friedan's eye. So why does Betty get blamed?

The food movement, with its insistence on how fun and fulfilling and morally correct cooking is, seems to have trouble imagining why women might not have wanted to spend all their time in front of the stove. Since scratch cooking today is largely a hobby or a personal choice of the middle class, many of us wish we could spend *more* time in the kitchen. But it's important to remember that this was not always the case.

It's easy to forget, in the face of today's foodie culture, that cooking is not fun when it's mandatory.

When much-lauded food writer Michael Ruhlman writes, "*I know for a fact* [emphasis added] that spending at least a few days a week preparing food with other people around, enjoying it together, is one of the best possible things in life to do, period. *It's part of what makes us human* [emphasis added]. It makes us happy in ways that are deep and good for us,"[20] he's writing from the point of view of a food writer, someone who enjoys cooking and has freely chosen it as his vocation. That's a privileged position, and a frankly absurd one. To borrow Ruhlman's wording, *I know for a fact* that plenty of people don't like to cook and it's not because they haven't been properly educated or had the "revelatory" experience of eating an exquisitely ripe peach or a simple-yet-perfect slice of sole meunière. *I know for a fact* that plenty of people aren't even that interested in the experience of eating, and I bet you do too: the absentminded friend who has to be reminded to bolt down a granola bar before heading to her after-work Italian class; the picky-eater sibling who, though grown, still happily subsists on spaghetti and bananas and diced red peppers. The term "foodie" was originally invented to describe people who really enjoy eating and cooking, which suggests that others do not. Yet today *everyone* is meant to have a deep and abiding appreciation for and fascination with pure, wholesome, delicious, seasonal, regional food. The expectation that cooking should be fulfilling for everyone is insidious, especially for women. I happen to adore cooking and eating, and nothing is more fun for me than sharing a home-cooked bowl of pasta puttanesca and a loaf of crusty bread with friends. Yet, I know for a fact that others would much rather go kayaking or read magazines or write poems or play World of Warcraft or teach their dog sign language. And, unlike Ruhlman, I don't suspect them of being less than human.

Before she was a professor, Arlene Avakian, food studies scholar and professor emeritus at U Mass Amherst, was a stay-at-home mom raising two young children in the early 1960s. She remembers a time when cooking was not fun or fulfilling at all. As a young wife, she was expected to cook nutritious meals day in and day out. She felt trapped, bored, and, as she says, she "began to go nuts."

Avakian, for one, is tired of hearing people moralize about the joy of slow cooking. "There's this romanticization of the family in which women do the nurturing, and Pollan is terrible about this," she says. "Because it's a very scary world, people want things to be the way they were. Or the way they never were."

The historically inaccurate blaming of feminism for today's food failings implies that women were, are, and should be responsible for cooking and family health. And, unsurprisingly, women are the ones who feel responsible.

## WOMEN, FOOD, AND GUILT: SUFFERING THE HIGH STANDARDS OF TODAY'S FOOD CULTURE

While women like Liz and Erika of the From Scratch Club may be finding fulfillment through deep involvement in sustainable food, others feel much more ambivalent about what they see as the unreasonably high standards promoted by today's food culture.

One might argue that making a healthy meal has never been easier: toss some prewashed spinach in bottled balsamic dressing and pop precut chicken parts in the oven, melt some cheese and leftover broccoli between two whole-grain quesadillas, toss whole wheat spaghetti with a jar of tomato sauce and a handful of cut-up red pepper. Yet, even as healthy food has become more convenient, diet philosophies have become ever more complicated.

These food philosophies don't always jibe with the reality of being a busy American. Locavorism, a nice idea, if hardly the solution for global warming, has become a rigid philosophy in many quarters. Genetically modified organisms (a.k.a. "GMOs," which are nearly ubiquitous in the American diet via modified corn and soybeans ), though widely considered perfectly safe by the scientific community, have been the subject of widespread food fears—recently *O, the Oprah Magazine* (circulation nearly 250,000) published a piece on "how to reduce exposure to GMOs."[21] Avoiding them, however, takes major doing—I talked to women who sought out and ground their own wheat just to be sure they were not consuming a product largely accepted by the medical community as perfectly innocuous. For mothers, the pressures to keep kids free from "toxins" by making your own baby food and growing your own veggies have been rising, and contrary to popular perception, these are not just concerns of a tiny elite. Suspicion runs deep, and the expert stamp of approval from doctors and researchers isn't enough to assuage fears.

These pressures can drain all the fun out of cooking and turn dinnertime into a referendum on good global citizenship, good parenting, good morals.

Addie, a twenty-eight-year-old newspaper reporter and mother of two in Austin, Texas, loves cooking but finds the high standards of today's food culture stifling. "Some people like Michael Pollan and Alice Waters set expectations so high that it sets women up to see themselves as failures if their kids aren't getting organic produce every day," she says. "We have become so obsessed with food, which I think on the whole is a good thing, environment- and health-wise. But people need a reality check about the effort it takes. It's expensive to eat that way. Feeding kids that way is hard too. You can't buy cereal at the farmers' market, and anyone who has kids knows that feeding them a frittata with local eggs and spinach is not realistic."

Marisa, the Philadelphia canning blogger and teacher, says the food blogosphere is guilty of perpetuating these unreasonably high standards, something she tries to work against in her own teaching.

"There are these very vocal women out there talking about how they make everything their kids eat and they're grinding all their own grains from scratch," she says. "Look, I have a grain grinder myself, but there's a certain point when you have to choose between making yourself crazy and saying, 'Okay, it's okay to buy a couple things at Trader Joe's.' There are a lot of women out there who have these food blogs where it's all homegrown and handmade, and they don't show the moments when they go to get fast food."

Rachel, a thirty-eight-year-old English professor in Fort Wayne, Indiana, spent years adhering to the DIY food ideology. She made all her own bread and all her own yogurt, and went to great pains to ensure that not a morsel of tainted nonorganic food passed her children's lips. Among her crunchy, child-focused peer group, the pressure to eat this way was enormous. Women judged each other for their DIY food skills— "Canning was some sort of gold standard of DIY-ing, this Everest," Rachel says. "I felt a real sense of obligation to choose the more natural, the organic, the more environmental, and I think that sense of obligation is very common."

This kind of lifestyle was possible when Rachel was a married stay-at-home mom, but once she got a full-time job—and subsequently separated from her husband—she simply didn't have the time. Attempting to juggle work, child care, and from-scratch cooking, she cracked.

"On my first weekend [after going back to work], I made yogurt and four loaves of bread. I busted my ass to keep up with these ideas about what I felt was important for eating good food, then Monday morning hit and I was exhausted. It was like, 'Oh, my God, I have the second week of my full-time job, and I spent my whole weekend cooking.' That was the moment of truth where I decided that there were things that were more important to me than making bread. I still cook a lot, because I like to and I like the food I make, but I definitely feel a sense of choice."

And what about those women who don't like to cook at all? These days, noncooks and "lazy" cooks are met with a disheartening amount of cultural guilt and judgment.

When Michelle Obama, a woman who has probably done more to promote healthy eating than any other public figure this decade, admitted to a reporter, "You know, cooking isn't one of my huge things," she might as well have said, "I enjoy crushing the skulls of kittens beneath my stiletto heels." Recrimination flew in fast and thick from all sides. Right-wingers took it as vindication of their belief that she was a ball-busting radical with a copy of the Black Panther manifesto hidden under her Prada jacket. Lefties wrung their hands over the fact that Obama had neglected an "opportunity" to show that cooking is always a joyful act of nurturing, never a chore (and she has such great *working-class* credibility, they whispered, as if Obama's tying on an apron would convince struggling black single moms to start spending their meager salaries on organic eggplants).

Virginia Heffernan, a *New York Times* reporter, took a public thrashing when she wrote about her slack cooking habits as well. Heffernan, whose main beat is technology, had written an opinion piece about how, since she doesn't like cooking, she substitutes "hacks" (in the techie sense) like 4-Minute Meals (a sort of NYC-only fresh-made microwave dinner), frozen broccoli, and takeout Indian.

*Times* readers were, shall we say, not sympathetic. Responses ranged from the scolding ("'Lazy' is the first word that comes to mind on reading this. Lazy of mind and of body. It would be even easier if someone else opened the can of peas for you, right?") to the smugly shaming ("I feel deeply sorry for Ms. Heffernan. She misses the essential point that it is elementally nourishing to both body and soul to prepare and serve food to others") to the downright brutal ("I wouldn't want you within 100 feet of my kitchen, my dinner table or my children").

Ouch.

Now let's make Virginia Heffernan a man. Can you imagine the same kind of spittle-flecked rage directed at a busy working father who admits to feeding his kids Annie's Organic Mac & Cheese?

"Cooking in the United States is very much considered to be mom's responsibility, not dad's,"[22] writes Sherrie Inness, a former English professor at Miami University who studies food culture, who points out that male home cooking is often seen as a hobby or weekend event, while female cooking is viewed as primally nurturing.

JJ, a thirty-two-year-old writer and mother of two in Los Angeles, finds herself constantly bucking against the social expectation that cooking pure, immaculately healthy food is the most important use of her time. As a new mom, she felt the pressure from her community of educated, liberal mothers to drop everything to make homemade baby food and scrutinize the ingredient list on every grocery store purchase. Even though she hated to cook, she felt like she had no choice.

"I'm a terrible cook, I kept burning things, but I felt like I had to do this," JJ says. "Like, 'I don't *know* what's in that baby food, I want my kids to have the most natural food.' It's this outgrowth of maternal protection."

Serving her child a snack of Cheetos was, in her circles, literally considered child abuse. These high expectations were part of a larger culture of "natural motherhood" (more on this in chapter 6), which, JJ felt, aggressively encouraged women to drop everything—career, sex, internal life—to provide their children with ideal environments.

"I am not into canning and I don't have chickens and most of my food comes from Trader Joe's already cooked," JJ says. "But I have a vigorous inner life and I've maintained my involvement in the culture and in intellectualism . . . But nobody sees that as noble. The noble thing is to cook your food from stuff you've grown yourself, not to cook your food from Trader Joe's so you can work on another article."

Despite being a zealous home cook who grows her own produce, Robin, a forty-three-year-old Silicon Valley mom, still wrestles with guilt over whether her efforts are good enough. "My values are such that I really want everything to always be organic and local, but the reality of my life is that sometimes I just show up at Trader Joe's," she says. "I have to keep reminding myself that I'm human."

Note to self: buy stock in Trader Joe's. But seriously, if we're living in a world where women feel that they've harmed their children by shopping at specialty grocery stores, never mind the consequences of going to ordinary ones, then something has gone awry. It's easy to dismiss these issues as "first-world problems," which, of course, they are. But they speak to a larger gender dynamic at work in this country, one that encourages women to adopt ever-higher standards of homemaking.

Our outsized expectations of what food can do lead to an outsized sense of guilt among the group traditionally responsible for food: women. If we truly believe that food is unsafe, that we can heal our children's illnesses through homemade food, that we were all better off 150 years ago, then it's no wonder that we feel like we should focus our lives around the stove.

It would be laughably retro to explicitly say that a woman's proper place is in the kitchen, yet women like JJ and Robin and Addie feel keenly the sense that a "good woman" focuses her energies on feeding her family only the very best, purest food. If food is so important, why wouldn't she? But in this brave new world of backyard chicken raising and homemade bone broth and hand-mashed baby food, the "best, purest food" is an ever-rising target.

# CHAPTER 6

# DIY Parenthood

It's midafternoon in Downers Grove, a quiet middle-class Chicago suburb. I'm sitting in the sunny second-floor classroom of the Bellies to Babies childbirth and parenting studio, a space of pale wood floors decorated with black-and-white photos of breast-feeding babies, listening to three women chat idly while their children play. Topics of conversation include: which iPhone app is best for charting ovulation, how big your nipples get during pregnancy, and what happens when an IUD "migrates."

Twenty-five-year-old Claire, wholesome and fresh-faced in a pair of chic cat's-eye glasses, carries her fourteen-month-old daughter, Rosemary, in a gray Boba wrap baby sling.

Gina, twenty-seven, has a short spiky hairdo and a retro-cool pink polka-dot sweater. Her two-year-old son, Cooper, scoots around the pale wood floor of the studio.

Anne, thirty-four, has curly black hair and a casual outfit of khakis and a cardigan. Her four-and-a-half-year-old son, Derek, runs around the room making whirring noises like an airplane taking off.

There is something incredibly cool and modern about listening to women talk so openly about their bodies. Veterans of 1970s-era consciousness-raising groups would, I think, be proud—these women don't need to be introduced to their cervixes with a hand mirror; they've already become intimately familiar with their own anatomy via "fertility awareness" (like checking your own cervical mucus with your thumb and forefinger for signs of ovulation) and drug-free childbirth.

At the same time, there's something deeply old-fashioned about the way the three women have thrown themselves so deeply into the role of mother. As partisans of what they call "natural parenting," the three breast-feed on demand, share beds with their children, carry them in slings rather than in strollers, and generally devote much of their time to providing their kids with the purest, most natural food and environments. The Bellies to Babies studio, where Anne is an instructor, is a gathering place for these kinds of parents, offering classes in breast-feeding, prenatal yoga, placenta encapsulation (i.e., turning your placenta into vitamin pills), baby massage, and holistic nutrition.

"This is how people have always parented," says Claire, handing Rosemary an apple slice from a glass jar she's brought with her.

Rosemary flashes a gummy pink grin and waves the apple slice above her head as if she agrees.

## THE RISE OF DIY PARENTING

The DIY ethos of New Domesticity truly flourishes when it comes to parenthood. Over the past decade and a half, hyperintensive parenting has become de rigueur for educated Americans. Some adhere to specific parenting philosophies like "attachment parenting," which emphasizes continuous physical closeness and immediate parental responsiveness to babies' cues. Others fastidiously monitor their children's environments, using cloth diapers, feeding children exclusively organic foods, giving them wood toys rather than plastic. Collectively, you might describe these intensive modes of parenting as "DIY parenting."

DIY parenting is about wearing your baby in a sling rather than pushing him in a stroller. It's making your own baby food rather than buying it at the store. It's homeschooling your child rather than sending her to public school. It's giving birth at home rather than relying on a hospital. It's about the idea that parents—usually mothers—know best and ought not to "outsource" care to day cares or food companies or schools if they can avoid it.

This type of "intensive parenting" has become "an imperative" for middle- and upper-middle-class families, says Janet Golden, a historian who has written several books about the history of parenting and baby care.

"It presumes you have the time and resources to devote to your own small family and that doing so is a way of developing their futures," she tells me.

As DIY parenting continues to rise in popularity, it's generated a scorching-hot debate. Is DIY parenting a sexist throwback, a way to push women into full-time domesticity by telling them it's what's natural and best for their children? Or is this truly a revolutionary way to parent, one that will benefit babies, mothers, and society at large?

## "IT FELT SO MUCH MORE NATURAL": THE APPEAL OF DIY PARENTING

Before she got involved in natural parenting, Anne was so anxious and unbalanced she regularly took antianxiety medication—"You name it, I was on it," she says. Working as a teacher, the native Chicagoan became friendly with a fellow instructor who was also a birth doula, who got Anne interested in natural childbirth and healthy living. Anne gave birth to Derek without painkillers, using the Hypnobabies self hypnosis program, followed by a daughter two years later.

When Derek arrived, breast-feeding was a nonnegotiable must—like any DIY parent worth her salt, Anne is a firm believer that breast-feeding is critical for healthy babyhood. But it didn't come easily.

"With breast-feeding, I struggled, as ironic as it is," she says, smoothing back her curly hair as she watches Derek careen around the room. "I always had latch problems. But I didn't care what I had to do—I was *not* going to feed him formula. It would have broken my heart if I couldn't breast-feed."

Anne and her husband still share a "family bed" with their two children.

"It felt so much more natural," she says. "I had a crib, but I never used it. I felt so awkward, my child not being with me."

When her son was older, she didn't feed him any jarred baby food, preferring the "baby-led weaning" method, which involves letting children go directly from breast-feeding to eating solid food on their own. Proponents say it helps with hand-eye coordination and ensures babies won't be overfed.

With her daughter, Anne was "so much more lax," feeding her boxed rice cereal.

"I won't do that again," she says ruefully. "She has so many more allergies."

Claire, who has been interested in natural parenting since college, gave birth to Rosemary at home, in a room specially decorated for the birth, after reading books about home birth and researching the topic online. With home birth, "I felt so much safer and more comfortable," she says, while hospital birth held "so much scarier consequences." She worried about being forced into medical interventions, like an epidural or a caesarian section, worried about doctors and nurses not sharing her values around breast-feeding and postbirth bonding.

Rosemary's home birth went perfectly, Claire says, and she plans on delivering her second child the same way—her loose shirt hides the bump of her current four-month pregnancy. Her parents, however, thought she was crazy. Claire's mother, in particular, doesn't understand her daughter's all-consuming brand of motherhood and frequently asks her, "If you stay at home, what's *your* identity going to be?"

"My mom wanted her [Rosemary] to cry it out!" says Claire indignantly, referring to the method, popularized by pediatric sleep expert Dr. Richard Ferber, of training babies to self-soothe by allowing them to cry them-selves to sleep for longer and longer time periods. For many DIY parents, crying it out is the moral equivalent of putting bourbon in a baby bottle.

"Gosh, that sounds like my mom!" says Anne with a sigh. "Mine are freaking out because she's not vaccinated," she adds, gesturing toward her daughter.

All three women nod.

The women, Gina explains, believe in vaccinating their children only on a selective or delayed basis. This often causes friction with their more traditionally minded families.

"My mother-in-law is head of infection control for one of the area's largest hospitals," she says, her sweater inching up to reveal a star tattoo on her wrist. "We just lie and tell her we're fully vaccinated."

"He's only been vaccinated once, because I felt pressured," says Anne, of her son. "I'm waiting until he's five. My feeling is that they can get their immunities from daily living. I don't trust what they're putting in those things."

"I don't know anybody who actually does every vaccine," says Gina.

"The CDC schedule?" Claire snorts, referring to the Centers for Disease Control's vaccine schedule, considered the standard by mainstream medicine. "Nobody. Among people like us, I'd be scared to say that she *had* had a vaccine."

Gina, a former sommelier whose short dark hair and tinkling laugh give her a pixielike demeanor, became interested in natural parenting when she became pregnant with her son. Scared by stories of awful hospital births—forced C-sections, women made to lie on their backs when they wanted to squat, unnecessary episiotomies—she began to research alternative methods.

"I wanted to own my own birth," she says as she scoops her son up and begins to breast-feed. "I guess that was my definition of feminism. Whatever I had to do to empower myself was what I was going to do."

That initial research into alternative birthing methods "completely changed the course of my life," Gina says. She became connected to a strong and vibrant community of like-minded women, women who were interested not only in alternative birth, but in all kinds of alternative parenting practices. She ended up giving birth with the help of a doula and a self-hypnosis program, laboring for thirty-eight hours without painkillers. Afterward, she was so impressed with the doula's work she decided to train to become one herself. She's now attended several dozen births in the Chicago area, and the natural parenting community has "completely taken over [her] life."

When the recession fell, Gina decided that perhaps this was a sign she should stay home. Though living on her husband's sixth-grade-teacher salary hasn't been easy, she feels she wouldn't be able to have as close a relationship with her son as she does if she were still working—at two, he still breast-feeds, and she tries hard to follow his feeding and sleeping cues. If she was working full-time she wouldn't be able to cook from scratch or use cloth diapers as easily, all important parts of natural parenting.

While she never envisioned herself as a stay-at-home mom, she loves it, she says. Embracing the role, she now blogs about motherhood, homemaking, and being a doula under the name Hipster Homemaker. She feels that by practicing eco-friendly natural parenting, she's part of a revolution.

"This is the new wave of feminism," she says, stroking her son Cooper's silky blond hair. "Women who grow their own food and make their own diapers. Women taking back the home. This is my domain."

## FROM BABY TRAINING TO BABYWEARING: THE RISE OF DIY PARENTING

The 1950s mom would have laughed at the idea of homeschooling or home birth. Part of living in an authority-loving, paternalistic society was deferring to experts like doctors and teachers. Part of living in a society where homogeneity was valued meant going with the flow. You gave birth at the local hospital like everyone else. Your kids went to the local public or parochial school, unless you were especially wealthy. In any case, the economy of midcentury America was less competitive and less "winner take all," so parents did not spend nearly as much time strategizing about how to get their children any possible advantage. In fact, parents usually spent less time worrying about their kids in general. Kids were expected to defer to all adults. Knowing your neighbor would discipline Johnny if she saw him playing in the road eased some of the burden off parents.

All this led to an attitude toward parenting that was somewhat more . . . relaxed than what you see today. That stereotypical 1950s homemaker drinking a cocktail while the kids played kick-the-can till dark? She really existed.

Today parents are expected to be the total authorities in their children's lives. Parents are taught to question everything they hear and make sure it "feels right" for their particular family. This can be empowering but also exhausting—every vaccine and preschool and baby-food brand must be rigorously vetted by Mom or Dad (usually Mom). A neighbor wouldn't dare discipline your child. Even if you know your neighbors—and many of us don't—you are likely to have totally different ideologies about discipline and child rearing. Increasingly, the neighbor won't even give your child a snack, since she doesn't know what dietary philosophy you might adhere to. Is sugar okay? Is gluten? Is meat? Motherhood becomes, in the words of academics Susan J. Douglas and Meredith W. Michaels, "an individual achievement, something you do alone, and you alone can screw up."[1] Mom is not just Mom, she's also teacher, nutritionist, doctor, cook, and so on. No wonder 70 percent of Americans say motherhood is harder today than it was twenty or thirty years ago![2]

The story of parenting in the twentieth century is about a slow move from a cold, expert-focused, authoritarian style of child rearing to the warm, ultra-intense, DIY style we see today. How did we get from there to here?

A hundred years ago, Americans were all about rigid, hands-off parenting. ("If you must, kiss them once on the forehead when they say goodnight. Shake hands with them in the morning," advised early-twentieth-century psychologist John Watson in his 1928 book of parenting advice.) Through midcentury, "scientific" child-rearing advice was all the rage. Experts advocated rigid regimens for sleeping, eating, and potty training. These experts lamented the "incompetence and inconsistency of mothers, and the social woes they caused," writes Ann Hulbert in her marvelous 2003 book *Raising America: Experts, Parents, and a Century of Advice About Children*.[3] Midcentury mothers were cautioned against "momism," the kind of overly close, overly protective parenting that would turn out sissies and weaklings—a real cultural fear in the paranoid, macho Cold War era.

Postwar parenting guru Dr. Benjamin Spock was the first to challenge this ideology. "Trust yourself. You know more than you think you do," he told mothers. He encouraged women to use their instinct to feed babies when they seemed hungry and comfort them when upset, ideas which were so revolutionary at the time that Vice President Spiro Agnew even took a pause from his busy schedule to accuse Spock of corrupting the youth with his permissiveness. The tides of parenting were clearly turning.

As part of the feminist movement of the 1960s and 1970s, women continued to question the paternalism of doctors and child-rearing experts (even Spock). In 1971, the Boston Women's Health Book Collective published *Our Bodies, Ourselves,* a health care guide written to help women empower themselves to make their own medical and childbearing decisions. The book helped launch the so-called women's health movement, which sparked interest in natural parenting techniques like home birth and extended breast-feeding.

At the same time, the idea of communal solutions for child care was receding further out of reach. In 1971, the Comprehensive Child

Development Act, which would have established a federally funded, locally controlled system of day care, passed Congress with broad bipartisan support. But Nixon vetoed the act, denouncing it as a Soviet-style threat to the nuclear family.

By the 1980s, parenting was becoming an increasingly anxious and intense activity. As mothers continued to enter the workforce, conservatives moaned about the decline of the American family and the media perpetuated endless cycles of panic about satanic day care operators and Halloween-candy poisoners. An increasingly competitive, "winner take all" economy gave rise to the idea that children must be carefully cultivated to be able to compete for the spots in elite colleges that would earn them decent jobs. Hence the "overscheduled child" being shuttled from soccer practice to tae kwon do to French lessons. Parents felt increasingly responsible for their children's success or failure, giving rise to so-called "helicopter parents" who are so consumed with their child's sense of worth that they might even do said child's homework for him.

Additionally, thanks to readily available birth control and greater access to education and jobs for women, the age of first-time parents had risen dramatically. In 1970, the average age of a first-time mom was 21.4; by the mid-1980s it was 24. By 2000, nearly 25. People are now having fewer kids—the average woman in 1960 had more than 3.5 children. By 1990, she had just over 2. Yet by 1997, there were 5 times more parenting books sold than in 1975.[4]

Older parents with fewer kids had the time and resources to invest heavily in the cultivation of their children. They wanted to do everything right. Throughout the 1990s, the general anxieties about the environment, the food supply, and the education system grew, hitting parents particularly hard. Many began investing larger amounts of time in protecting children from the outside world. Everything became suspect—food, vaccines, public schools, day care. The media and corporations encouraged this kind of suspicion, often stepping in to sell products—organic baby food! Baby Einstein!—meant to fill the gap that public systems like the FDA and the public schools were supposedly leaving open. All this led to the growth of what historian Stephanie Coontz calls "the myth of parental omnipotence."[5]

"As a historian, I suspect that the truly dysfunctional thing about

American parenting is that it is made out to be such a frighteningly pivotal, private and exclusive job," Coontz writes. "Modern discussions of maternal employment, day care, divorce, and single parenthood are distorted by the myth that parents can or should be solely responsible for how their children grow."[6]

As psychologist Madeline Levine put it: "Never before have parents been so (mistakenly) convinced that their every move has a ripple effect into their child's future success."[7]

Then came Dr. Sears.

## ATTACHMENT PARENTING: THE APOTHEOSIS OF DIY PARENTING

If you live near any major or medium-sized city or college town, chances are you've seen parents walking around with their babies tucked snugly into cloth slings tied to their chests. This may just be for convenience— look, Ma, no hands!—or it may be that these parents are AP-ers.

Attachment parenting (or "AP" among the cognoscenti) has become the dominant parenting philosophy in many parts of America in the early twenty-first century. In her memoir *Poser,* Seattle writer Claire Dederer recalls her own experience as a new mother: "There were many ideas extant about parenting, but you wouldn't know it to visit North Seattle (or, based on friends' reports, West Los Angeles or Brooklyn or Portland, Oregon, or any other liberal bubble town). In North Seattle, there was attachment parenting, and that was about it."[8]

Dr. William Sears, the father of modern attachment parenting, is the most influential parenting guru of the new millennium, the Dr. Spock for Gens X and Y. The California pediatrician first introduced his philosophies in 1992's *The Baby Book,* which has sold more than 1.5 million copies. He later codified these philosophies in 2001's *The Attachment Parenting Book,* which introduced a generation of parents to the "7 Baby B's" of attachment parenting: birth bonding (mother and baby should be together 24/7 for at least the first six weeks of life), breast-feeding (extended, if possible), babywearing (carrying your baby on your body rather than putting him in a stroller or baby seat), bed sharing (sleeping with baby in the adult bed), belief in baby's cries (crying is a sign of baby's distress; never let a baby "cry it out"), beware of baby trainers (don't try to put a baby on a sleep or eating schedule for your convenience), and balance and boundaries.

Sears claims the Baby B's help create secure "attachment"—a durable parent-child bond that will supposedly protect children from the slings and arrows of life. Expounding on what's known in psychology as attachment theory, Sears theorizes that if some attachment is good, more is better. A parent's job is to carefully pay attention to baby's "cues" in order to more immediately meet their needs. "The first step in learning to guide your child is becoming an expert in your child," he writes.

In addition to *The Baby Book* and *The Attachment Parenting Book*, "Dr. Bill," as Sears calls himself, has published twenty-eight other child-rearing books, including the evangelical-oriented *The Complete Book of Christian Parenting and Child Care* (Sears and his wife, Martha, are Catholics turned evangelical Christians turned Catholics again). He is a consulting pediatrician for *Parenting* magazine (official circulation 2.23 million,[9] but read by anyone who's ever waited in an ob-gyn office) and the official pediatrician of the website Parenting.com. The Sears empire includes Sears's three physician sons, seen on the home page of Sears's extensive website wearing stethoscopes over their necks and smiling kindly like younger, handsomer Marcus Welbys. "Dr. Jim" Sears is a cohost on the popular CBS medical talk show *The Doctors*. "Dr. Bob" Sears, who has written a bestselling antivaccine book, appears regularly on shows like *The Ellen DeGeneres Show* and *Dr. Phil*. "Dr. Peter" Sears, the coauthor of two Sears-brand books on childhood nutrition, is the most recent addition. William Sears's reach also extends to food and child care products—Sears sells an extensive line of natural child care items, such as Cool Fuel "all-natural" kids' snack bars ($16.99 for eighteen bars) and supplements like Immune Pom-Blueberry Fruit Chews with "Wellmune" ($22.95 for a one-month supply). For $595, you can sign up to become a Sears-certified healthy-living coach; classes are taught via Sears's "eCampus." Graduates who hope to set up shop as healthy-living coaches can buy, for an additional fee, marketing materials for their new businesses.

It is impossible to be a new parent today and not have been influenced by Sears's ideology. Sears's ideas—keeping babies in slings, co-sleeping, extended breast-feeding—have become thoroughly part of the norm for educated parents, even those who don't actually practice AP (attachment parenting, like ballet or Mandarin, is always "practiced"). It has, as parenting-book author Pamela Druckerman noted, become the "new common sense" for American parents.[10]

Many of the DIY parents featured in this chapter practice some form of attachment parenting, or at least have been influenced by the philosophy. Attachment parenting fits right into the twenty-first-century progressive ethos of self-sufficiency, sustainability, and the elevation of the "natural." For eco-conscious parents, cloth diapering and making DIY baby food are appealing. For parents disgusted with the modern rat race, ancient practices like babywearing and co-sleeping seem to offer a connection to a simpler way of life. For children of stressed-out baby boomers, the idea of a slower, more instinct-based way of parenting makes sense.

## SMARTER, HAPPIER, BETTER: THE CLAIMS OF DIY PARENTING

The claims for DIY-parenting styles such as AP can sometimes sound as bombastic as a late-night infomercial. Attachment parenting, Sears writes, "immunizes children against many of the social and emotional diseases which plague our society," producing children who are "compassionate," "caring," "admirable," "affectionate," "confident," and "accomplished" ("faster than a speeding bullet," "more powerful than a locomotive," and "able to leap tall buildings in a single bound" seem to have been left off the list!). As Sears openly states, children raised with the AP method are "smarter" and "will turn out better than if you hadn't practiced attachment parenting."

Mothers who practice extended breast-feeding are promised results ranging from better emotional health to fewer allergies.

"Breast-feeding a toddler helps with the child's ability to mature," says La Leche League. "The closeness and availability of the mother through breast-feeding is one of the best ways to help toddlers grow emotionally . . . Your milk continues to provide immunities and vitamins, and can help protect your toddler from illness and allergies."[11]

Diaper Free Baby, a website dedicated to "elimination communication" — allowing babies to go diaperless by watching their faces for signs of potty need, then holding them over a bowl or plastic potty—touts the "75 benefits of elimination communication." These alleged benefits range from "Reduces the risk of diaper rash" to "Encourages the development of a trusting relationship" to "Supports babies in developing self-confidence from infancy."

Though elimination communication may seem marginal, it's grown increasingly common in recent years. Since its inception in 2004, Diaper Free Baby has established support groups in thirty-nine states and sixteen different countries.

DIY parents are also promised closer relationships with their children. "I feel emotionally invested in my children," says one parent quoted in Sears's *The Attachment Parenting Book*. "I have spoken to other parents who don't seem to be as emotionally invested in their children, and I think they are missing out on one of the best experiences in life." Economic and environmental benefits are also a draw. "Attachment parenting is better for parents, better for babies and better for the earth. It really IS a much better way!" reads the tagline of A Much Better Way, a popular "natural family living" site. The site features articles on topics like the negative environmental impact of formula feeding, frightening videos of traumatic-looking hospital births, and sales on products like "Swaddlebees Econappi" cloth diapers.

Since the benefits of DIY parenting are thought to be so huge, it's not surprising that other types of child rearing are considered lacking, perhaps even harmful. And with DIY parenting, the easy or convenient option seems almost inevitably the bad one. Yes to extended breast-feeding. No to formula. Yes to home birth or natural birth. No to hospital birth with painkillers. Yes to co-sleeping. No to letting baby "cry it out" as they fall asleep.

*Mothering* magazine, the publication of record for DIY parents, warns of the dire consequences of letting babies cry it out: "there is no doubt that repeated lack of responsiveness to a baby's cries—even for only five minutes at a time—is potentially damaging to the baby's mental health . . . possibly leading to feelings of powerlessness, low self-esteem, and chronic anxiety later in life." Yikes.

Mothers who don't breast-feed are warned that they're making their children obese, stupid, sick, or worse. Claire, the Chicago mom, mentions how sad it is that women don't know that breast-feeding can reduce your risk of breast cancer by 60 percent (according to the American Cancer

Association, "some studies have shown that breast-feeding slightly lowers breast cancer risk, especially if the breast-feeding lasts 1½ to 2 years").[12]

Hospital births are often portrayed as Dantean trips into an underworld of screaming women; callous, Pitocin-pushing nurses; and knife-happy obstetricians.

In Ricki Lake's influential 2008 documentary, *The Business of Being Born,* a French obstetrician is brought before the cameras to claim that C-sections prevent moms from bonding with their babies. "It's simple," he says. "If monkeys give birth by Cesarean section, the mother is not interested in her baby."

No wonder women like Claire are scared to give birth in hospitals.

In the past few years, the term "birth rape" has even been thrown around to describe traumatic, disempowering hospital births. Sheryl, the owner of the A Much Better Way website, characterizes her first birth that way.

"The birth was an unnecessary induction at thirty-eight weeks," Sheryl tells me. "It was violent, traumatic, and one I definitely characterize as birth rape (in every sense of the word). I had flashbacks for years. It changed everything about who I am."

Her second birth was a "UC"—natural-mom slang for "unassisted childbirth," or home birth without a midwife or attendant.

It's not hard to see why so many parents gravitate toward DIY parenting. The way these parenting styles are promoted, it seems that the stakes are high, the results black-and-white. An unmedicated childbirth is "calm and natural," while a C-section leaves you unable to bond with your baby. Extended breast-feeding will produce a secure, happy toddler, while early weaning leaves a sickly future obese person. Carefully controlled diets give children the immunities to eschew vaccines, while rice cereal introduced a bit too early leaves a child ridden with allergies.

If you could control these things, why wouldn't you?

## FROM HOME BIRTHING TO HOMESCHOOLING: MOTHER AS EXPERT

Skepticism and suspicion toward communal institutions—doctors, schools, public health organizations, day cares—are central to the

DIY-parenting philosophy. When you don't feel safe giving birth in a hospital, when you don't trust your pediatrician or the CDC's vaccine recommendations, when you don't trust commercially available baby food, when you don't believe in day care or think schools are adequate, what do you do?

You do it yourself. Hence the dizzying rise of practices like home birth, homeschooling, vaccine refusal, and DIY cooking and gardening, and the increasingly negative attitude toward communal solutions like day care and public schools.

Sears and other DIY-parenting gurus encourage skepticism by privileging the idea of maternal instinct over the knowledge of experts like pediatricians or child-development researchers: "'What I learned from attachment parenting is that there is no expert better than me for my baby,'" Sears writes, quoting an AP parent.

"Doctors are just technicians in white coats," says Shannon Hayes, the Radical Homemaker—we'll meet her in chapter 8. "I'm the mother."

Home birth is a prime example of the "mother knows best" philosophy. Once considered extremely fringe, the domain of the kind of women who roll their own tampons out of wheatgrass, it's now become an aspirational goal of the educated classes. Rates of home births rose 20 percent between 2004 and 2008, with a 94 percent increase among white women—in 2008, 1 in 98 white women had their babies at home (compared with 1 in 357 black women and 1 in 500 Hispanic women).[13]

The popularity of home birth is driven by a profound and widespread dissatisfaction with the current standard of care in American hospitals. Many believe that hospital births are overmedicalized, with doctors and nurses pushing for unnecessary medicines and procedures to speed up the process. Home-birth advocates point to the United States' climbing C-section rate (32 percent of all births in 2010)[14] as evidence of the problems with contemporary obstetrics. Many also say that hospitals are simply unnecessary for healthy women and that birth should not be treated as a medical emergency.

DIY-parenting culture has embraced the idea that the medical system is impossibly flawed and the best solution is giving full control back to Mom.

For some mothers, a devotion to DIY covers up gaps in our country's social safety net. Janelle, a thirty-three-year-old mom of four in the

Philadelphia suburbs, can't afford health insurance. Janelle's a stay-at-home mom, while her husband is a self-employed tiling installer whose employment has been sketchy since the recession hit. But, she says defiantly, she doesn't need insurance anyway.

"We consider our insurance taking care of ourselves, being healthy, and eating organic foods rather than spend a ridiculous amount of money we don't have each month," she says.

And while she and her husband can't afford private school, Janelle says she will "never" send her kids to public school because she doesn't "agree with the public school system at all." She believes in "gentle" education that allows kids to learn at their own pace and develops their creativity. So she, like a growing number of other mothers, doesn't send her children to school at all.

## MOM AS TEACHER: HOMESCHOOLING AS DIY PARENTING IN ACTION

When I was a kid in the 1980s, the only homeschoolers I ever met were the children of religious extremists (and this being the South, the bar for religious extremism was set pretty high). These homeschoolers dressed funny, were clueless about pop culture, and generally didn't fit in with the little Baptists and Methodists on our YMCA basketball team.

Today, however, a homeschooled child might well be the whimsically named spawn of educated creative-class city dwellers (the number of homeschoolers in New York, for example, grew by 36 percent in the past eight years).[15] And they will be in good company.

The number of homeschooled American children leapt from 850,000 in 1999 to 1.1 million in 2003 to 1.5 million in 2007,[16] though actual numbers may be much higher. As Stanford political scientist Rob Reich writes, "Once a fringe phenomenon, home schooling is legal in every of the fifty states and is widely considered the fastest growing sector of K–12 schooling."[17]

Indeed, homeschooling is growing fast among educated, liberal parents, the type most likely to embrace hyperattached parenting styles. For many, homeschooling is a logical next step on the natural-parenting path.

Claire, the mom from the Chicago birth center, plans on "unschooling" her children. Unschooling is an increasingly popular method of homeschooling that involves, in a nutshell, allowing kids to learn about whatever they want to, whenever they want to. And, conversely, not forcing them to learn anything they don't want to until they're "ready" (and therefore want to).

"It's like homeschooling, except I'm not the teacher, she is," Claire says, nodding toward fourteen-month-old Rosemary. "This is the way I wish I had been allowed to learn—complete and total freedom to study however you want."

Sheryl, the forty-one-year-old owner of the A Much Better Way natural-parenting website, also unschools her children.

"I feel that school is an extremely unnatural environment for children," she says. "They only get one childhood and I want it to be full of lizards, mud, puddles, leaves, and trees."

It sounds nice, and that kind of pastoral vision of childhood is part of what makes homeschooling and unschooling so appealing. For Gen X and Y parents who remember being unhappy in school, homeschooling has an especially emotional pull.

"I hated school when I was growing up," says Jen, a thirty-eight-year-old homeschooling mom in Boulder, Colorado. "I couldn't figure out why I needed to do it, why I should be excelling at these arbitrary things . . . I wanted to really give [my kids] a chance to love learning and not just memorize things. Why shouldn't kids just be able to learn to sail a boat if that's what they want to do?"

Jen and her husband initially sent their son to Montessori school, where he was anxious and unhappy. So Jen began homeschooling, which she plans on doing through high school.

In Jen's progressive community of Boulder (the kind of place where people boycott Whole Foods for being "too corporate"), most of her friends are stay-at-home homeschooling moms, all of them well educated with interesting careers behind them—writers, newspaper reporters, ER nurses. These women all turned away from their careers to throw themselves fully into the lives of their children. What was more important? they asked. Having a high-powered career or raising the happiest, healthiest children by having the time to meet their individual needs on a one-on-one basis?

Courtney, a thirty-one-year-old crafty, gardening, from-scratch-cooking stay-at-home mom in Iowa City, says she's interested in exploring homeschooling when her son's old enough, since she's concerned about the school environment.

"I'd worry about what my son was eating at lunch, and the advertising at schools, and the pop in vending machines, and the cleaning solutions they use on the floors," she says. "I kind of want to opt out because it's easier to maintain a little bit of a bubble at home."

Many of the homeschooling parents I've talked to seem to simply be loath to give up quality time with their kids. After all, when you've nursed a child through toddlerhood, sending her off to preschool might seem like an untenable separation. Plus, for women who have centered their entire lives around intensive child rearing, homeschooling keeps a void from opening up.

"I really, really believe that kids need their parents," Janelle says. "So many of our society's problems are stemming from the fact that from six weeks on we stick our kids in child care, they go to school at five, and they go off to college at eighteen."

## "YOU JUST HAVE TO FOLLOW YOUR OWN HEART": DIY PARENTING AND THE ANTIVACCINE MOVEMENT

The "mother knows best" attitude of DIY parenting that leads to parents opting out of traditional establishments can take a dangerous turn. The prime example of this is the antivaccine movement. This is not to say that all parents who practice natural or attachment parenting are against childhood vaccines. But many are. And, like DIY parenting itself, antivaccine attitudes are spreading.

A twenty-nine-year-old friend of mine recently brought her baby daughter to her Chapel Hill pediatrician for her first round of vaccines. Before they could even sit down, the doctor launched into a defensive dialogue about the importance of vaccines for preventing deadly diseases. "Uh, of course," agreed my friend, who happens to have a degree in public health.

"Oh, good," the doctor said, sighing. "I have to deal with so many parents who fight me every step of the way."

Vaccine refusal has become its own epidemic in America over the past decade. Initial fears about a vaccine-autism connection were sparked by a single 1998 paper by British doctor Andrew Wakefield, who was later found to have fabricated data and subsequently lost his medical license. Though numerous studies have since failed to find any connection between vaccines and autism, fears about immunization have metastasized. Today antivaccine parents cite everything from worries about mercury in vaccines to the idea that contracting a disease "naturally" is better for a child's overall health. While these fears are roundly dismissed by the scientific and medical community, they continue to influence millions of parents. No amount of reassurance from experts seems to help, and skepticism of vaccines has become a common thread linking many natural parents.

Numbers of unvaccinated children have spiked in the past ten years, especially in progressive, affluent parts of the country like Northern California and Boulder, Colorado. In California, for example, numbers of schoolchildren with "personal-belief waivers" excusing them from vaccines doubled in the first decade of the twenty-first century. In some crunchy Northern California counties, the number of kids with these personal-belief waivers exceeds 10 percent. At some progressive private schools, unvaccinated kids are the majority—at one San Diego–area private school, for example, 83 percent of the kids have personal-belief waivers.[18]

Since a vaccine's success depends on so-called herd immunity, about 90 percent of the population needs to be vaccinated in order to prevent outbreaks. As percentages of vaccinated children drop lower, outbreaks of preventable childhood diseases have begun to occur with increasing frequency. In 2011, measles cases *quadrupled* in the United States, a situation blamed on vaccine refusal.[19] In 2010, the worst whooping cough epidemic in sixty years broke out in California. Ten babies were killed, most of them still too young to be vaccinated and therefore reliant on herd immunity; the outbreak was blamed on the state's low vaccination rates. Similar outbreaks have been seen in Virginia, Minnesota, Chicago, Colorado, and other areas.

These antivaccine parents aren't stupid. Like most DIY parents, they're often highly educated, highly thoughtful people whose very thoughtfulness leads them to question authority.

"I feel like people are getting smarter. They're standing up for themselves and they're making decisions based on knowledge instead of following everybody else," said one antivaccine California mother quoted in a news story.[20]

Like many antivaccine parents, Janelle, the Pennsylvania mom, talks about her decisions in terms of freedom, personal choice, and being empowered to make her own decisions. As an attachment parent who believes in primal motherly instinct, she felt comfortable listening to her gut when it came to immunizations. When she took her oldest daughter to get her DPT vaccine, the toddler looked at the needles, looked at her mother, and said, "Don't do this to me."

Janelle felt her gut wrench. "I was like, 'Oh, you're right. My heart's telling me not to do this,'" she recalls.

Her conclusion: "You just have to follow your own heart" when it comes to medical decision-making.

She didn't have her other children vaccinated, and she's come to believe (contrary to accepted mainstream science) that vaccines are full of antifreeze and heavy metals, and that a healthy lifestyle will provide her children with strong enough immune systems to fight off disease.

For Janelle and several other mothers I talked to, vaccines are seen as a dangerous shortcut to health, a way of abnegating the real responsibilities of motherhood. The proper way to achieve health, according to Janelle, is a careful regimen of exclusive breast-feeding and organic foods.

"You need to take responsibility for your life," she says.

It's easy to look at someone like Janelle or the Chicago moms and say they're irrational, irresponsible, hippies. But at the same time, it's easy to see how they came to their conclusions.

Dr. Sears and his sons have had a major part in spreading antivaccine attitudes. In 2007 Sears's son Robert Sears published *The Vaccine Book: Making the Right Decision for Your Child,* which advocates a reduced schedule of vaccinations. In the book, Sears suggests that public health agencies like the CDC are dangerously cavalier about vaccine side effects, that vaccines should not be mandatory, and that "natural" immunity is better than vaccine immunity (hence the rise of so-called "pox parties" to infect kids with chicken pox the old-fashioned way). The book sold more than forty thousand copies, and "Dr. Bob's Alternative Vaccine Schedule" has become a mainstay of progressive parenting. Mainstream physicians, however, view this alternative schedule as dangerous nonsense. "Sears' misrepresentation of vaccine science misinforms parents trying to make the right decisions for their children," reads an aggrieved article in the journal *Pediatrics*.[21]

In vaccine skepticism, we see two larger social trends that influence New Domesticity come together: (1) the growing distrust toward conventional medicine and science, and (2) the idea that individuals—like mothers—should follow their instincts rather than defer to authorities.

On the one hand, the idea of questioning authority and doing your own research rather than blindly deferring to experts is a worthy one. In the 1950s, paternalistic doctors amputated legs and lopped off breasts without even bothering to tell patients they had cancer. The subsequent backlash—the insistence on patient autonomy and informed consent— has clearly changed our medical system for the better. The women's health movement of the 1970s, which empowered women to ask questions and challenge authority when it came to their own bodies, was revolutionary; the idea that parents would educate themselves about medical issues is a huge step forward.

But it seems clear that, at least when it comes to vaccines, this attitude has gone too far.

Advocates for "vaccine choice" defend the individual rights of the parent above any community health considerations. Peggy O'Mara, the longtime editor of *Mothering* magazine, tells me she believes in "trusting women as experts" and teaching parents to do their own research rather than simply deferring to authority. For her, professionals like pediatricians and public health researchers should be used only as "consultants." O'Mara has stuck to this attitude, even when it's generated huge controversy for *Mothering*. The magazine has regularly been criticized by public health officials as being antivaccine. In 2001, the magazine featured a heavily pregnant Christine Maggiore on the cover, next to the headline "HIV+ Mothers say NO to AIDS Drugs." Maggiore, an HIV-positive activist who believed that HIV doesn't cause AIDS, was praised in the magazine for her independent thinking, portrayed as a fierce woman warrior fighting against a patriarchal medical establishment. It also praised her decision to breast-feed her two children, despite ample evidence that breast-feeding transmits HIV from mother to child. Maggiore and her baby daughter have both since died of AIDS.

Still, to O'Mara, a mother's choice is paramount. "You have to decide for yourself," she says.

## YOU MAKE ME FEEL LIKE A NATURAL WOMAN?
## DIY PARENTING AND FEMINISM

Many wonder whether DIY parenting is problematic when it comes to questions of gender equality. Do DIY parenting's ideals require that a woman subordinate herself to her family? Does the fascination with the idea of what's "natural" lead to a "biology is destiny" philosophy at odds with egalitarianism?

To begin to answer these questions, we first must understand the two different lenses through which most people view these issues. The first lens is what's often termed "liberal feminism." The second is what's often called "cultural feminism." Liberal feminism suggests that most gender inequality is culturally based. When faced with a question like "Why are women only 4.2 percent of Fortune 500 CEOs?" a liberal feminist might respond: "Because girls are socialized to be less competitive than boys, female businesswomen are punished for ambition while men are praised for it, companies don't accommodate women's needs by offering reasonable maternity leave, women still shoulder the majority of the child care," and so on.

Cultural feminism is the idea that some gender inequality is actually just "gender difference" and that we should honor women's (and men's) natural, inherent natures. When asked the CEO question, a cultural-feminist might respond: "Women are naturally less competitive than men, and why is that a bad thing? Why should 'success' be measured on a male-designed scale—why should we view a CEO as more successful than a mother of four happy, well-cared-for children? The fact that we don't honor women's natures as nurturers is frankly sexist."

In some aspects of New Domesticity, especially when it comes to parenting, we seem to be seeing a shift away from liberal feminism toward cultural feminism. In *The Paradox of Natural Mothering,* academic Chris Bobel writes about the dominance of the cultural feminist attitude in the natural-parenting community. "When I asked women to explain why they constructed a child-centered, mother-dependant, simplified lifestyle, I heard a similar refrain: natural mothering respects and reflects our nature as females," she writes. "Women are designed, with wombs, breasts, and 'the mothering hormone' (oxytocin) to nurture children. Men are not."

Many of the women I've interviewed have similar attitudes:.

"It seems like such a natural thing for a woman to do, to care for children and the home and so forth," says Sofya, the Wisconsin blogger. "I guess, maybe as a result of the feminism movement—which is good in so many ways—it came to be something people viewed negatively."

In an e-mail, Claire, the mom from the Chicago childbirth center, eloquently describes her choices as an expression of her feminism:

> Because my working mother offered me few practical skills beyond sewing on a button and reheating processed food in a microwave, I have used my time since leaving the academic sphere to re-acquire knowledge and abilities that women throughout history have taken for granted. It actually requires a decent understanding of scientific method, philosophy, education, politics, psychology, nutrition, medicine and spirituality to run a household with confidence, joy and wisdom. So am I unfulfilled and limited, when I believe I am at the forefront of a revolution in my children's learning, our country's food system, the faith of my childhood, the nourishment of our marriages, a crisis in our economy? Absolutely not. To tackle these issues and more on a daily basis from the command center of my quaint suburban home is more exciting and meaningful than I know how to communicate. And while my willingness to sacrifice my own career in favor of my husband's may be more June Cleaver than Betty Friedan, in light of the direction I see our nation's families and communities going, nothing could feel more right or more poignant to me.
>
> Choosing a simpler life does not offer me a paycheck, a pat on the back from the parents who paid for a "wasted" education, or reassurance from my feminist upbringing that screamed "You can be anything you want to be—and you damn well better want a career because we FOUGHT to shatter that glass ceiling for you, honey!" But what it does offer is worth more than any amount of money or recognition to me—the chance to fight for a shockingly healthy,

lasting marriage, the opportunity to sit and sip tea while my child brings me book after book to read to her rather than hearing her day recounted to me by a daycare worker and the endless putterings and ponderings that my kitchen, my community, my Netflix subscription, my library and my backyard have to offer. Do I sit in my pajamas some days and eat homemade ice cream and accomplish very little? Absolutely. But am I blissfully happy, intellectually fulfilled and physically healthy while doing so? I'd have to say, resoundingly, yes. So no, my feminism is not squelched, but rather best expressed through an occupation that I find vital to the authentic sustenance of my family and community.

Natural mothering does have its roots in a reaction against 1960s and '70s liberal feminism. Peggy O'Mara, the editor of *Mothering* magazine, points out that *Mothering* was founded in 1976, at a time when, as she says, "the act of mothering was being really maligned by the feminist rhetoric."

But many don't agree that "biological equals natural equals best." Some experts, in fact, think it's a flat-out wrong. We don't go around killing our rivals just because it's natural, they say. We don't smile upon men who cheat on their wives with younger women, even though such behavior might be evolutionarily adaptive. Evolutionary and biological answers only get you so far; the reliance on them is a glib and shallow, if undeniably popular, way of understanding human behavior.

"Although we tend to think that, perhaps because of hormones, there is something natural about fathers being more hands-off, biology offers us a lot more flexibility than we might think," points out psychologist Cordelia Fine, a sharp critic of biology-as-destiny thinking.[22]

As Chris Bobel writes, the goal of natural parenting—"cultivating a gentler, less material, more family-centered social climate"—is worthy, but the philosophy can reinforce sexist, limiting visions of womanhood. "The natural mothering rationale accommodates patriarchal visions of women and mothers," she writes. Reinforcing the idea that women are simply natural caregivers is basically a modern take on the "a woman's place is in the kitchen" blather of yore. Venerable French thinker Elisabeth Badinter made international waves in 2012 with her ferocious anti-natural-parenting polemic *The Conflict,* in which she suggests that "women are falling victim to sociobiological fictions that reduce them to the status of female mammals."[23] She describes natural parenting as "a movement dressed in the guise of a modern, moral cause that worships all things natural."[24]

According to Badinter, by buying into natural parenting women are voluntarily holding out their wrists for a new kind of shackles. This time, instead of being oppressed by men, they're allowing themselves to be oppressed by babies and by the ever-higher bar of Good Motherhood. Time-consuming natural mothering—the cloth diapers, the constant attachment, the obsessive controlling of their children's environment— limits women's ambitions and turns them into servants to their children. Since they believe it's "natural," they find it hard to question.

In reading Sears's book, it's not hard to see why some parents find attachment parenting oppressive. The goal of Sears's attachment parenting seems to be a near-supernatural melding of mother and baby. Sears talks frequently of developing a "sixth sense" or being completely "in tune" with a baby, and writes that when an AP mother is separated from her baby "she feels as if part of herself is missing." He writes approvingly of mothers who can bear to be apart from their children for only short time periods and "can't imagine anything that's more fun or satisfying" than being with baby. He glowingly describes how his own wife always sets her watch to California time when she travels, to keep herself connected to her children and know what they're doing from minute to minute. While Sears claims to support working mothers, he's also written that moms should ideally work from home and that mothers who choose to work might simply not "understand how disruptive that is to the well-being of their babies."[25] Sears and his wife have also suggested that moms borrow money in order to quit their jobs. In fact, they gave money to their sons' wives to allow them to stay home. "It was the least we could do," said Martha Sears in *Time* magazine.[26]

"Basically, I think the idea of attachment parenting is a way to force women to cut back on their role in the workplace," says sociologist Louise Roth, herself the mother of three young children.

Reading things like the following, from natural-parenting guru and La Leche League affiliate Dr. George Wootan, can indeed make one more than a little queasy:

> Let me submit to you that the need for mother is as strong in a toddler as the need for food, and that there is no substitute for a securely attached mother . . .

If he scrapes his knee, or gets his feelings hurt, he can't put his need on hold for two hours until Mommy is home, and the babysitter—*or even Daddy* [emphasis added]—just won't do as well as if Mommy was there . . . I believe that many women return to work not out of necessity, but because they (or their spouses) want to maintain the two-income lifestyle to which they've become accustomed. These parents need to do a little soul-searching about what they really need and not sacrifice their child's best interests.

Mother is better than Daddy? Really? This raises another important question: does natural parenting, with its emphasis on mothers' natural role, discourage egalitarian parenting?

JJ, a thirty-two-year-old writer and mother of two in Los Angeles who calls herself a "natural parenting dropout," thinks that attachment parenting asks more from mothers than from fathers and tends to erode gender equality in relationships. With its focus on motherly instinct, "motherly hormones," and exclusive breast-feeding, it can be hard for Dad to find his role.

"A lot of attachment parenting—though it explicitly says otherwise—becomes very much about mom's monopoly on the babies," she says. JJ also thinks that the "rigid structure" of attachment parenting discourages dads from feeling competent and confident with their own children. "If you want men to be involved in child care, you can't tell them exactly how to do it," she says. "If there's only one way for a father to properly interact with his children, he's probably going to check out."

"Attachment-parenting philosophies really are mom-centric," agrees her husband, Alden, thirty-four. "They do somewhat disenfranchise the father."

In New Zealand, La Leche Leaguers rallied against an antismoking ad featuring a celebrity rugby player tenderly bottle-feeding his infant daughter. One might think that an ad showing such a stereotypical beefcake nurturing a child would be welcomed for promoting shared parenting.

But to hard-core Leaguers, the breast is always best. So Mom must feed, not Dad.

Melanie, the thirty-eight-year-old mom and PhD student in Austin, says "attachment parenting is the most antifeminist parenting strategy you could practice" and points out that the ideology of natural parenting can sound awfully similar to right-wing fundamentalist ideas about the sanctity of motherhood as a woman's highest calling. "You're so liberal you've swung around to where you're not that different from that Duggar woman," she says, referring to the notoriously fecund Michelle Duggar of TLC's *19 Kids and Counting* fame. The Duggars, fundamentalist Christians from Arkansas who don't believe in birth control, live a frugal, family-centric lifestyle, complete with DIY laundry detergent, homeschooling, and (in the case of the Duggar grandchildren) home birth. The Duggars may be working in the service of God, while the natural moms in this chapter are working in the service of Nature. We'll talk more about the parallels between the extreme right and the extreme left in chapter 9.

## "IF I DON'T DO THIS, I'LL BE THE WORST MOTHER EVER": THE PRESSURES OF DIY PARENTING

Through the past half century, parents have wrenched control away from patriarchal "experts" and proclaimed the validity of their own instinct. But with greater control comes greater responsibility—too much, for some.

Few understand this better than JJ, the thirty-two-year-old "natural parenting dropout" from Los Angeles.

When she first had her daughter, now three, it was a foregone conclusion that JJ would practice attachment parenting. Raised in a middle-class home in Northern California, JJ often felt neglected by her own working parents, who "paid no attention to whether I was coming or going." She vowed that when she had kids, she would give them all the attention she felt she'd missed out on. That, plus her natural inclination toward all things crunchy, made attachment parenting the obvious choice. Really, it was hardly a choice at all—everyone in JJ's social circle practiced attachment parenting, or at least claimed to.

"Attachment parenting is sort of conflated with social class," says JJ, who describes herself and her husband as living a "lean lower-middle-class existence" in status-conscious L.A. "So when you roll with educated liberal types in the big city, attachment parenting is what people do."

JJ thinks today's mania for DIY parenting is the result of the boredom felt by creative, educated women when they quit or pull back on their careers to raise children.

"Being a stay-at-home mom to one child, a baby, when you're a mom of one is not really a full-time job," she says sotto voce, as if revealing a dirty secret. "You've got a lot of other time. I think that's where all the canning and the cloth diapering and that frenzy comes in. You have this time vacuum. It really isn't that hard to look after one kid all day long."

So why did JJ and so many of her friends give up their jobs? I ask her. "It was always financial," she says, explaining that she had to leave a good university teaching job because she couldn't afford day care. "You just can't pay for child care, and you lose the career, whether you want to or not," she says.

Friends of hers who made healthier salaries still found themselves blocked by lack of maternity leave and workplace flexibility, she says.

"It's really awful to go back to work full-time when you have a six-week-old baby," she says. "When you have to choose between going back at six weeks or quitting their jobs, a lot of women chose to quit their jobs. It is really awful to go back so soon. If this was Canada and we had that yearlong leave, it would be very different for a lot of people."

But we're not Canada. And so JJ and many of her friends found themselves stay-at-home mothers, whether or not they'd ever intended to be. And, like JJ, many of them found themselves at loose ends. Immersion in high-intensity parenting seemed to fill some of that vacuum, and the idea of doing something that was better for everyone—your baby, yourself, the environment—was highly appealing to JJ's set of socially conscious peers.

But JJ quickly began to feel that she was falling short of natural-parenting ideals. Shortly after her daughter was born, JJ discovered she had insufficient milk supply for exclusive breast-feeding. Since breast-feeding is central to DIY parenting, she felt like a terrible parent.

"I thought, 'If I don't do this, I'll be the worst mother ever,'" she recalls. "[Breast-feeding] was the crucible. If I didn't, I was going to be a failure."

So JJ, like many young mothers today, went to "extraordinary lengths" to breast-feed. She worked with lactation consultants, attended breast-feeding support groups, and pumped breast milk with a mechanical pump on a nearly constant basis.

"I was pumping around the clock, every three hours," she says, groaning at the memory. "All night and all day, I was hooked up to a breast pump. I was feeding her from a bottle while I was pumping, sometimes simultaneously, then washing the pump. You have to sterilize it, so I'd spend fifteen minutes pumping, fifteen minutes sterilizing, then have two and a half hours to rest before going back through the whole process."

This obsession with being able to breast-feed wasn't just physically and emotionally taxing for JJ. "It really precluded bonding with my daughter," she says. "I could have just been feeding her formula and not dying inside."

In retrospect, JJ sees her interest in attachment parenting as being tied up with her own class anxieties. "It was like when smoking was an upper-class thing to do, and then upper-class people stopped smoking and it became a lower-class thing. [Breast-feeding] became the thing to do when you're culturally aware. It fed into my own class anxieties. Like it's trashy to buy your baby's food at Target. If you're a good and classy and clean upscale lady, then you'll make your breast-feeding work."

Exclusive breast-feeding has become symbolic of a certain kind of parenting, giving the practice a moral weight far beyond the reality of its health benefits. Recently, there's been a move by some women to question this breast-feeding mandate. In an (in)famous 2009 *Atlantic* story, "The Case Against Breast-feeding," Hanna Rosin writes that "in certain overachieving circles, breast-feeding is no longer a choice—it's a no-exceptions requirement, the ultimate badge of responsible parenting. Yet the actual health benefits of breast-feeding are surprisingly thin, far thinner than most popular literature indicates."

The extreme proponents of breast-feeding have indeed become fairly notorious for pushiness and judgment as of late (the fact that terms like "lactivist" and "breast-feeding Nazi" even exist illustrates this point), leaving women like JJ bereft when they're unable to measure up.

Suzanne, a thirty-four-year-old Los Angeles mother of two, also had trouble nursing and wound up bottle-feeding her babies. She quickly learned that this was the moral equivalent of slapping them in public. Strangers at the store would scold her about her formula use. "It was like, 'Oh my God, why aren't you breast-feeding?'" she recalls grimly. "'Aren't you worried?! Are you sure you should take him outside? Aren't you worried his immune system is compromised?'"

Though groups like La Leche League, originally started by a group of

Catholic housewives in the 1950s, have been promoting breast-feeding since then, the pressures didn't use to be nearly as intense.

"My mom didn't breast-feed any of her three children, and she basically thought I was crazy for being hung up on this," JJ says. When her sisters had their babies a decade or so ago, it was not a big deal. But by the time her middle sister had her son two years ago, her "class-conscious" husband pressured her to breast-feed.

Eventually, JJ decided that the pressures of DIY parenting were bad for her and bad for her children. She went back to work as a writer and has taken what she describes as a pragmatic approach to motherhood. This has meant losing certain friendships with women who remained wrapped up in all-consuming child rearing.

"This really time-consuming parenting precludes Mom having a life and precludes Mom maintaining a sense of self," she says. "Women become totally subservient to their role of mother, and they become mothers [above] all the other parts of their identity . . . It's maddening to watch how many women become erased by motherhood."

Ultimately, JJ thinks the judgment surrounding parenting choices comes from fear.

"We're all very insecure," she says. "Maybe it's different in small towns, but in L.A. none of us are going about parenting the way our parents raised us . . . I'm making it up as I go along. So everything is a choice. And when everything is a choice, it means you could have chosen something different. That makes mothers desperately insecure, myself included. What if I'm making my kids stupid for feeding them jarred foods? What if there's more BPA in there than I had understood? What if they're right and I'm wrong?"

## BUT IS IT REALLY BETTER?

At the end of the day, there's very little evidence to suggest that DIY parenting benefits children more than other loving parenting strategies. Some of the foundational principles of DIY parenting—breast is always best, "crying it out" is bad, day care is harmful—seem to be based on faulty or nonexistent data.

Critics point out that Sears's attachment-parenting philosophy is derived from attachment theory, the mid-twentieth-century idea that children need to form secure attachments to their caregivers. No one disputes this. But attachment theory studied children who were severely neglected or institutionalized, not kids whose parents failed to co-sleep or babywear. Just because neglect is bad doesn't mean hypercloseness is best.

"There is a very big difference between neglecting a child and not being with the child all the time," sociologist Louise Roth tells me.

Extended breast-feeding, the topic of much teeth-gnashing for stressed-out new moms, has surprisingly thin data. While it's clear that breast-feeding can confer some important immunological benefits to babies, the idea that it's "liquid gold" that will make for smarter, thinner, healthier adults has little evidence to back it up. But the idea that it might has generated a massive amount of guilt for moms, especially working moms. The idea that allowing babies to cry it out will cause brain damage, central to attachment parenting, is not scientifically supported. In fact, a recent study in the journal *Paediatrics* reported that allowing for controlled crying reduced infant sleep problems and cut down on maternal depression, and that children left to cry it out did not show any long-term physical or mental health effects.[27]

Yet the media continues to take advantage of the emotional issue with alarmist stories of little scientific merit. The fact that crying raises cortisol (a stress hormone) has led to headlines like "Avoid putting the under-threes in daycare if you can."[28] Yet many things raise cortisol levels (like brushing your teeth), and there's no evidence that this causes harm. And children placed in quality day cares have consistently been shown to do just as well as children who stay at home.[29]

The claim that DIY parenting is simply a return to our roots—"this is the way people have always parented," as Claire said, or, in the words of Attachment Parenting International, "Attachment Parenting isn't new. In many ways, it is a return to the instinctual behaviors of our ancestors"—is also disputed by experts.

Anthropologist David Lancy, author of *The Anthropology of Childhood*, points out that in developing countries mothers may frequently nurse their babies but otherwise pay them "relatively little attention."[30] In fact, he says most developing-world mothers practice what he calls "detachment parenting," taking a utilitarian view of babies as future workers and investing relatively little in them emotionally, since they often die from disease at an early age. And while American attachment parents believe that stimulating babies is crucial and natural, Lancy notes that mother-child play is considered "absurd" in much of the developing world.

In Lancy's view, attachment parenting is little more than a "secular religion," based on a confused interpretation of mid-twentieth-century attachment theory.

While kids clearly need love, nutrition, and security, it doesn't seem to matter much exactly how this is given. A kid who grows up co-sleeping, eating homemade bread, and being homeschooled is unlikely to have any clear advantage over a kid who grows up crying it out, eating Jif peanut butter sandwiches, and attending decent public schools.

Yet DIY parenting has grown so popular because it seems to fill a deep-seated need for parental control in an anxious world. It attempts to fill a gap left by our often-lacking social safety net, which doesn't provide us with safe enough food systems, good enough schools, or a responsive enough medical system. It also seems to offer an "out" for women who can't or don't wish to find outside employment. If it's "necessary" to stay home and bond with baby, then of course Mom isn't working. It also seems to appeal to creative, educated moms, who are used to cerebral work and constant stimulation, something traditional homemaking and child care don't necessarily provide.

## "I DON'T NEED THE GOVERNMENT TO LOOK OUT FOR ME, BECAUSE I CAN LOOK OUT FOR ME": IS DIY PARENTING SELFISH?

As is the case with vaccine refusal, there are ways in which DIY parenting can privilege extreme individualism at the expense of the group. So we must ask ourselves whether, by focusing so much attention and energy on the minute needs of one's own child, the larger society suffers. For example: when affluent, educated parents decide to homeschool, public schools lose out on involved PTA parents and capable school-improvement advocates. Or when parents spend all their money and energy searching for the best organic baby products, there's little energy left to lobby for consumer product regulations that might benefit everyone.

In her book *Perfect Madness,* about the rise of obsessive, time-consuming parenting, Judith Warner writes, "Our neurotic quest to perfect the mechanics of mothering can be interpreted as an effort to do on an individual level what we've stopped trying to do on a society-wide one."

Back at the end of the nineteenth century and the beginning of the twentieth century, everyone's kids, rich and poor alike, were vulnerable to the same problems: a banker's child could die of listeria from unpasteurized milk just as easily as a chimney sweep's child. Therefore, parents with high socioeconomic status—the ones with the greatest social and political clout—advocated for policy changes that ultimately benefited everybody. These policy changes included the creation of the federal United States Children's Bureau (1912) to deal with child welfare and health needs; the passing of the Pure Food and Drug Act (1906), which banned the sale of mislabeled and adulterated food products; and the passing of a number of school-reform bills. It was during this period—now known as the Progressive Era—that high school education became widely available to the middle class, that federally funded prenatal clinics were built across America, and that the profession of social work was born. Infant mortality took a steep decline, diseases like diphtheria and typhus decreased sharply, and day-to-day food safety increased hugely. In 1880, a bag of candy might contain lead, mercury, or chromium, while milk could be diluted with water or adulterated with chalk.[31] Half a century later, consumer protection laws meant a mother could serve her children store-bought milk without worry.

Ultimately, the Progressive Era gave way to pressure from business and political interests, who warned that such collective reforms were dangerously socialist and undermined economic interests. That attitude has more or less informed the way the United States has dealt with progressive reforms ever since—as a battle between private business interests and public good.

Historian Janet Golden observes that we've abandoned the idea of communal good in favor of individual, family-focused solutions. "We don't have a collective political sense that *all* of our children are our future citizens," she says. "We twenty-first-century dwellers have been waiting over one hundred years for universal prenatal care. We don't have that. We don't have a movement for universal subsidized high-quality day care . . . I don't see people out there demanding that anymore." That's a scary thought.

The rise of DIY parenting means that there are fewer people fighting for institutional changes like better EPA and FDA oversight, volunteering to improve the public schools, working to improve health care for everyone, etc. Ironically, much of today's "progressive" parenting is more about deregulation than regulation. While, in the words of historian Glenna Matthews, "faith in the capacities of the expert was one characteristic of the Progressive generation," today we see the exact opposite.[32] The kind of people who, one hundred years ago, would have pushed for the Pure Food and Drug Act are now advocates of making raw milk unregulated. Parents who would have crusaded to develop new vaccines to beat diseases like diphtheria and polio are now loudly proclaiming that the government has no right to force them to vaccinate their own kids. Women who might have fought for federally funded day care now say things like "I don't want strangers raising my children." In über-crunchy Portland, Oregon, a parent-led protest nearly derailed a city plan to add fluoride to the water in 2012. Though the city's lack of fluoridated water (Portland was the largest city in America without fluoride in the water) had led to rampant tooth decay, especially among the children of the poor, the suspicious antifluoride faction felt their right to keep fluoride away from their own families was paramount.

"We have the right to raise our families the way we want," says Janelle, the Pennsylvania mom, who says she does her best to educate fellow parents on their right to not vaccinate their children.

"I feel strongly that short of checking for signs of abuse or neglect, the government should entrust families to make their own decisions concerning both education and health care," says Claire, the Chicago mom.

Claire, of course, is an educated woman who cares deeply about her daughter and goes to great lengths to keep her safe and healthy. Her homeschooling is informed by her familiarity with educational theorists like John Holt and thinkers like Ivan Illich. She's done her homework, and it makes sense that she thinks the government doesn't have the right to second-guess her.

As Golden explains, "people with political power don't feel that their own children are at particular risk" these days. We've moved far away from the world of the late nineteenth century, when disease knew no social bounds. For a dramatic example, look at the presidents of the

United States. In the decades leading up to the Progressive Era, *every single* American president suffered the death of at least one young child, usually due to infectious disease. The death of a president's child today would be a frightfully rare and shocking incident, as would the death of any child born to parents of middle or high socioeconomic status.

The United States still has one of the worst infant mortality rates in the developed world, and African-American babies are nearly twice as likely as the average to die within the first year of life.[33] An educated Caucasian like Claire, the young woman who felt that hospital birth held "so much scarier consequences" than home birth, is the kind of woman most likely to worry about her birth experience. She's also the kind of woman who, by dint of her social class, is by far the least likely to experience the tragedy of a baby's death.

Golden sees parental uninterest in collective solutions as part of a larger "decline in the social contract," one that happens to be particularly evident in the world of children. "As a scholar, I'm very disturbed that we have more [media] articles about toxins in the home than the fact that we live in a country where we don't have universal prenatal care," she says. "We've moved from collective concern about infant and child welfare into this very privatized focus on 'my child' and this intensive child-rearing."

Carolyn Hough, an anthropologist who has studied modern motherhood, agrees. "I can so relate to that frustration and that feeling that the system is broken," she says. "There's no collective sense of responsibility, so there's been this kind of trend toward ramping up expectations on parents—mothers specifically."

This ramping up of expectations is extremely class based, she points out. If only middle- and upper-class parents have the resources to meet these higher expectations, then they become symbols of status. Since extended breast-feeding is hard to balance with full-time work, it suggests that the mother is wealthy enough to stay home. Organic foods suggest money and educated tastes.

Chris Bobel, the author of *The Paradox of Natural Mothering,* blasts the progressive shrugging off of government oversight as privileged class "narcissism."

"What would turn you off government oversight?" she asks. "Because *you* don't need it. You can educate your own children, you can feed your own children and protect them . . . You can live in a community with clean water and clean air and clean soil. [You can think], 'I don't have to worry about disease in the way a poor family does. I can prevent illness by the very choices I'm able to make and expose my child to. My child has pretty severe dyslexia—I can hire tutors. I don't need the government to look out for me, because I can look out for me.'"

So in the twenty-first century, parents with resources and education feel they can best protect their child by "opting out" of the system. If the government isn't doing a good job at regulating the food supply, then parents with money and education can buy organic, local food from the farmer's market. If the schools aren't good, parents can homeschool or choose a charter or private school—wealthy parents are "abandoning public education," Golden says. If parents worry about chemicals in household products, then those with the time, money, and inclination can make their own cleaning products or buy pricey VOC-free rugs and paints. Which is all well and good, but these options are not so freely available to working-class parents with less time and money. They're the ones who will be left behind if we collectively abandon the effort to push for better social and governmental solutions.

# The Emergence of the "Hipster Homemaker": How New Domesticity Appeals to a Generation of Mothers Unhappy with the Workplace

Emily got her first newspaper job the Monday after college graduation; her University of Michigan diploma hadn't even arrived in the mail yet. The ambitious and "very competitive" daughter of a lawyer mom and physician dad from the liberal college town of Ann Arbor, Emily had her eyes on a full-time writing job all through college. Now her dream was beginning.

As a cub reporter covering the "cops and courts" beat for the tiny *Sandusky Register* in Sandusky, Ohio (population 25,793), Emily quickly got hooked on the rush of investigative journalism. She caught the assistant police chief in a cover-up scandal, exposing him as a liar to the entire community.

"That was a revolution for me," says Emily, thirty-three, her green eyes widening with pleasure at the memory. It was a great feeling to know she could make a genuine difference through her writing.

Her hard work earned her a job at the much-bigger *Charlotte Observer* in Charlotte, North Carolina, where she found her niche writing about wrongful death-penalty convictions. To her, this kind of social-justice journalism seemed like the highest possible calling, giving "voice to the voiceless" and getting real-world results.

"Two people I wrote about were let out," she tells me proudly.

When her Charlotte successes landed her a coveted job at the *Chicago Tribune,* one of the country's most important papers, Emily thought it was a "match made in heaven." It was 2008, and the city was "electric" with excitement about its favorite son, Barack Obama. She was working among some of the best and brightest people in the industry, people who cared passionately about their work.

Emily was just as passionate. When she began getting serious with her boyfriend Erik, she warned him that her career was "the most important thing in my life" and she would never quit.

Less than two years later, Emily wrote a column for the *Tribune* that began with the following sentence: "When people ask me what I'm going to do now that I've quit my job, I sometimes just blurt out, 'I'm going to grow tomatoes,' and am greeted with understandably confused looks."

## "I WANTED TO REMOVE MYSELF FROM THE CORPORATE CULTURE AT LARGE"

When I visit Emily at her Charlotte home, in a tidy 1950s-era suburb of modest single-story houses, she opens the door holding baby Luke, a gurgling blond four-month-old dressed in a yellow onesie. Tabitha, two, is down for her afternoon nap. Emily's now-husband, Erik, who works in Internet technology, is headed out the door for some Saturday-afternoon "man time."

Emily, dressed casually in jeans and a turquoise T-shirt, her auburn curls hanging down over her shoulders, welcomes me inside. The house smells of buttery pastry from the quiche Emily just baked in her small kitchen. The kitchen overlooks her tangled half-acre garden, where, yes, she does grow tomatoes, as well as zucchini, peppers, winter squash, onions, and a variety of kitchen herbs.

Sitting down on the tan couch in her living room and beginning to breast-feed Luke beneath a purple patterned nursing cover, Emily explains how she got from newshound to latter-day hausfrau.

As excited as she'd felt to join the *Chicago Tribune,* Emily began to feel disillusioned as the environment at the paper shifted rapidly away from what she had expected. The paper was facing continuous budget cuts and layoffs, and the remaining reporters were pushed to fill the website with a constant parade of minor stories rather than work on the longer, more satisfying (but less lucrative for the paper) investigative stories.

Emily felt that newspapers were simply part of a larger, culture-wide problem: a sped-up, unsustainable work culture that demanded more and more from its workers while offering less. Because of the recession, paths to promotion were blocked. Raises were less than the cost of living. Layoffs were rampant. A senior *Tribune* editor likened the situation to being in a canoe and needing to "paddle faster." From what Emily could see, this was true of other industries as well.

As an ardent environmentalist, Emily also worried constantly about how her fast-paced schedule was forcing her into un-eco-friendly choices—ordering takeout dinners, buying new work clothes, commuting long distances. She began to feel disgusted by the amount of consumption needed to fuel her lifestyle.

And then—most important—there was the question of kids. She and Erik, whom she'd met in Charlotte and who had moved to Chicago with her, were beginning to talk about marriage. This prompted Emily to start "thinking really critically about how I wanted to live my life."

Nearing her thirtieth birthday and influenced by media stories about career women who waited too long to try to get pregnant, Emily worried about infertility. And despite what she had been told about being able to "have it all," she didn't see much room in the world of journalism for women with children. Her female coworkers who had children either dropped out or hired nannies; Emily's newspaper job and Erik's work-from-home IT job didn't earn enough to hire full-time child care. Emily remembers watching a female coworker scramble to finish a tax story by six P.M. so she could catch the last train home and see her child awake for the only time that day.

"I remember thinking, 'A tax levy story's not worth that,'" Emily says.

So Emily, formerly so full of passion for her work, decided to quit.

Some might see Emily as part of the much-ballyhooed "opt-out revolution" of highly educated young women quitting prestigious jobs to stay home with their children. But Emily sees herself as part of a very different revolution: people rejecting an all-consuming work culture in favor of slower-paced, DIY-infused stay-at-home lives.

"I was thinking critically about how much of my health and finances are really in the hands of the large corporate forces that don't give a shit about me," she says, burping Luke on her knee. "I wanted to remove myself from the corporate culture at large."

The very day (give or take) her quit-my-job column came out, Emily got pregnant. She was nine weeks along when she and Erik celebrated their marriage with ice cream and barbecue on an Asheville mountaintop. They left Chicago and moved back to Charlotte, where they bought a 1,200-square foot house that cost a fraction of their Chicago rental. There, she began to live a very different life. A downsized life. A slow life. A stay-at-home life.

Instead of using gas by commuting to work, Emily stays home with her children and freelances a few hours a week for a book company. Instead of ordering takeout, she now cooks from scratch as much as she can, gardens intensively, and trades stuff like honey and backyard chicken eggs with like-minded friends. Instead of buying commercial laundry detergent, she makes her own—a box of 20 Mule Team Borax sits on top of her washing machine. Some of her homemaking choices—like leaving the thermostat at a chilly fifty degrees in winter, hanging laundry on the line, and sewing up torn curtains rather than buying new ones—serve both environmental and budget purposes; after all, they're living on one salary now. Other things are purely environmental: When Emily first moved to Charlotte, she tried to recycle everything—"and I mean *everything*," she says—even putting dog hair from her dog's grooming sessions in a basket so birds could use it to make nests.

Though Emily's not working, she's clearly working hard. "It definitely takes all day," she says of her routine. "But this stuff has become my new normal."

## A NEW OPT-OUT REVOLUTION

For a generation of young women (and a growing handful of young men) disenchanted with or displaced from the workplace, New Domesticity offers a new sense of purpose. If the stay-at-home mom of the 1990s used her MBA to micromanage PTA meetings, today's supermom bends her considerable creative energies toward an intensive eco-friendly lifestyle.

This new style of home-focused, sustainability-minded living seems to offer an answer to the opt-out question for creative, educated women. Now they don't need to worry that they'll wind up as bored and frustrated as the women in *The Feminine Mystique;* New Domesticity moms imbue their days with meaning and purpose in doing not only what's right for their family but what they believe is right for the entire world.

As we've seen, several facets of New Domesticity are rooted in workplace dissatisfaction. The indie craft movement has grown enormous because of the appeal of working with one's hands instead of in an office and the desire to have a flexible, family-friendly career rather than work for a corporation. The foodie movement is also motivated by workplace unhappiness, as evidenced by the surge of artisan food businesses and the "femivore" phenomenon. The new, intensive mothering philosophies we read about in the previous chapter offer women an "out" from careers they're not that happy with anyway.

"There's this dissatisfaction with work that professional women find," says Melanie, the thirty-eight-year-old writer and PhD student in Austin. "This return to what my adviser would call 'the sister arts'—fiber arts, cooking, canning, quilting, knitting. You see it reflected in chick lit— *Friday Night Knitting Club, Circle of Quilters.* There's sort of this cultural zeitgeist where women are feeling unfulfilled by work, so they seek out this romanticized vision—'my grandmother, my great-grandmother did that, and it was such a simpler time.'"

This dissatisfaction is born of disappointment, Melanie says. "Second-wave feminism promised us that we'd be able to break through the glass ceiling, and so then we all went to work and our mothers went to work and 'Oh, this sucks. I don't have enough parental leave, I can't have it all, there is no such thing as work-life balance, so I'm going to go can some peaches.'"

## "THIS ISN'T HOW IT WAS SUPPOSED TO BE": WHY YOUNG WORKERS ARE SO UNHAPPY

Young employees of both genders are facing a very different working world than their parents did. Even before the recession hit, the idea of stable lifelong employment at the same company was already about as retro as office smoking lounges. Workers today are being asked to do more—work longer hours, answer their e-mails at night, come to the office when they have the flu—and all of this for less reward. Wages have been stagnant at best, opportunities for advancement blocked and replaced by the need to cling to whatever form of employment is possible. Benefits like health insurance have begun to feel like luxury perks rather than givens.

Generation Y-ers, raised to expect great things from themselves, have quickly become disillusioned with this kind of workplace. Very few workers in their twenties and thirties see their current jobs as "careers." Many have simply not been able to find jobs at all—the percentage of young adults, ages eighteen to twenty-four, who are employed (54 percent) is the lowest recorded since the government began keeping records in the 1940s.[1] And an enormous number of them plan to quit their current gigs within the next year. Fewer are interested in moving ahead, perhaps since they don't think it'll be worth it: since the 1990s, the number of young people interested in more career responsibility has declined precipitously.[2]

Young women, saddled with the prospect of figuring out "work-life balance" in addition to the work itself, have been particularly vocal in expressing their dissatisfaction with jobs—62 percent of Gen Y women don't want to have the long-hours careers of their mothers' generation.[3]

"[Gen Y women] are wary that they can, in fact, have it all," notes a study on Gen Y women and career attitudes, which found young women to be extremely skeptical that the superwoman ideal even exists.[4]

In 2012, former State Department higher-up Anne-Marie Slaughter took to the pages of the *Atlantic* to point out this same fact. While older women hew devotedly to the belief that balancing career, family, and a personal life is doable, if only you just *try harder,* young women, Slaughter says, are calling that bullshit. "When many members of the younger generation have stopped listening [to older women], on the grounds that glibly repeating 'you can have it all' is simply airbrushing reality, it is time to talk," she writes.[5]

The article clearly hit a nerve, becoming the topic du jour among so many people it is said to be the most-read article in the *Atlantic*'s 150-plus-year history. I personally received links to the story from no fewer than a dozen acquaintances, ranging from my sixtysomething aunt to a friend in her early twenties.

Though Slaughter suggests that through careful planning (such as freezing your eggs) and sweeping policy change, women may indeed be able to "have it all" in the future, many Gen Y-ers—women *and* men—still feel that they'll have to make unappealing choices between family and career.

And, when faced with a choice, today's twenty- and thirtysomethings say they'll choose family. Generation Y-ers and X-ers, male and female alike, are more likely to describe themselves as "family-centric" than baby boomers, who are more likely than Gens X and Y to call themselves "work-centric." In addition, Gen X and Y women simply have a far less rosy view of the workplace than older women did. Raised watching their mothers struggle to balance their lives, they've grown up to see "having it all" as a 1990s-era joke, a vestige of a time of padded shoulders and Murphy Brown. Young women know that the workplace hasn't changed—it's still a very, very difficult place for women with young children.

JJ, the Los Angeles "natural parenting dropout" we met in the previous chapter, says many of her friends are disillusioned by the fact that, despite all the gains of feminism, it's still so hard to balance work and family.

"Why does it have to be all or nothing?" JJ asks, frustration in her voice. "Why do I have to be working eighty hours a week as a lawyer or not at all? A lot of the resentment is that the workplace is so unfriendly to mothers. I can't even tell you how many times I've been at a mommies' play group and heard 'Oh, I've got a master's and now I have to wipe asses all day. This isn't how it was supposed to be. Hey, this was all a lie—you *can't* do it all.'"

Things were supposed to be . . . different. Feminism raised women's expectations for career satisfaction, but the larger culture didn't rise up to meet these expectations. In fact, American culture at large has failed working mothers.

## HOW CORPORATE AMERICA SCREWS OVER WORKING MOMS

Some disturbing facts:

The United States is the only country in the developed world without guaranteed paid maternity leave (the tiny handful of other countries that don't have paid maternity leave include Lesotho and Papua

New Guinea, not exactly known for their progressivism or modernity).[6] Our closest neighbors are light-years ahead: In Canada, the government guarantees at least fifteen weeks of paid maternity leave, combined with another thirty-five weeks of parental leave, which can be shared by the mother and father. In Mexico, women get paid leave for six weeks before and six weeks after childbirth.[7] We're also the only country in the developed world without guaranteed paid vacation. (By contrast, the French have thirty days, the hedonists! Even the stereotypically nose-to-the-grindstone Japanese have ten days minimum.)[8] Sick leave? Ha. While guaranteed sick days are an unquestioned right in all other developed countries, many U.S. workers are left to sneeze all over their keyboards.[9] And while many other countries offer leave days for parents of sick children—a benefit that largely helps mothers—the United States has no such policy. Additionally, mothers are straight-up discriminated against in terms of hiring and salary: moms are 79 percent less likely to be offered jobs, according to one study, and are offered $11,000 per year less.[10] The Cornell researchers who made this shocking discovery theorize that mothers are simply perceived as less committed and less capable by employers. In their paper reporting their findings, they quote a real-life employer saying exactly this: "I find myself choosing men here every day over a woman with a child. If I had kids, I might not have made the same commitment to my job."[11]

Young American mothers and wannabe mothers have become painfully aware of their second-class status. Among my circle of friends, threatening to "move to Sweden" to have children is a frequent, only half-joking cry. There's the sense that somewhere, but not here, mothers might actually have the support necessary to "do it all."

"More countries are providing the workplace protections that millions of Americans can only dream of," said Jody Heymann, director of the Institute for Health and Social Policy at Montreal's McGill University.[12]

"We give so little support to mothers who work, and we have so little social provision for children in general," Judith Stacey, a sociologist at NYU, tells me. "It puts enormous pressure on women, who find themselves in very conflictual situations. It's pretty staggering, compared to in France, where they have a nurse come out from the hospital for every newborn [to evaluate both mother's and baby's health] and public crèches [day care centers]. There's just enormous social support there."

Since women are still overwhelmingly the primary caregivers of children, unforgiving work schedules affect them disproportionately. And just to be clear: women *are* still almost always the primary caregivers. While people today talk big about the rise of "stay-at-home dads," the numbers tell a different story: Though men are clearly taking greater part in child rearing these days, stay-at-home dads account for only 3 percent of all stay-at-home parents.[13] And when mothers do work (as most do), societal expectations mean that they—but not their male partners—feel guilty about it. Women are stressed and unhappy in record numbers, and overall female happiness levels have declined since the 1970s.[14]

"Women in the United States and Europe are shouldering major responsibilities at home and at work simultaneously, and this makes for stress and a low quality of life," reported the lead author of the "2010 Corporate Gender Gap Report" of the World Economic Forum.[15]

"The difficulty is in changing a work environment and a work rhythm that's based on a full-time male breadwinner model," economist Nancy Folbre tells me. "It makes it very hard for women who want to achieve more work-family balance to achieve that."

Sarah, the Portland investment banker/IT exec turned crunchy, gardening, bread-baking stay-at-home mom, used to adore her career.

"I really actually loved working in investment banking, despite the fact that it gets a bad rap," she says. "I was putting together large loans for companies, working with company management, developing proposals. I love strategy—I'm a strategy geek . . . Figuring out how to meet the needs of the market was really interesting and fun."

But she was fired from her job shortly after her first son was born. "My kid was seven months old, and my boss and my other male colleagues were like, 'She's not pulling her weight,'" Sarah recalls. "He was seven months old, and I was working as hard as I could!"

Later, working for AOL after her third child was born, Sarah got fed up with corporate culture once and for all. "You have all these times when your baby is sick and your boss wants you to turn in some really brainless [task] that has no impact on the world, and you're like, 'Okay, I'm letting my kid cry while I finish this stupid spreadsheet, and nobody is going to care about this spreadsheet,'" she says. "And I'm working for AOL, whose CEO is doing this list of stupid things that are destroying shareholder value, so why does it even matter?"

So she quit. Wanting to spend more time with her kids and create a healthier home was a genuine desire, but she might not have done it if she hadn't been so frustrated with corporate culture.

She'd only had six weeks of maternity leave and felt run ragged. If she'd had more, things might have been different, she says. "A year or two of maternity leave, that would make a huge difference."

"The labor market is extremely hostile to anybody with primary caregiving responsibilities," says Joan Williams, from the University of California's Center for WorkLife Law. "Women have a series of unappealing choices. They can perform as 'ideal workers'"—i.e., work sixty-hour workweeks—"they can not have children—and many of them do that regretfully. They can, quote, try to 'do it all,' but without the domestic service that men enjoy" (i.e., wives).

Or they can, as Williams says, "take their ball and their bat and go home."

And many of them have done just that, either quitting jobs or (more likely) scaling back to part-time or work-from-home schedules. Mothers today are significantly less likely to want full-time jobs than they were in the 1990s. "In a notable shift during the past decade, working mothers overwhelmingly view fewer work hours as the best option for their busy lives with young children," says *The Washington Post,* reporting on a Pew Research Center study.[16] Though the majority of women do work, the number has declined from its peak in the late 1990s and remained fairly flat ever since. More women today stay home full-time with their children than did twenty years ago. In 1994, 19.8 percent of married-parent families with children under fifteen had a stay-at-home mother. By 2008, it was 23.7 percent of families.[17] In a 2012 Forbes Women Survey, an astonishing 84 percent of working women said they aspired to stay home with their children.

"Over the past three years we've seen highly educated women—who we'd imagine would be the most ambitious—who are going through med school, getting PhDs with the end-goal in mind of being home with their kids by age 30," said Leslie Morgan Steiner, the former author of the *Washington Post*'s work-life balance blog.[18]

With the recession and subsequent lack of opportunities, ducking out of a full-time or career-track job seems like less of a gamble to many; a certain fatalism about future opportunities for career fulfillment within the mainstream framework makes alternatives like self-employment seem more appealing.

"Women are realizing, 'Ambition is nice, but the job market is crappy, so I might reimagine what my career will be like'—it's not as big a trade-off as it was ten years ago," says Alana, the thirty-three-year-old Duke PhD student who dedicates her free time to reclaiming traditional women's crafts.

Alana would desperately love a job in academia, she says. After all, she's spent the past fifteen years of her life working toward that. But she's seen the way mothers are treated in the increasingly competitive working world, and she's not sure she'll be able to make the trade-off if she does have kids one day. She's been talking and thinking about other options— an off-the-grid house with a huge veggie garden. An Etsy shop.

"The question for women of our generation is, can we have both a domestic life and a career?" she says. "I do worry."

As Alana points out, this is not just an issue for moms, either: she knows several other unmarried women and men without kids who are chafing against the expectation of an all-consuming work environment. In the course of interviewing for this book, I met plenty of other nonparents equally disinclined to bend their lives to the status quo of current work culture—a Web designer turned farmer, a (male) nonprofit worker more interested in sewing and raising chickens than working a nine-to-five, several former professionals who have crumbled under the pressures of corporate culture and wound up trying to parlay their domestic hobbies into businesses—just to name a few.

A cruddy economy. A generation of young workers who demand meaning and fulfillment. Lack of maternity leave and other workplace protections. Sexist expectations. Guilt. A sense that we've been fighting for two generations and still haven't won even basic concessions like paid maternity leave.

No wonder domesticity has been looking so rosy lately.

## THE MODERN HOMEMAKER EMERGES

In 1999, when Cheryl Mendelson published her best-selling *Home Comforts: The Art and Science of Keeping House,* she made domestic chores sound about as illicit as glue sniffing:

I am a working woman with a secret life: I keep house. An off-and-on lawyer and professor in public, in private I launder and clean, cook from the hip, and devote serious time and energy to a domestic routine not so different from the one that defined my grandmothers as "housewives." . . . Until now, I have almost entirely concealed this passion for domesticity.

Mendelson's book turned out to be the first in a long series of "reclaim domesticity" books. As the idea of homemaking-as-progressive-political-act gained steam, a slew of books with titles like *The Hip Girl's Guide to Homemaking* and *A Householder's Guide to the Universe* and *Making It: Radical Home Ec for a Post-Consumer World* hit the market, offering tips on how to clean the bathroom with a lemon or how to cook a "grandma-style" stew.

These books often dramatized the degree to which women have "lost" their traditional skills. In one such book—2009's *How to Sew a Button: And Other Nifty Things Your Grandmother Knew*—writer Erin Bried recalled serving her dinner party guests a homemade "rhubarb" pie accidentally made with look-alike Swiss chard. One might chalk this up as a simple goof (hey, they've both got red stems!), but Bried saw her mistake as something much more serious, writing, "When did I lose my ability to take care of myself? . . . What is simultaneously comforting and alarming about my domestic incompetence is that I am hardly alone. I'm joined by millions of women, Gen X-ers and Gen Y-ers, who either have consciously rejected household endeavors in favor of career or, even more likely, were simply raised in the ultimate age of convenience and consumerism."

This vision of what it means for a woman to take care of herself was either radically new or incredibly retro. Bried was a senior staff writer at *Self* magazine—a job many young women would kill their grandmas to get—yet she was framing her ability to take care of herself around her ability to bake a pie.

Many thinkers and writers began to heavily promote the idea of eco-conscious homemaking as a fuck-you to a greedy consumer culture. In 2011's *Making It: Radical Home Ec for a Post-Consumer World*, husband-and-wife duo Erik Knutzen and Kelly Coyne tell readers that DIY homemaking (window-box gardening, making your own peppermints, etc.) can change the world: "Our guiding principle is the adage that all change begins at home . . . We realized we were part of a wave rising through the culture, a network of backyard revolutionaries who weren't content to buy into a 'green lifestyle' based on a slightly tweaked version of consumerism but instead were challenging the foundations of 21st century consumer culture itself."

Most of these books proudly flew the flag of feminism. The 2004 knitting manifesto *Stitch 'n Bitch,* from *Bust* magazine editor Debbie Stoller, explicitly suggests that "reclaiming" housework is a feminist act—though Stoller suggests early feminists were the ones to blame for making homemaking look bad in the first place: "Taking their cue from Betty Friedan's influential book *The Feminine Mystique,* feminists were claiming that anyone who spent her days cooking and cleaning and her nights knitting and sewing, all in an effort to please her husband and her children, was frittering her life away . . . All those people who looked down on knitting—and housework, and housewives—were not being feminist at all. In fact, they were being anti-feminist, since they seemed to think that only those things that men did, or had done, were worthwhile."

Even the most basic how-to craft and cooking guides began to adopt a "you go, girl" feminist rhetoric. You could hardly browse a knitting pattern without talk of "reclaiming" and "sustainable living" and "taking back our grandmothers' skills."

Attitudes about homemaking had clearly done a 180-degree turn. In fact, the very word "homemaker" had become politicized. Writers took a defiant stance toward the word, claiming it had been unfairly maligned. Even the word "housewife" took on a new shine.

In Barbara Kingsolver's massively influential 2007 homesteading memoir, *Animal, Vegetable, Miracle,* Kingsolver writes about being called a "real housewife" by a supermarket employee awed by Kingsolver's cheese-making abilities.

"It has taken me decades to get here, but I took that as a compliment," she writes.

The mushroomlike spread of blogs with titles like *Hausfrau* and *Evolving Homemaker* and *The Radical Housewife* told the story of the growing "reclaim homemaking" movement. Many ordinary women embraced this new style of domesticity; some even began to talk about a return to "what's natural."

A popular blogger who calls herself Calamity Jane succinctly captures the zeitgeist: "I could have, after 3 months, put my daughter in day care and gone about my life. But the truth was I secretly wanted to be a housewife. Some part of me still thought making and keeping a true Home was about as good as it gets. What could possibly be more feminist than to embrace the natural female quality of nurture? It seems to me that to truly honor 'woman,' we must also honor her biological role as mother."[19]

Like many of the women in this book, Calamity Jane considers herself part of a growing "DIY housewifery" movement, which includes, in her words, "digging dirt, tending vegetables, Dumpster diving, punk sewing projects, household fix-its, salvage construction, cooking something delicious and nutritious almost every night and raising up little ruffians who frequently overtake the entire caper."

It's no coincidence that this image makeover took place just as women were beginning to feel disillusioned by the workplace. New Domesticity has made being a stay-at-home mom a palatable option for women who are unhappy with their jobs, but who would rather chew broken glass than sit around watching soap operas and ironing curtains like their grandmothers did. Today's neo-homemaker is no longer a drudge—she's an eco-warrior, an attachment mom creating a better breed of child, a blogger with a huge following, a food producer.

## NO SOAP OPERAS, NO BONBONS: TODAY'S "MODERN HOMEMAKER"

Carla's grandmother was the kind of 1950s housewife who vacuumed in pearls and high heels (seriously) and had a fully cooked dinner waiting on the table the very moment her husband walked in the door.

Carla, twenty-nine, adored her grandmother, but she would like you to know that she's not *that* kind of homemaker.

Carla would also like to point out that she's not a Mormon (or a religious person of any kind), and she's not a hippie, either. Also, she's not wealthy—her husband's a plumber, and they live with their two-year-old son in a humble one-thousand-square-foot house in Northern California.

She wants to say all this because people sometimes don't understand why she jettisoned her promising career to stay home with her son, sew, and cook. They assume that she must be some kind of brainwashed

Stepford wife, or a fundamentalist committed to some retro version of biblical womanhood.

Like any college-educated woman, Carla had a vast number of career possibilities. After graduating from the University of California at Santa Barbara, she took a job in newspaper sales. Later, she tried her natural charm in the public relations field.

But she says, "I just felt like it wasn't fulfilling me." She also began to wonder if her career in ad sales and PR really jibed with her morals. She wondered if her life was going to consist of "selling people stuff they don't need." At the time, she had several slightly older friends who were ambitiously working their ways up the career ladder but often discussed why they felt miserable. One eventually quit her job as an accountant to take a much-lower-status job as a part-time aesthetician and care for her two young sons. Carla took that as a warning and—before ever having children—made a "conscious decision to not follow a career."

"I'm a tiny bit defensive," admits Carla, a punky brunette with long bangs. "Like, I *should* go to school, I *should* have a career . . . don't think that I'm not educated and ambitious, because I am all of those things. I've just decided to channel that energy more domestically than work for somebody else . . . It's not like, oh, my son just goes down for a nap and I sit on the couch and watch soap operas."

To put space between herself and 1950s housewife stereotypes, Carla calls herself a "modern homemaker," which she feels captures the spirit of her life better than any other term. "'Homemaker' is very old-fashioned," she says. "But it fits better because I'm not just a housewife or just a mom. I am a maker of my home."

Judging from Carla's full plate of homemaking activities, it's clear that she couldn't possibly be watching soap operas. In fact, it's hard to see how she even has time to sleep. For Carla, making her home means—in addition to chasing after her energetic son—from-scratch cooking, gardening, crafts, home renovation projects, and lots and lots of sewing. She's an incredible seamstress, whipping up toddler jeans out of her old jeggings, sewing bow ties, and making kid-sized chef toques for her son to wear while "helping" her cook.

"Having a home fulfills me," she says. "It makes me feel rewarded in a way I didn't when I had a job."

Carla's mother, who fought for women's rights in the 1970s but never got the chance to go to college herself, wanted to see Carla pursue a career. Though the two are close and her mother is "super proud" of Carla, it's still "weird" to have rejected all her mom's generation fought for.

"We were supposed to be the ones that did it all," Carla says of her generation, slightly wistfully. "I'm not quite sure where we got the idea to say 'screw that.' But we did."

Courtney, a thirty-one-year-old stay-at-home mom in Iowa City, says she's always considered homemaking her vocation. She's always been crafty, and she loves to cook and decorate. But until she had kids, she didn't think it was socially acceptable to stay at home. After all, she had a graduate degree!

"I feel that having a baby has justified a desire to work in the home that I have always had," she says. "In the fifteen years that I have been employed in the formal workforce, I have gone through over twenty-five jobs. This isn't because I'm a bad worker—I've never been fired. I just get really bored and really hate the idea of going to work every day and so I have always inevitably quit. I've always wanted to stay home. But to do that without a child brings up all sorts of negative connotations of being a kept woman. I think all I've ever really wanted to do is the work of home-keeping."

Interestingly, plenty of men tell me they'd like to stay home too. Jason, Carla's husband, said he'd be a stay-at-home dad "in an instant" if Carla hadn't beaten him to the punch. A college dropout who was never much interested in a career, he stumbled into being a plumber solely as a way to support his family. But cooking, gardening, and hanging out with his son are his passions.

Jason admires Carla's grandmother, who he thinks was living the dream. "If you watch *Mad Men*, that was their life," he says in his California surfer-boy drawl. "But the only thing that wasn't accurate to her was that she wasn't unhappy. I think the myth of the closeted, horribly unhappy, and cloistered housewife is kind of a fallacy."

To Jason, the life of a middle-class 1950s homemaker sounds "awesome." Carla's grandmother got to stay home all day and cook and hang out with her friends, things Jason wishes he had more time for.

Jason thinks New Domesticity is a reaction against the materialism of the 1980s and 1990s, and a reaction against our baby boomer parents who always seemed so miserable and lost.

"We're seeing a lot of the problems that our parents have had, as far as emotional problems, having trouble finding something that makes them happy, reaching middle age, and not being prepared for it at all," he says.

Women like Carla and Courtney view their lifestyles as a rejection of both the workplace *and* the stultifying enforced domesticity of 1950s homemaking. After all, they say, this was their choice. They're reenvisioning homemaking *as* work. The divide between "work" and "homemaking," which first opened during the Industrial Revolution when men left the homestead, is artificial, they say. This claim might have been hard to believe a half century ago, when homemaking meant stirring boxed cake mix and driving carpool. But today, what with all the backyard chicken raising and sewing and homeschooling, it's easier to see homemaking as a vocation.

Some women even try to make good on the idea that housework ought to be paid (a popular view with 1960s and '70s feminists) by thinking of their work in terms of cash value. Saskia, an "urban homesteader" in Anchorage, tells me her vegetable garden is worth $5,000. So while her husband, who conducts energy audits for a living, earns the income, Saskia feels her gardening is her own way of contributing monetarily to the household. Of the women I spoke with who were stay-at-home mothers, many said their old jobs weren't "worth it" financially, since most of the income would go toward paying someone else to watch their child. They considered their stay-at-home motherhood as "earning" back the price of day care.

## IF WORK SUCKS ANYWAY, WHAT'S THE POINT OF GENDER EQUALITY IN THE WORKPLACE?

Most of us kids of progressive baby boomer parents have grown up on the notion that "getting women into the boardroom" should be a major and ongoing goal. Women are barely represented at the pinnacle of power, whether in finance, law, government, business, or technology. In a very real way, men still rule the world. That's wrong.

Right?

In fact, within the culture of New Domesticity, there's the growing idea that this is the wrong way to think about things. Why is "outside work" so important? they ask. Isn't it sexist to denigrate homemaking as less valuable than being a CEO?

These attitudes take on extra weight when paired with the belief that eco-friendly homemaking is the key to a just and sustainable world.

"The feminists, they had it right that the suburban housewife was in a bad position," says Sara, a twenty-nine-year-old stay-at-home mother of two in South Dakota. "That was not good for any sort of human being to be living in that sort of isolation and meaninglessness, but they got the answer wrong. The answer wasn't for everybody to go out and get a job. That's not really giving anybody necessarily any more purposeful work."

Sara, whose husband, Jake, is a graduate student, is deeply involved in the New Domesticity ethos of handmade, DIY, organic, sustainable. She knits, she cans tomato sauce, she sews her daughters' clothes, bakes her family's bread, and blogs about her attempts to create a "down-to-earth, back-to-the-earth, simplified, handmade, from-scratch kind of life for our family." Sara, who has a college degree, says she's "so thankful" to feminism for giving her things like the right to vote and the right to an education. But she's not so keen on the idea that only "outside work" is real work. She thinks the real answer to today's societal woes is to go back a few hundred years in history (without taking away women's rights to vote or get an education, she is quick to say) to an era where homemaking was more valued, people lived more lightly on the earth and relied less on corporations, and family and community came first. If people—both men and women—spent more time at home and became more invested in DIY, they might not have to work as much, she says. Though she doesn't go as far as to say that all women are better off being homemakers, she does say she hopes her daughters choose the same path she has chosen.

"I think I would prefer if they decided to be homemakers, at least when they have children at home," she says. For Sara, "purposeful work" is found in her style of intensive homemaking. A longtime environmentalist who ran with the hippie crowd in college, she spent her early twenties reading Wendell Berry and learning to sew her own clothes rather than buy corporate goods. An English major who planned on being a librarian, she married young and, once her first daughter was born, found herself increasingly interested in natural homemaking. She started reading blogs like *Soule Mama,* and through them began to see crafting and DIY as more than hobbies. Instead of "going and buying something off a shelf," she makes it herself. Instead of buying convenience foods or eating out, Sara opts for a labor-intensive diet of grain soaking and gathering local eggs and veggies.

Since this kind of homemaking is labor-intensive and, often, saves money, Sara sees it as "work," just like going to an office.

"I came to this point where I realized that work could be meaningful and not something to be dreaded," Sara says. "And that work could be done at home."

Mallory, a thirty-eight-year-old mother of two in the Albany suburbs, is the model New Domesticity homemaker, down to the home-baked bread and the homeschooled children. A women's studies major in college, Mallory now thinks many of our current societal woes—environmental degradation, chronic stress, high divorce rates—can be traced back to feminism and women joining the workforce.

"I'm not blaming women," says Mallory, a tall woman with a neat pageboy and the glowing complexion of a movie milkmaid. "I'm just looking at the time line."

Mallory thinks her eco-conscious homemaking and mothering is a way of giving back to the larger community. She sees herself as not just a stay-at-home mom but "an activist for food and the environment." In fact, she thinks eco-conscious homemaking is a particularly noble calling because "women have more influence over how we treat our earth and the environment."

"What I'm doing is better," she says, sipping tea on the couch in her beige living room as her small daughters play with blocks on the landing. "I'm focusing on my children and my home and I do have time to cook from scratch and I'm not abusing the earth."

She hopes that her daughters will follow in her footsteps and become eco-conscious stay-at-home mothers. "I think it would be better if they were like me," she said. "If you're just going to the grocery store and shuttling your kids from place to place, what's the point?"

As for men, Mallory doesn't see much hope for their participating equally in housework and child care—nor is she convinced that they should.

"I do think that a lot of things are biological," she says. "A lot of tendencies to be more caring and protective of children are biological. My husband *likes* going to work—it's partly biological."

Even those who don't believe that women are naturally better nurturers are calling into question the valuing of "outside work" over homemaking.

Take forty-one-year-old Ruben. A former industrial designer in Victoria, British Columbia, he left his government job a year ago to stay home, garden intensively, cook, care for his stepdaughter, and take care of various household DIY projects like his backyard rabbit hutches. While his wife, a wine and liquor sales rep, earns the income, Ruben makes his own cheese, picks local apples for cider, cans tomatoes, and bakes bread.

"We call it 'working in the household economy,'" he tells me with a hint of a smile in his voice.

Ruben, who repeatedly refers to all employment as "shitty office jobs," considers himself a feminist but says those who are trying to get women into powerful careers are simply looking at things the wrong way.

"The goal of getting women into the boardroom was wrong," he says. "It seemed right at the time, but it was the wrong question, the boardroom is the wrong path . . . so if the question of getting women into the boardroom is taken off the table, then what is the question we're asking?"

To Ruben, achieving gender equality in the workplace is not an important goal, because the workplace is fundamentally a "shitty" place anyway. At Ruben's old job, he felt like a nameless widget in a giant machine, rarely able to see or enjoy the fruits of his labor.

"We spend our time driving to shitty office jobs to make money so someone else can cook our food," he says. "It feels like everybody knows that the way we live isn't working."

Ruben, like so many stay-at-home moms before him, has had some trouble adjusting to his new role in the home. It hasn't been easy on his ego to go from a job with a "fat government paycheck" and conference invitations to being a stay-at-home gardener and stepdad struggling to grow tomatoes in the Canadian climate.

But Ruben is adamant that home-based, DIY-centric lifestyles—not high-powered office jobs—are the key to a sustainable world and a happy life.

As cozy as this idea of "working in the household economy" is, it's also troubling on a number of levels.

Social critics like Susan Faludi would say that Sara and Jillian and Ruben have simply bought into the "Big Lie" that feminism has made women unhappy by forcing them into the workplace. The problem, they would say, is that feminism and workplace reform haven't gone far enough.

As social critic Elisabeth Badinter writes, many younger women are bitter that the workplace isn't all it's cracked up to be: "Among this new generation many women also had scores to settle with their feminist mothers, and they were quick to answer the siren call of the natural. If the world of work lets one down, if it fails to offer the position one deserves, if it provides neither social status nor financial independence, then why give it priority?"[20]

Badinter has an answer to her own question: jobs are essential for independence, both financial and emotional.

Rachel, a thirty-eight-year-old ex-homemaker turned English professor in Indiana, also groans at this new "home is better than work" narrative. She understands it, having once been a bread-baking, yogurt-making stay-at-home mama who fantasized about a rambling farmhouse with six kids. In this former life, she considered work crass and competitive. Even though she had a PhD, she purposefully didn't look for an academic position, because she'd heard so much about how greedy and backstabbing it was.

"It's a seductive idea," she says of the modern homemaker narrative. "Because it really is pleasant. It is much more pleasant, there is less struggle at home than at work, and there is more payoff in that you can start a task and you can finish it with something to be proud of."

But women who buy into the idea of homemaking as a valid form of "work" are asking for trouble, she says. She laughs at the idea of veggies being worth cash.

"These stories about 'Oh, a homemaker's worth one hundred thousand dollars, if everything she did could be paid for by the market economy.' Well, that's not going to happen. If you're quitting your job to focus on the domestic sphere, you're saying, 'No, no, no, we're separate but equal.' It's a fact that if you sign up for that you're putting yourself at huge risk. Because if you get divorced, he's going to be fine and you're not. You're not going to be able to do it on Etsy, period."

Having had plenty of "shitty office jobs" myself, I completely understand that the workaday grind can be a miserable way to live. Who wouldn't rather garden and grocery-shop and play with their kids than shuffle papers behind a desk in a fluorescent-lit office building?

But the idea that a job is just a way to "earn money to pay for things you could just do yourself" seems curiously without imagination. It seems almost self-explanatory that all jobs, even the least prestigious, serve some function. Unless we're all going to go back to yeoman farming (as some of the people in the next chapter want to do), we need nurses and grant writers and teachers and waitresses and mattress salesmen and auto repairwomen and dentists and janitors.

Even if we think housework should be paid, it's not. So money remains a necessity for those of us not born to inherit aerospace fortunes, and financial independence should be a concern for anyone, even within a committed relationship.

And, on a deeper level, what about the idea that career ambition, the desire to make a mark on the world, is an honorable thing? Has "ambition" itself become a dirty word in our cozy, small-scale, DIY-loving world of New Domesticity?

## THE OPT-OUT STORY: HOW THE MEDIA ROMANTICIZES THE IDEA OF QUITTING WORK

It's clear that young Americans, male and female alike, have plenty of valid reasons for being dissatisfied with the workplace. It's also clear that mothers have particular reason to be unhappy with their career options. But there's something else at play here, something else that accounts for the omnipresence of the "moms are happier at home" narrative: the media.

The media did not invent female workplace dissatisfaction. But it has enshrined the idea that work-life balance is impossible and that mothers generally find it more satisfying to stay home. For decades, mainstream American newspapers and magazines have harped on the impossibility of "having it all" and delivered dewy-eyed "opt-out" stories about stay-at-home moms "so in love" with their babies that they can't possibly imagine going back to work.

This is not to say that these stories are not based on truth—as we know, "having it all" is extremely damn difficult, and many mothers, for many reasons, choose to stay at home with their children. And, obviously, many of them are perfectly happy. The problem is that the media rarely discusses the real reasons behind why women leave their jobs. We hear a lot about the desire to be closer to the children, the love of crafting and gardening and making food from scratch. But reasons like lack of maternity leave, lack of affordable day care, lack of job training, and unhappiness with the 24/7 work culture—well, those aren't getting very much airtime.

The story of the United States' shameful lack of support for working parents is rarely the tale that gets told in our newspapers and magazines. We don't read much about young working-class moms who have to quit their much-needed jobs because they can't afford day care. We don't read about moms who have to quit beloved careers because their companies don't offer time off to deal with sick kids. We certainly don't read about the executives and CEOs who are bemoaning the loss of a growing section of the workforce or the economic impact of an increasing number of families going to a one-salary income. Instead, we hear endless stories about privileged young women who freely reject a vast range of career opportunities to bask in the rosy glow of the children.

The term "opt out" comes from an infamous 2003 *New York Times Magazine* story by Lisa Belkin called "The Opt-Out Revolution," which profiled Ivy League grads who had ditched high-flying careers to stay at home with their children. Women, Belkin said, weren't just hitting a glass ceiling. They were consciously rejecting the workplace because they wanted to embrace their female natures.

"I think some of us are swinging to a place where we enjoy, and can admit we enjoy, the stereotypical role of female/mother/caregiver," says one subject, a former publisher. "I think we were born with those feelings."

This story spawned dozens upon dozens of lesser imitators. Publications from the *New York Times* to the *Wall Street Journal* to CNN have made a cottage industry out of these opt-out stories, which present work-life balance as an unwinnable goal for women and focus disproportionately on the benefits of leaving the workforce in favor of spending time with family. A scholarly analysis of these stories by the Center for WorkLife Law showed that only a tiny fraction of them (12 percent) mentioned the negative economic impact of women leaving the workforce; 74 percent focused on the "pull" of home and hearth when describing women's decisions to leave the workforce, rather than the "push" of a family-unfriendly corporate culture.[21] Pamela Stone, a sociologist, has noted the rise of stories about stay-at-home moms as "the latest status symbol" and working moms as "passé."[22] She points out how the opt-out story always tells the same narrative: "These stories are remarkably similar: the women love their jobs, they have great employers who accommodate their family responsibilities, but motherhood is the most rewarding job in the world, children the greatest love affair of their lives, there is no such thing as quality time, they need to 'be there' for them."[23]

When articles about working mothers *do* appear, they tend to focus on the onerous grind of work-life balance. In 2012, the *New York Times* published a story about how working mothers deal with traveling for business. The story profiled exhausted women who leave long grocery lists, printouts of doctors' phone numbers, and itineraries of soccer practices for their apparently hapless male partners.

A lawyer quoted in the story says she makes sure to "include some sweetness" for her husband when she texts him instructions from the road, "so he doesn't feel like an employee."

Oh, please.

These journalistic choices are dramatic enough to cause talk of conspiracy theories. Syndicated columnist Bonnie Erbé writes about the *New York Times*'s series of opt-out stories as a "bizarre and suspiciously predetermined editorial effort to talk women out of working."

When we combine very real workplace inequalities with these romantic opt-out stories, the idea that "having it all" is a laughable goal becomes enshrined as immutable truth. And when we portray opting out as a simple matter of "choice," we ignore the systemic problems that make combining work and motherhood so difficult. Things like lack of affordable day care. Like the fact that many people still describe fathers providing child care as "babysitting." By suggesting that women stay at home because it appeals to their feminine nature, we're subtly implying that the women who stay in the workforce are somehow kidding themselves or are going against nature. Through these opt-out stories, women are encouraged to view their workplace decisions as "personal choice." This benefits companies— after all, if women are simply "choosing" to stay home because they prefer it, then companies don't need to make larger institutional changes to accommodate the changing needs of their employees. These needs go beyond child care—plenty of nonparents or older parents, both male and female, need flextime to care for sick spouses or elderly parents. But companies have been glacially slow to acknowledge this. The narrative that caregiving responsibilities are something an employee should deal with on their own time suits them much better.

These romantic opt-out stories can make work seem even less appealing than it really is. When the media portrays working mothers as harried, exhausted, and miserable, is it any wonder workplace negativity among women is at an all-time high? After years of being inundated with media stories about how much happier women are when they stay home with their kids, is it any surprise that so many women are embracing lifestyles like attachment parenting that enshrine stay-at-home parenting as natural and noble?

"The media loves the 'opt out' story," says Arlene Avakian, the University of Massachusetts professor emeritus. "It's important to think about how this shapes the rhetoric. Even if a woman can't do it, she starts to think about how that's a great way to live."

As far as science is concerned, there's no evidence that women are actually happier at home. In fact, numerous studies show that working moms are happier and more fulfilled than stay-at-home moms. I'm not pointing this out to knock stay-at-home motherhood, only to note that there are dangerous consequences to allowing only one kind of narrative on the topic.

As Susan Faludi pointed out in *Backlash,* these newspaper trend stories—even when they're not true—influence the way people act. A spurious 1986 *Fortune* magazine cover story about female MBAs "bailing" on their degrees promoted a real decline in female MBA applicants the following year.

For my generation, weaned on "you can't have it all" opt-out stories, it's no wonder we view domesticity as such an alluring alternative.


## WE CAN'T HAVE IT ALL: FATALISM ABOUT CAREERS

In the evenings in Chapel Hill, I often walk with a group of old friends, mostly professional women in their late twenties and early thirties. A few have babies, a few don't. As we walk, we talk about our lives—work, relationships, kids. But one of the topics that comes up over and over again with increasing frequency is the topic of work-life balance. And the overwhelming consensus is this: it's impossible.

The academics among us talk about how difficult it is to vie for tenure while raising children. One friend rails against the university where she's earning her PhD in biology, which offers no maternity leave for students and saddled her with unexpected new teaching duties two weeks after her daughter was born. If it weren't for her mother and mother-in-law, who care for her baby while she's working, she would have to drop out, she says. Maybe she will drop out anyway, she says. She's doing okay now, but it's almost inevitable that the stress will get to be too much, right?

Those of us who don't have kids but want them someday repeat secondhand horror stories: "At my friend's newspaper, only one of the eight female senior editors had children. And they were all over forty!" When I tell these stories to my husband, he looks at me with puzzlement and tells me I'm cherry-picking the most negative scenarios, then rattles off a list of dozens of women in his field who have both children and massive career success.

When I consider it, all this negativity strikes me as a bit odd. Because, at the end of the day, everybody in that walking group is doing okay. Yes, it's hard. Yes, it's really stressful. But the moms among us are surviving and maintaining happy-enough-seeming families. Many of us grew up with working mothers. We all have job mentors who balance career and family. We are all lucky and privileged enough to have the kinds of careers that offer a reasonable amount of autonomy, unlike, say, having to punch a time card in a factory or sweep floors on the night shift.

Yet over and over again we say this: "I don't know how anybody does it."

But we do know! We've seen it in action. We're doing it ourselves. So why the overwhelming feeling of negativity and doom and imminent failure?

It's clear that my friends and I have been deeply affected by the attitude shift from the "have it all" mantra of the eighties and nineties to the "balance is impossible" narrative of today. So even as we successfully balance work and family, we are just waiting for it to come tumbling down on our heads. I wonder how much of this will turn into a self-fulfilling prophecy. How many of us, plagued with the idea that you can't have it all, will end up quitting our much-loved jobs at the first sign of opposition?

Rebecca, twenty-nine, a business writer and mother of two in Raleigh,

North Carolina, is a prime example of someone who's affected by negative rhetoric about working mothers. A curly-haired brunette with an easy manner and a ready laugh, Rebecca used to hang out with a crowd of crunchy stay-at-home attachment mothers. These women, she said, looked at working moms with the greatest pity. It was conventional wisdom within the group that jobs were soul sucking and family destroying, at best a necessary evil, Rebecca explains, holding her two-year-old daughter on the living room couch at her Raleigh bungalow. Bosses were cruel creatures who wouldn't let you off to take your child to the doctor. The only reason women would work was greed—how could money compare to the pure joys of watching your baby take his first step?

Rebecca, a college dropout who was living on her student husband's paltry income, did everything she could to avoid a conventional job. She made all her food from scratch, scrupulously avoided eating out or buying new clothes, never hired a babysitter. She sewed her son's pajamas out of old shirts, made her own laundry detergent from Borax and heavy yellow bars of Fels Naptha soap grated with a cheese grater. She was convinced that this lifestyle was the noble path—best for her kids, best for the environment, best for society.

When Rebecca finally did earn her college degree (she'd dropped out to get married and "live the simple life") and got her first regular nine-to-five job, at a Raleigh-area software company, she was shocked. Her colleagues were nice, her bosses flexible, and the forty-hour-a-week schedule relatively undemanding, compared to her housework routine.

"Up until then, it had never occurred to me that you could have a job that you like," she says, wonder in her voice as she sits on her couch with her legs tucked underneath her. "You're not a slave to the Man if you like what you do. And there are a lot of perks to working for someone else, like sick leave and paid vacation."

What's more, the extra money made her life immensely easier. Instead of making everything from scratch, she could go out every once in a while if she wanted to.

"Eating in a restaurant is not wasting money," she says. "That's a higher standard of living. Money gives you options."

Need I even point out how ironic it is that Rebecca, a twenty-first-century woman, experienced the exact same mythology of the noble homemaker as a 1950s housewife?

Like a 1950s woman, she grew up reading media stories about the unhappiness of working moms and the primal satisfactions of being home with baby. Like a 1950s woman, she had a peer group who denigrated working moms and valorized homemaking as the most noble thing possible. Like a 1950s woman, she was shocked to learn the working world could be freeing.

# CHAPTER 8

# A Woman's (*and* a Man's) Place Is in the Home After All: The Rise of Homesteading

Shannon Hayes is standing barefoot in the kitchen of her upstate New York farmhouse wearing an orange apron, explaining what's wrong with the world.

The list is long.

We've moved away from our agrarian roots. We used to make things at home, things like food, clothes, soap, but now our homes are places for consumption. We've "outsourced" our families—putting our children in day care rather than caring for them at home, relying on experts like doctors and professors at the expense of traditional wisdom and personal intuition. We've given away our lives to corporations that work us like slaves and give us nothing in return. We've developed an "extractive" economy that destroys the environment, local communities, and our very souls.

The solution? Screw it all and go home. Women, men, kids, everyone.

"Developing domestic skills gives you the power," Hayes says as she stirs a pot of soup made from homemade stock. The soup contains chunks of lamb from Hayes's own herd of sheep and vegetables from the root cellar. Stacked on the kitchen counter are several marble-white slabs of butter wrapped in paper, which she got from a neighbor in exchange for some chickens.

With her long pale red hair tied back in a loose knot and a freckled oval face devoid of makeup, thirty-seven-year-old Hayes looks every inch the placid earth mother. But as she talks, her blue-green eyes take on an avid glow, like an Irish farm girl who's just seen the Virgin Mary appear in the cowshed.

It's easy to see why many people consider her a guru. The author of a 2010 book called *Radical Homemakers: Reclaiming Domesticity from a Consumer Culture,* she's given a cohesive philosophy to many of the ideas that have been flying around in the past few years. Ideas about sustainable living, self-sufficiency, the value of DIY. Ideas about the importance of home and family and a slowed-down life.

Radical homemakers, who can be male or female, reject the standard two-career, upwardly mobile American Dream in favor of frugal, small-footprint, DIY-loving, home-based lifestyles. Radical homemaking is, in Hayes's words, "homemaking as a vocation for saving family, community, and the planet."

*Radical Homemakers* has become a touchstone of the growing "homesteading" movement, a movement that takes today's ethos of frugality, self-sufficiency, and domestic DIY to its ultimate extreme. It's New Domesticity on steroids, the apotheosis of the sentiment "All change begins at home." Today's neo-homesteaders are raising chickens in their backyards, turning their front lawns into vegetable gardens, and then pickling and canning the products of these gardens, making their own soaps and shampoos and laundry detergents and homeopathic remedies. They're mobilizing friends to build their houses rather than paying contractors. They're bartering homemade jam for fresh goat milk. They're homeschooling their children or organizing local school co-ops. They're producing their own energy with solar panels and wind turbines, going completely off-grid.

If the 1960s counterculture mantra was "back to the land," today's most radical mantra is "back to the home."

## BACK TO BASICS . . . AGAIN: THE ROOTS OF THE TWENTY-FIRST-CENTURY HOMESTEADING REVIVAL

The idea of going back to basics is nothing new. And the hippies of the 1960s and 1970s didn't invent the concept, either. It's much, much older than that.

Thoreau went to Walden Pond to "live deliberately" back in 1845, and Helen and Scott Nearing promoted "the good life" from their rustic New England farmhouse in the 1930s, influencing a generation of idealistic young Americans to take up woodworking and gardening. The back-to-the-land movement of the late 1960s and early 1970s had young people poring over the *Whole Earth Catalog* and flocking to rural communes, hoping to build a simpler, better world away from the constraints of what they saw as a sick mainstream society. Perhaps it was the drugs, perhaps it was the overly idealistic nature of some of these communes ("free love" tended to create commune-destroying jealousy; poverty was rampant), perhaps it was just the natural cycle of things, but the movement didn't last long and had pretty much petered out by the end of the 1970s.

"As the 1979 energy crisis waned in the following years, so too would the accompanying desire to live more simply," writes Melissa Coleman, the daughter of 1970s homesteaders, in her memoir, *This Life Is in Your Hands*. "By the 1980s oil glut, jobs and opportunities would become so plentiful in the cities that few could resist the pull to return."[1]

The past few decades have been solidly urban, consumerist, and technology oriented, and the idea of "back to nature" seemed passé and laughable to many, a patchouli-scented relic of a foolishly naive era. But then, starting around the early 2000s, fears about food safety and climate change began to drive a new interest in DIY food cultivation. The recession, with its subsequent reevaluation of the American Dream, helped all these trends begin to gel into something larger.

Hayes calls it radical homemaking. Others call it "simple living," "intentional living," "sustainable living," "slow living," "voluntary simplicity," or "downshifting," all terms that have entered or reentered the lexicon in the past few years. But "homesteading" seems to have emerged as the modern term of choice for this new kind of self-sufficient, home-focused, frugal, slowed-down lifestyle.

It's difficult to say exactly when the word "homesteading" started to be thrown around in its current form. By looking at Google Trends, you can see that the word was practically never used in searches before 2007, but it really took off in 2008, the year the recession started and the Institute of Urban Homesteading was founded in Oakland. Around this time, a parade of neo-homesteading books began to pour into bookstores, from Abigail Gehring's *Homesteading: A Back to Basics Guide to: Growing Your*

*Own Food, Canning, Keeping Chickens, Generating Your Own Energy, Crafting, Herbal Medicine, and More* (2009) to Carleen Madigan's *The Backyard Homestead: Produce All the Food You Need on Just a Quarter Acre!* (2009) and dozens more—my local Barnes & Noble has an entire shelf dedicated to these books (and their resultant memoirs), nearly all published between 2009 and the present. In 2010 a Pasadena family trademarked the term "urban homesteading" and began to send cease-and-desist letters to bloggers, setting off a firestorm in the now-robust homesteading community. Around that time, major media outlets like the *New York Times* began to pick up on the phenomenon: "'Urban homesteaders' are farming in San Francisco," reported the paper in April 2010. "I went back to the land to feed my family," proclaimed a Brooklyn writer-slash-urban-homesteader in a 2011 *New York Times* op-ed. The movement, it seemed, had arrived.

In my town, it is completely normal to keep chickens in your backyard. I frequently see a pair of goats wandering up the road near my old apartment, just around the corner from the Harris Teeter supermarket and the CVS pharmacy. If you're not familiar with downtown Chapel Hill, this is *not* the kind of place where you expect to see goats while you're walking home with your groceries. Drunk UNC students stumbling around holding giant red Solo cups, yes. Goats, not so much. But this is our new normal. Since 2008, we've even had an "urban farm tour," where you can wander around your neighbors' backyards inspecting their coops and doing workshops on composting and honey harvesting.

Tim Kasser, a psychologist at Knox College, studies this kind of "downshifting." According to his studies, about a quarter of Americans have at some point voluntarily simplified their lives by taking a pay cut or cutting home spending, while perhaps 10 to 15 percent of the population practices hard-core types of voluntary simplicity such as homesteading. And it's not just us. A study in Australia showed that nearly a quarter of Aussies have "downshifted," defined as "those people who make a voluntary, long-term lifestyle change that involves accepting significantly less income and consuming less."[2] According to one study, over a quarter of British adults ages thirty to fifty-nine have voluntarily moved to lower-paid jobs to spend more time with their families. The author of this study says these people are part of an entirely new social class who "consciously reject consumerism and material aspirations."[3]

"This isn't a fringe thing anymore," simple-living guru Wanda Urbanska told *O, the Oprah Magazine*. "There is a shift going on. When I first started talking about this in 1992, I was seen as a wacko zealot. Now simple living is fashionable."[4]

The movement is not only fashionable. According to research by Kasser and others, it may in fact produce happier people. According to psychology research, voluntary simplifiers earned $15,000 less than their fellow citizens (about $26,000 compared to $41,000) but were found to be "significantly happier."[5] The same study showed that more than a quarter of Americans had already taken voluntary income cuts in favor of lifestyle.

"Not only were the voluntary simplifiers living in a more eco-sustainable way than mainstream Americans," Kasser tells me. "The voluntary simplifiers were happier than the mainstream population."

## REJECTING THE AMERICAN DREAM: SHANNON HAYES'S STORY

The afternoon sun is shining through Hayes's dining room window as we sit down at the long wooden table overlooking the fruit orchard. It's a gorgeous, unseasonably warm fall day in rural Schoharie County, and the fields glow like spun gold.

Hayes's home might be described as "rustic hippie chic." The airy tiled kitchen opens into a high-ceilinged dining room, which is decorated with quilts, dried Indian corn, and Latin American dolls. An enormous stone fireplace divides the dining room from the living area, which leads to a mudroom where Hayes and her two daughters dry their homemade soap on big trays. A staircase leads to the upstairs sleeping area. The floor is brick, warm to the touch, laid by Shannon's husband. Everywhere, large windows offer sweeping views over the wooded hills.

Hayes offers me a glass of raw milk, then, sniffing the jar, realizes it's gone off. "It'll have to become yogurt," she murmurs, tucking it back in the fridge and pouring a glass of home-fermented kombucha tea for herself. We start in on the meal—homemade soup and bread, a wedge of local cheese, and homemade baked apples from a nearby orchard.

Hayes's life was not always this golden idyll, she tells me.

"There was a time when lunch for me was Oreo cookies with Peter Pan peanut butter, which was made by Philip Morris," she says (at one point Philip Morris, the cigarette company, owned Kraft, which makes Oreos), wrinkling her smooth oval face at the memory.

Back in the days when she ate Oreos for lunch, Hayes was your average ambitious, overeducated American, she says. Raised in upstate New York by two "avid professional" parents, she "charged through high school and college at full throttle, ravenously ambitious, eager to start my own career as soon as possible."[6] Her first college paper was—cue irony—about "the psychological benefits of enrolling children and babies in day care" (Hayes now believes that babies' "limbic brains" don't develop as well if they have multiple caregivers).

She spent a year teaching English in Japan and worked at a program for flood victims before being accepted to Cornell and earning a PhD in sustainable agriculture by the time she was twenty-seven. By this point Shannon had met her husband, Bob Hooper, a county planner with an outdoorsy bent.

Though Hayes could have had a coveted academic career, by the time she graduated from Cornell she and Hooper were both starting to have second thoughts about the whole job thing. The pair did a calculation, Hayes said, and realized that the extra costs involved with a two-career family, costs like child care and an extra car and gas for commutes, would eat up much of the extra income. And when they looked around at the trappings of the American dream—SUVs, McMansions, private schools, designer clothes—they realized they didn't want those things anyway.

So they made a radical decision.

They would start working at Hayes's parents' small hobby farm in Schoharie County. They'd live simply, cheaply, and pursue their passions— Hayes as a writer, Hooper as an artist. If it didn't work, they could always go back to conventional life.

Today Hayes and Hooper work the family farm, sell veggies and homemade soap and lip balm at the farmer's market, and make just about everything themselves. They only have one car ("I love the inconvenience of it," Hayes says, sighing happily). Over the years, they transformed their home from a 750-square-foot cabin to their chic lodge-style abode, using sweat equity and the help of friends. Where other families go to the movies, Hayes, Hooper, and their daughters stay home and "read long novels aloud at night, play music and sing by the fire, enjoy cider and popcorn while playing games."[7]

At the moment, Hooper and the girls are off processing the family's turkeys at the processing plant. The girls, who are four and eight, are homeschooled and spend much of the year helping with farm production.

"I started feeling that school was training kids to be employees," Hayes explains. "I want to train them to be entrepreneurs." Entrepreneurship, resourcefulness, and self-reliance are big parts of Hayes's philosophy. Plus, they're not vaccinated—Hayes does not believe in "outsourcing" medical decision-making to doctors, whom she calls "technicians in white coats," and says she's done her own research into vaccines and now believes they contribute to autoimmune disorders. So while the other kids in the county study phonics and long division at Schoharie Elementary, Hayes's girls process turkeys and help make jelly and beeswax soap and lip balm to sell at market.

Amazed that she and her family could live so plentifully on less than $40,000 a year, Hayes wanted to spread the word about her simple, home-centered life. She put out a call on her website looking for people who were living similar lifestyles and was flooded with responses. Hayes traveled around the country interviewing these fellow radical homemakers—a single mom raising her son in an off-grid cabin, several couples who rejected suburban lifestyles for extreme simplicity, a chemical engineer who was fired when she had a baby and turned to stay-at-home motherhood and part-time farming, a stay-at-home dad who built his family's house by hand.

Though self-published, *Radical Homemakers* has become a hit. It has now sold more than fifteen thousand copies and has been blurbed by the likes of venerated environmentalist Bill McKibben. Suddenly, Hayes found herself as one of the major voices of the homesteading movement.

At first, Hayes was wary of promoting her lifestyle. Was she, a self-professed feminist, comfortable with the idea of promoting domesticity to a mass audience, lest it be interpreted as a call to return to retro gender roles?

"I was terrified to write it," Hayes says, of the book. "Terrified of questioning, 'Is it right for a woman to be in the home?' . . . I do get hate mail. I know there are nasty things written about me on Amazon and feminist theorists psychoanalyzing me. But I also get letters of thanks from readers, people who were already living this way and felt guilty and ashamed. People who chose to not have a job, to not be career professionals."

Homesteading is clearly the way of the future, Hayes says. People are sick of the workplace, sick of the food system, sick of being sick and fat and overworked.

"We are seeing support for the system erode," she says. "People are starting to question it . . . Ten or twelve years ago, Bob and I were this curious aberration. Now I know tons of people who are doing this . . . I don't think we've scratched the surface yet."

## LAURA INGALLS WILDER, ECO-WARRIOR: THE APPEAL OF MODERN HOMESTEADING

When I was a kid, my favorite books involved scrappy frontier heroines. I wanted to milk cows and make pies like Laura in *Little House on the Prairie*, hunt like Caddie Woodlawn, bake bread like Anna from *Sarah, Plain and Tall*. When I was eleven, I begged my parents to send me to a summer camp on a farm in the North Carolina mountains. I'd seen its brochure, which featured a girl feeding a baby bottle to a tiny calf. I wanted to feed a calf with a baby bottle!

Visiting Shannon Hayes's house makes me kind of jealous. Her life appeals to some kind of primal, pastoral urge. Screw this computer—I want to make some soap!

Plenty of others feel the same way. In her 2011 memoir, *The Wilder Life: My Adventures in the Lost World of Little House on the Prairie*, writer Wendy McClure embarks on a quest to enact her childhood fantasies of living in "Laura World." In Laura World, McClure would "make candy by pouring syrup in the snow . . . Sew a seam with tiny and perfectly straight stitches. Have a man's hands span my corseted waist, which at the time didn't seem creepy at all . . . Keep a suckling pig as a pet."

The homesteading movement is so appealing because it combines the common yearning for a hands-on life with the notion that such lives are morally, economically, and environmentally superior. You can quit your boring job to live your Laura Ingalls Wilder fantasy, and now nobody will look at you like you're a nut job!

"When people feel a little betrayed and alienated from companies and the outside world, there's a tendency to focus on your immediate surroundings," says Jennifer Reese, the author of *Make the Bread, Buy the Butter,* a cookbook-cum-warning about the absurdities of getting too deeply obsessed with DIY homemaking. "It's a little pastoral fantasy. You're playing *Little House on the Prairie*—you've always wanted to do this!"

When Reese lost her job in 2008, she sat on her front porch drinking tea and staring at the apple tree in her front yard. "Who needs a job when you have an apple tree?" she remembers thinking. "They didn't have jobs in *Little House in the Big Woods*."[8]

The way our culture has been going, homesteading begins to look like good common sense. Many elements of neo-homesteading are already thoroughly mainstream. Working from home is on the rise—more than thirty-four million Americans work from home at least part-time[9]—as is self-employment. Gardening has exploded. DIY is huge in all areas of life, from crafting to home cooking to learning how to fix your own lawn mower.

"Our guiding principle is the adage that all change begins at home," write urban homesteaders Kelly Coyne and Erik Knutzen in their 2011 book, *Making It: Radical Home Ec for a Post-Consumer World.* "The larger forces of politics and industry may be beyond our control, but the cumulative effects of our everyday choices have the power to change the world."

Viewed optimistically, as a growing handful of economists and social scientists do, the homesteading movement is a positive move away from feckless consumerism and toward a more sustainable world—overly idealistic, perhaps, but still valuable. In her 2010 book, *Plenitude: The New Economics of True Wealth,* Boston College economist Juliet Schor promotes a lifestyle she calls "plenitude," which sounds almost indistinguishable from Hayes's radical homemaking. Plenitude involves four major principles—reducing work hours and reclaiming free time, "self-provisioning" (growing your own food, fixing your own car), environmentally sensitive consumption, and a reinvestment of energy in local communities. It's a lifestyle that many are beginning to embrace, Schor says, as the recession and the inevitability of climate change are beginning to make the status quo unsustainable. Snarky observers call this effect "Portlandification," a dig at the über-green, hyperlocal lefty culture of Portland, Oregon, where people all seem to work only part-time, ride bikes, and spend all their money buying their friends' homemade organic chocolate bars. Though it's easy to make fun of this stuff as a silly hipster trend, it's much larger and more widespread than that. "Portlandification" isn't just in Portland, and it isn't just for hipsters anymore.

## "IT FELT VERY UNEMPOWERING TO DEPEND ON ALL THESE SYSTEMS": THE ALLURE OF SELF-SUFFICIENCY

A few hours west from Hayes's house, not far from the Vermont border, Jenna, twenty-nine, is trying to herd her sheep in the rain. Her sheepdog, Gibson, is new at this. He bounds around the muddy pen with a look of pure doggy bliss on his face, sheep scattering every which way. "That will do, Gibson," calls Jenna as Gibson skitters gleefully down the steep, mud-slicked hillside.

Jenna, a forthright sparkplug of a woman in a plaid shirt and square-framed glasses, is fairly new at this too. Just a few years ago, she was a Web designer living in a funky city apartment in Knoxville, Tennessee. But weekend trips to the nearby Blue Ridge Mountains got her to thinking about how resourceful people used to be: the early settlers of the mountains were, by necessity, nearly self-sufficient.

"I realized that I couldn't do any of this stuff," she says. "I had no idea how to grow a salad or make clothes. It showed me how little I knew how to take care of myself. It felt very unempowering to depend on all these systems."

This is why we've seen the rise of the DIY movement, the books about the moral value of pie-making, the evangelism of community gardening, the talk of how "scary" it is that we've lost our great-grandparents' self-sufficiency skills. This idea—that it's disempowering to be disconnected from the preindustrial skills of our great- or great-great-grandparents—is one of the common threads connecting the many aspects of New Domesticity, and it's one of the driving ideas behind the neo-homesteading movement. Our mothers' generation may have judged their independence by their ability to make their own money, but many members of my generation seem to have a different standard. For those of us who came of age in the 9/11 era, who spent formative years worrying about terrorism and global warming and running out of oil, and who now, in these recession-plagued years, fear there will be no jobs left for them, the idea of "self-sufficiency" via old-fashioned, hands-on skills seems incredibly reassuring.

Annie, twenty-four, is busy canning tomatoes when I call her on the phone. A recent college grad, Annie is spending her summer studying at the Driftless Folk School in rural Wisconsin, one of several such institutions set up in the last few years to teach people the basic skills of two hundred years ago. At Driftless, Annie is learning canning, cheese-making, blacksmithing, and farming techniques, skills she hopes to use one day on her own mountain homestead.

"We need to be able to be self-sufficient," Annie says, explaining that she believes the world will soon deplete its oil reserves, potentially causing a breakdown of society. "It's important we think about it now while we still have the resources and the Internet and all that. If we're not learning the homesteading and self-sufficiency skills, I can imagine people not knowing what to do and starving.

"Convenience," Annie says ominously, "is not going to be in our future."

"Everybody knows the way we live isn't working," says Ruben, a forty-one-year-old homesteader in western Canada. Basic resources are becoming more scarce, the supply chain for goods like food or electronics is unimaginably long and complex, and production has been taken out of the hands of the average citizen, Ruben says. This order of things won't last. "I think it's inevitable that we will return to a much simpler life. I don't think we have a choice."

Jenna also thinks the era of convenience is over. "The convenience we're so used to is such a fragile system, based entirely on cheap fuel," she says. "In ten years, you're not going to find a home that isn't somehow going to be providing for itself. I think homesteading is absolutely going to change from being a novelty to being a necessity."

## "LIKE GETTING A MERIT BADGE TOWARD BEING A REAL PERSON": A LONGING FOR AUTHENTICITY IN A HIGH-TECH WORLD

The rain turns sleety as Jenna finally wrangles the sheep into the pasture. She spreads straw in front of the chicken coop, checks on her piglets, and leads Jasper, her balky new cart pony, into the paddock. Jasper was a reject from an Amish community, too jumpy to be good with children. Jenna picked him up at an auction for $500 and hopes to use him as an alternative transportation method to get to the village just down the road. I stand to the side of the paddock, holding Gibson on an improvised twine leash. Gibson's tail beats arrhythmically on the wet ground as he strains toward the pony, his black eyes gleaming with delight.

We head back into the small, creaky farmhouse where Jenna lives with Gibson and two older dogs. It was built in the mid-1800s and she bought it with a USDA loan; it has the low-beamed ceilings and slightly sloping floor of another era. Jenna has played up the old-timey look with antique record players, mounted deer heads, and retro woodblock prints. In the kitchen, a pot of beef chili bubbles away in a slow cooker. Jenna throws some logs on her wood-burning stove and we sit down with mugs of coffee—me in a big armchair, her on a squeaky old daybed covered in a vintage quilt—and Jenna begins to tell me about the first time she baked bread.

"The fact that I did that with yeast, water, and flour . . . ," she says, her voice trailing off with wonderment. "It was like getting a merit badge toward being a real person. Food was, to my parents, something you bought." She shakes her head as if this is still slightly bizarre to imagine. "It was a chore for them. We ate prepared foods—canned Ragú, boxed spaghetti. I never grew up with homemade bread or handmade pie. I was never taught to can tomato sauce." She pauses, her face growing darker. "Up until a few generations ago, most women knew how to cook, clean, and sew. I grew up my whole life pushing buttons and flicking switches. I grew up with microwaves and the Internet and Saturday-morning cartoons. I was taught and raised my entire life to not value homemaking—it was something you paid someone else to do."

When Jenna moved to Knoxville for her first real postcollege job, she began to read up on homesteading and re-skilling, poring over farming books in Barnes & Noble. A short time later, when she was offered a job at a company in rural Idaho, she jumped at the chance to put her book-learned skills to the test. She rented a farmhouse, got some chickens and rabbits, and began to learn to garden, bake, and preserve food. The experiment in semi-self-sufficient living went so well she moved on to a rental farmhouse in rural Vermont, then to her current farm, just across the state line in New York's Upper Hudson Valley. She's been living here alone, commuting across the border to work four days a week at a Web-design job at Orvis, the fly-fishing company, at its headquarters in Manchester, Vermont. That's only temporary, she hopes—the farm's not making money yet, but she hopes it will. Soon.

But for Jenna, her lifestyle has as much to do with a search for authenticity and meaning as it does necessity. This search was the topic of her first memoir, *Made from Scratch: Discovering the Pleasures of a Handmade Life,* which chronicled her awakening as a newbie homesteader.

"When you start producing your own food, even the simplest plot of potatoes, your life regains some of the authenticity we've all forgotten about," she writes.[10]

The fact that Jenna's "career girl gone *Green Acres*" story has earned her not one but two memoir deals (her second, *Barnheart: The Incurable Longing for a Farm of One's Own,* came out in late 2011) speaks to the fact that this lifestyle has a powerful appeal for ordinary people. Though most of us aren't actually ditching it all to become farmers, of course, it's certainly a common fantasy. Jenna spends much of her time online chatting with readers and fans: her blog gets more than one hundred thousand hits a month and earns her a healthy secondary income. Many of her readers are interested in exploring the homesteader lifestyle themselves. "I can't tell you how many e-mails I get a month from women whose husbands don't want them to get chickens," she says.

Other homesteaders also rhapsodize about the authenticity of their lifestyles.

Saskia, an urban homesteader in Anchorage, Alaska, grew 1,622 pounds of vegetables on her average-size city lot last year. Some go in the root cellar, others are jarred during marathon end-of-summer canning sessions with her husband, while others are eaten fresh—Saskia likes to cook from scratch, and the average lunch might include sandwiches on homemade bread with homemade cheese and garden veggies.

She sees her lifestyle as a bridge to an older, slower, more traditional way of doing things.

"In the past twenty or thirty years, people have devalued growing and preparing their own food," she says. "It's become the thing to go out to restaurants and get takeout or whatever, and just buy things from the grocery store. That's just such a shallower existence in so many ways."

Lately, Saskia's seen many of her friends start dipping their toes into homesteading—getting chickens, starting a beehive. She hopes that more people will become self-sufficient.

"I feel like we as a society should be striving to work less and do more of our own stuff, instead of trying to keep up with the Joneses."

"What is true happiness, what does constitute success?" asks Jen, a thirty-eight-year-old Colorado urban homesteader who gave up a career to live frugally, homeschool her kids, and turn her lawn into a garden. "I am asking this as someone who gave up a journey to typical success."

## A FARM OF ONE'S OWN: HOMESTEADING AS FEMALE EMPOWERMENT

In the 1960s and 1970s, female back-to-the-land homesteaders were often seen as mere helpmeets for males—"they ended up washing the nappies while the men opined politics and talked about changing the world," says historian Rachel Laudan. But today's neo-homesteading movement is distinctly female led, and many of the women pursuing this kind of lifestyle describe it explicitly in terms of feminist empowerment that has nothing to do with being a wife or mother, let alone a "helpmeet." What's more empowering, they ask—working for the Man, or being self-sufficient by raising your own food and making your own clothes?

Megan, a thirty-one-year-old urban homesteader in Brooklyn, is a prime example of this kind of new thinking. With her pixie-cut hair and inked-up biceps, Megan looks like she should be fronting an indie rock band. But her daily life more closely resembles a nineteenth-century farmwife's than a rock star's. When I arrive at her tiny Greenpoint apartment one morning, the whole hallway smells like homemade granola, and a pot of dried beans sits soaking on the stove. A book called *Country Wisdom & Know-How: Everything You Need to Know to Live Off the Land* sits on the counter by a white vintage KitchenAid mixer; a collection of aprons hangs on a hook.

Megan, who is dressed in a red 1940s-style housedress, has been up for hours tending her animals. She greets me warmly, then leads me down into the building's low-ceilinged communal basement to show me a plastic bin of composting worms, then into her little postage stamp of a backyard.

Here, three large rabbits sit trembling rabbitishly in wire hutches—Megan plans to breed them for meat—while a clutch of chickens (two Rhode Island reds, an Australorp, and a Polish standard with a poofy feathered crown) peck at the bare fall grass.

Megan grew up in Baltimore, where her divorced mom worked two jobs and left Megan alone much of the time. "I was a latchkey kid," she says. "I ate a lot of crappy convenience food." When Megan moved to New York to work at a children's clothing company, she found herself unhappily sitting behind a desk, feeling restless and unfulfilled. Her cooking and gardening hobbies began to take on new importance in her life, and she soon found herself deeply involved in the city's burgeoning urban homesteading movement.

Recently, Megan left her job to pursue this homesteading full-time. She grows about a quarter of her own produce—potatoes, tomatoes, squash, huckleberries, garlic—and hasn't bought eggs from a store in two years, she tells me proudly as I admire the raised vegetable beds she's built out of industrial metal cylinders. Recently, she's challenged herself to eat only meat she's killed herself: "I feel like I can trust myself more than I trust anybody else," she says. "The commercial food system is in a pretty precarious place; a lot of people are getting sick. I like the idea of not having to depend on it at all."

A few years ago, Megan's friends thought she was nuts. Now, with the economy stagnating and career disillusionment growing, they all want to imitate her. So do plenty of others—her classes on urban food production sell out, and she's been commissioned to write a book for a major publisher about city beekeeping.

Most of the other urban homesteaders Megan knows are female, and she gets e-mails "all the time" from young women who want to apprentice with her. "Women find this lifestyle very empowering," she says, bending down to adjust the Critter Canteen water bottle on the rabbit hutch. "Some people assume that this is a backlash against the feminist movement, but I see it as a continuation of it."

To Megan, homesteading is an extension of her feminist values— independence, self-sufficiency, the need for intellectual challenge. "Growing your own food is a powerful thing," she says. Since leaving her day job, she spends her days baking bread, writing, tending to her animals, salvaging scraps from local businesses to reuse on the homestead (she feeds her chickens spent grain from a local brewery), blogging about beekeeping, attending local food swaps, and teaching and attending classes related to homesteading. "If anything, this just means progress [for women]," she says. "I think most of the women who are doing this now are tremendously resourceful—they're out there making homemade cleaning products and selling them on Etsy . . . I think of them as businesspeople."

While her live-in boyfriend pulls a healthy salary from his IT job, Megan prides herself on her ability to live off the $1,000 a month she earns from teaching and writing about homesteading (the couple splits their expenses evenly). She sees women's lesser attachment to the status of "breadwinner" as a positive—it allows her a freedom her boyfriend can't enjoy, she says.

Though her boyfriend is supportive of her homesteading, she says, "He's not always that keen on getting super-involved. He does feel this kind of herd pressure—he needs to be the breadwinner, he needs to be the stable one."

As she stands in the yard with the chickens she rose at dawn to feed, a flicker of pity flashes across her face. "It's kind of strange," she says. "It's like, you spend so much time sitting behind a desk, doing something usually kind of abstract, and there's never really any reward. You end up using that paycheck to buy the things you could totally grow."

Male homesteaders, perhaps because of homesteading's close connection to domestic work, often face more raised eyebrows than women. A female homesteader, especially if she has kids, more or less looks like a stay-at-home mom with a gardening habit, a cultural type people are familiar and comfortable with. But a single guy who rejects careerism to can jam? That's weird!

Ryan, a twenty-eight-year-old urban homesteader in Charlotte, North Carolina, got hooked on self-sufficiency as part of the "tiny house" movement. Tiny houses—anything from wee little wood cabins to Airstream trailers retrofitted with solar panels to yurts—are having a vogue these days among environmentalists interested in smaller eco-footprints. Ryan is currently working on designs for his own tiny house, which he hopes to "park" somewhere in Charlotte.

Tiny houses were a "gateway drug" into the world of homesteading, Ryan says.

"You tackle sustainable housing, and you realize that's one part of a larger system, and that's quickly tied to things like food and environmental changes and being a better citizen in the earth and the world," he says.

He started gardening, though he had no clue what he was doing at first. Later, he got chickens, then quails, all on the lot of his suburban Charlotte home. He learned about keeping bees and started canning his own jam. He started meet-up groups for other Charlotte dwellers interested in sustainable living, which now have some four hundred members.

Most of them are women, Ryan says. In Charlotte, a Southern city anchored by the classically macho banking industry and surrounded by traditional-minded small farming towns, a man doing organic gardening and canning raised a few eyebrows.

"These are extremely basic life skills that you need to live," Ryan says, scoffing. "Everybody has to eat—you should know how to cook, male or female."

Ryan thinks gender roles are "blurring"—his last girlfriend "literally didn't know how to boil pasta," while Ryan has known how to sew since adolescence. But it's not happening quickly enough.

"Eventually, hopefully, we'll get to a lack of these divisions, but it's going to be forever," he says. "I can't imagine that happening in one hundred generations."

The title of Jenna's second memoir—*Barnheart: The Incurable Longing for a Farm of One's Own*—is revealing. It echoes, of course, Virginia Woolf's famous essay "A Room of One's Own," one of the most important feminist writings of the twentieth century. In it, Woolf declared that women needed two things—money and a room of their own—to be able to let their creative lives flower. The room of one's own equals freedom. To Jenna, that's what the farm represents. The question then is, what made Jenna—and Megan, and Saskia, and Jen—feel they needed this freedom? Wasn't that exactly what their mothers had fought for?

## I DON'T WANNA WORK FOR THE MAN: HOMESTEADING AS WORKPLACE DISENCHANTMENT

To homesteaders like Megan and Jenna and Shannon Hayes, it's not the home that oppresses women; it's the workplace. If second-wave feminists envisioned careers as a source of personal fulfillment, many neo-homesteaders seem to see conventional jobs in the mostly blackly negative terms. This is a continuation of the antiwork attitude we saw in the last chapter, but it's not limited to women with children.

"The workplace, particularly corporate America, treats most women poorly," writes Shannon Hayes. "If we had a boyfriend or spouse who treated us this badly, most of us with healthy self-esteem would peg him as an abuser and dump him."

Hayes, the daughter of professional parents, remembers how the adults around her—many of them feminists who fought for the right to join the workforce—used to claim to enjoy their careers. In retrospect, she views these claims with suspicion: "It was like this mantra: 'I like my job,'" she tells me as she chops carrots. "It was promoted in the culture—the successful, happy, two-career family. Our mothers fought very hard. After they fought so hard, *of course* they're going to say they like it."

Weaned on these careerist values, Hayes grew up equally ambitious—hence the PhD at twenty-seven. But as a student at Cornell, Hayes first began to question whether the working world was really all it was cracked up to be. Academia was "brutal," she says, especially toward women with children. Not only that, but Hayes was beginning to see that the relatively stable corporate life her parents and in-laws enjoyed was not going to be around anymore—benefits were being slashed, pensions gutted. "You can be thrown out like a used hankie," she says.

Nowhere is this as starkly obvious as in Hayes's old stomping ground of academia, where the security of tenure has largely been overthrown for a system of low-paid, nonpermanent adjuncts and lecturers, who now make up some 70 percent of college teachers.[11] A generation ago, a tenure-track job meant lifelong security. Now, many newly minted PhDs grovel and scrape to teach classes for a few thousand bucks a pop, no benefits, while working in restaurants or bookstores or day care centers to pay the bills.

Small changes in work culture—more maternity leave, less pay discrimination—aren't good enough, Hayes says. In fact, she thinks spending time fighting for these small changes is "like a therapist working with a wife-beater to at least stop smacking her around on Sundays."[12]

In Hayes's worldview—and the worldview of many of the homesteaders I talked to—opting out of the traditional workforce becomes not just a valid option but a feminist necessity.

As one "simple living" blogger writes:

> You won't find me slaving away at a day job to make money (most of it for someone else) while waiting for some corporation to deliver my food to the grocery store and hoping that the baby formula isn't contaminated with lead . . . You'll find me sweating over the oven, making the best bread, instead of sweating over the credit card payments . . . And one day, hopefully not so far away, you'll find a beautiful, happy child, sucking some good old-fashioned mother's milk from me instead of the modern world sucking the life out of me.[13]

It's a poetic verse, but it makes me squirm. It's hard not to see this as a rehash of the Cult of Domesticity: Women belong at home, protecting the family from the dirty world of commerce.

I ask K. Ruby Blume, the director of Oakland's Institute of Urban Homesteading, whether she worries that this radical homemaking is part of a retreat of smart, capable women from the workforce. She tells me, with obvious annoyance, that I'm asking the wrong question. People—both men and women—*ought* to retreat from the workforce, she says.

"Am I going to stay home and grow some food or am I going to go out and work for Bank of America?" she says.

This is a false dichotomy, of course—even if we presume that working for Bank of America is, in fact, evil, it's certainly not the only kind of job there is—but Blume's statement is emblematic of an attitude I hear over and over again as I interview self-described radical homemakers and neo-homesteaders: work sucks, so we need to reclaim the home as a source of fulfillment and moral living.

Jennifer, a fifty-year-old "reformed" executive turned suburban homesteader in California, offers a mea culpa for her generation and says she's glad her daughter's generation sees things differently.

"I'm definitely a baby boomer," she says. "Life was all about climbing that corporate ladder and having more toys than anybody on the block. Lots of my friends are like that. Move up, make millions, show off. We were the epitome of the consumptive generation. My daughter's generation, they don't care about that."

In fact, today's homesteaders are going back to a very 1950s idea of "what makes women happy." They'll add, though perhaps with less conviction, that this makes men happy too. Since homesteading—like much of New Domesticity—is not an exclusively female pursuit, it's easy to use men's participation (even if marginal) as a way of negating claims of sexism or retro thinking.

Later, Blume writes me and adds this:

> I also think that women—no—*people*—like to be in the home, raise their kids, etc. It's only when there is no other option and they are isolated in such a role that it becomes a problem. As someone who has been in the work force now for over 35 years, if I had a guy (or gal) willing to support me as a homemaker, I would dive on that in a hot second.

## HOMESTEADING, MONEY, AND CLASS

For years, it's been the conventional wisdom that women—like men—can derive a huge sense of satisfaction and self-worth from careers and that homemaking, while important, is not really fulfilling or intellectually stimulating as a full-time gig. It's also been the conventional wisdom that letting your partner support you is the road to loss of independence and potential financial ruin. But radical homemakers have an answer to that too:

Homesteading proponents suggest that depending on a partner is far less risky than depending on a corporation (despite the fact that your partner is probably depending on a corporation for his or her income, and you're depending on the partner, so . . . ). There's this idea, heavily promoted in Hayes's book, that homesteading is actually a road to financial independence: "Money becomes a marginal chit when a family can cultivate self-reliance and community interdependence," writes Hayes. It's easy to see the appeal of this line of thinking. Instead of working a cruddy corporate job, you can stay home and save money by baking delicious—and healthy!—bread rather than going to the store. And by doing so, you're helping the earth, promoting sustainable local econo-mies, and giving a big fat middle finger to the Man. Makes sense, right?

"I'm really doubtful that tiny, small-scale homesteading is going to be economically viable for most people," says historian Rachel Laudan. "Are you going to be able to put the kids through college on this?" The 1960s and 1970s back-to-the-landers learned just how difficult homesteading is, she says, and "the movement rather fizzled out."

"I think there are some pretty serious economic constraints on it as a viable model," economist Nancy Folbre says drily. "Even if people want to be fairly self-sufficient in terms of the way they grow their own food and take care of family members, people still need cash in a modern economy to get really basic things like health care . . . Most people who do successfully live off the grid have a source of income that enables them to do that." This source of income, Folbre says, could be a partner's income, or a piece of land, or some family money.

In fact, nearly all the homesteaders I talked to have at least one of the above.

For Hayes, it was her family's farm—rather than starting from scratch, she and her husband moved to Hayes's hometown and started helping her parents run their preexisting hobby farm. For Jenna, it's her own day job—"It'll be enough money before I make enough money here [on the farm]," she says. Megan has no additional income but lives close to the financial edge on her $1,000-a-month (in New York City!) budget. Saskia's husband works full-time.

Even with these staple sources of income, these homesteaders often practice extreme measures of frugality. To save money, Hayes and her husband do things that most of us would be terrified to even consider: They've gone without insurance (their kids are insured through the state's Healthy NY program for lower-income families and small-business owners). Her husband makes a one-month supply of insulin for his type 1 diabetes last for six months. They've stopped putting money in their daughters' college funds; though Hayes has a traditional education—public schools, undergrad at SUNY Binghamton, a PhD in sustainable agriculture from Cornell—as does her husband, she says college is a "dying phenomenon" that will soon be replaced with online learning and apprenticeships anyway.

## WHAT'S NATURAL? GENDER AND HOMESTEADING

In other contexts, encouraging women to quit their jobs to stay home would be considered unacceptably retrograde and sexist. But since radical homemaking is not just for women, adherents say there's nothing retro or backlash-y about it. Men can be—and often are—equally involved in homesteading, if not in the same numbers as women. At the same time, the very idea of radical homemaking brings up some potentially problematic gender issues.

Homesteaders, almost by definition, tend to be preoccupied with "natural" versus "unnatural" dichotomies. Genetically modified soybean seeds are "unnatural," while heirloom tomatoes are "natural." The petrochemicals in drugstore shampoo are "unnatural," while olive oil soap is "natural."

So it shouldn't be terribly surprising that this interest in defining what's "natural" should extend to people. Yet, as I talked to more and more homesteaders, I was still a bit taken aback at the old-fashioned gender essentialism many of them seemed to espouse.

When I ask Megan why homesteading is so female driven, the word "natural" comes up almost immediately. "I think for women, it does come naturally—we are naturally more nurturing," she says. "Maybe it doesn't interest men as much. Maybe it doesn't come to men as quickly."

At first, Jenna tells me she doesn't think homesteading or radical homemaking should be gender-specific at all. And she certainly doesn't think women should not have careers if they want them. But then she says this:

"I think it is our biological role, homemaking and caring for children. As females, we are biologically programmed to be protective and nurture and take care of things. We are animals. It's a pretty noble role. I don't see it as my biblical role or my societal role. I see it as my *biological* role to be a homemaker.

"I'm actually a very traditional woman," she adds, "though it may not seem like it."

It's hard to know what to make of this attitude. There's nothing at all oppressed or subordinated about Jenna's badass, farmer-girl life, and there's nothing oppressed or subordinated about Jenna as a person: she struck me as one of the toughest, most independent-spirited people I've ever met. Though she claims what she's doing on her farm is incredibly traditional—"what people have been doing since time out of mind," she says—it's also clearly quite radically modern. A young single woman, moving—against the strenuous disapproval of her family—to a remote part of the country to live alone and raise sheep? It's hard to think of a more independent, scrappy thing to do. So it's interesting—and puzzling— that she puts it in terms of a return to a more traditional, biologically determined style of femininity.

Of course, when "homemaker" means spending your day carding wool to sell at the farmer's market, trading chicks for blog ad space, and taking digital photos of your sheep, it's hard to know what "traditional" really means.

As a single homesteader, Jenna is a bit of a rarity. Most of the homesteaders I've heard of or talked to are partnered. And when it comes to partnerships, it's clear that homesteading, despite its progressive nature, has not yet transcended traditional gender divides. Since most radical homemakers still do need one steady income, the choice to pursue homesteading often has the effect of reinforcing traditional breadwinner-homemaker divides, even when that's not the intent.

"I feel like, in our relationship, it just happened that he's become the primary breadwinner, though we both really believe in this [homesteading]," says Saskia. "I don't feel like our roles are totally traditional, but at the same time I'm the one that's ended up doing the garden and whatnot, because I have the time to do it. Maybe that's the reason it [homesteading] has been more female led—because women haven't been the primary breadwinners."

Jennifer also thinks homesteading is a natural role for women, a role she describes as heroic. Echoing a sentiment promoted by many of the environmentalists I've talked to, Jennifer says that women, naturally more sensitive than men, are better able to identify and implement the lifestyle changes that are becoming increasingly necessary as the environment and economy collapse. It's the "mom as sustainability warrior" paradigm.

"The moms of the world, the women of the world, they see what's on the horizon," she says, explaining that she sees the world as on the verge of an environmental and economic collapse. "Women tend to take care of what they see as a coming problem a lot sooner than guys do . . . I definitely see this as a women-led movement."

Given how economically marginal homesteading is, it's hard for me not to worry about it being embraced as a "woman's thing."

In her famous 1968 essay on hippie culture, *Slouching Towards Bethlehem,* Joan Didion sits down to eat macrobiotic apple pie with a San Francisco hippie woman named Barbara, who is embracing what she calls "the woman's trip"—i.e., traditional caretaking duties like cooking and housekeeping—"to the exclusion of almost everything else," including all but the most marginal paid employment.

"Doing something that shows your love that way," Barbara tells Didion, "is just about the most beautiful thing I know."

Later, Didion muses thusly:

> Whenever I hear about the woman's trip, which is often, I think a lot about nothin'-says-lovin'-like-something-from-the-oven and the Feminine Mystique and how it is possible for people to be the unconscious instruments of values they would strenuously reject on a conscious level, but I do not mention this to Barbara.[14]

## WHERE HOUSEWIFE MEETS HOMESTEADER

One of the reasons homesteading is so female led is because it's a natural progression for stay-at-home moms of a certain crunchy, eco-conscious bent. For creative, educated women looking for deeper engagement and self-sufficiency yet not interested in full-time employment, homesteading can appear to offer the perfect solution.

Mallory, whom we met briefly in the previous chapter, does not look like a woman who would want to raise chickens. A fresh-faced thirty-eight-year-old with glossy chestnut hair and preppy square glasses, she greets me at her front door in a cardigan and crisp trousers that say "accounts manager" more than "organic farmer." Her home, in a middle-class subdivision outside Albany, features your standard-issue American Suburban Interior: beige wall-to-wall carpet, tan walls, tidy bins of children's toys in the living room. A plate of fresh-baked muffin bread sits on the counter. Mallory's two young daughters, four and six, both dressed in fairy costumes, play on the landing.

Though Mallory might seem like the average suburban mom, she doesn't see herself that way. This explains the For Sale sign in the front yard. Mallory, see, is hoping to sell the house and move to a small farm nearby. There, she plans to grow most of her family's veggies, raise the aforementioned chickens, and let her homeschooled daughters run around in the dirt.

"It will be *very* labor-intensive," she says, picking up a mug of tea as she makes her way to the living room.

Mallory must catch my skeptical look as I scan around her pin-neat living room trying to imagine her mucking around in a compost heap. Because she immediately hastens to explain that this was not the way she expected her life to turn out, either. A former Web designer with a degree in history and women's studies from the University of Connecticut, she expected to live out her life as part of a standard two-car, two-career suburban family. After all, that's what her own working mother and all her college professors expected of her.

"My teachers were graduates of the women's lib movement and they drilled it into us that you have to work, be a professional," she says. "But as soon as I had Emmy I just knew I just didn't want to be away from my baby. It was primal. So my husband goes to work, and I stay home. My professors would be horrified to see me now.

"In the beginning, I was a typical middle-class American mom," Mallory explains further, sitting down on the couch, legs crossed. "Mom's groups, all the preschool stuff."

But Mallory found life as a typical suburban stay-at-home mom underwhelming. Looking for stimulation, she began to read and watch documentaries about sustainable living. She started reading New Domesticity blogs like *Hip Mountain Mama* and watching documentaries condemning the industrial food system. Eventually, she began to be disgusted with the "blatant consumerism" and "plastic crap" involved in standard middle-class parenting. She quit her mom's groups because she "only wanted to be friends with people who were supporting my lifestyle," she says.

Within a few years, she was homeschooling her two daughters; cooking almost all her family's food from scratch, down to the homemade bread; and blogging about natural homemaking.

But as dedicated as Mallory is to full-time New Domesticity homemaking, she's beginning to find it . . . less than completely satisfying.

"Even having this setup isn't enough for me," she says, gesturing toward her spacious kitchen and the bread cooling on the counter. "That's why I want to move to a farm."

When the house sells, Mallory hopes to move to a small, sustainable farm, where she'll grow the bulk of the vegetables her family eats. In preparation, she's been working at the farmer's market, attending beekeeping school, and learning about chickens. Mallory hopes that homesteading will give her a greater sense of purpose and that growing vegetables will give her a sense of "contributing to my family emotionally" if not financially.

Revealingly, the idea of returning to preindustrial homemaking for fulfillment is not new. In fact, it was attempted during the very era that today's homemakers find so awful: the 1950s. In *More Work for Mother*, historian Ruth Schwartz Cowan notes that nostalgic preindustrial homemaking had a vogue among the unhappy homemakers of the 1950s:

> If women who lived before the Industrial Revolution had led happy, fruitful, and productive lives (as the sociologists were suggesting), then it seemed reasonable to assume that modern discontents could be wiped away if women would return at least to some of the conditions that had pertained in Martha Washington's day. In communities across the land (especially in those that were particularly affluent and, therefore, farthest removed from the horrors of pre-industrial conditions), people were acting out the sociologists' prescriptions by bearing numerous children . . . by breastfeeding those numerous children, raising vegetables in their backyards, crocheting afghans, knitting argyle socks, entertaining at barbecues, hiding appliances behind artificial wood paneling, giving homemade bread for Christmas presents, and decorating their living rooms with spinning wheels.

In *The Feminine Mystique*, Betty Friedan even interviewed a wealthy housewife with a hand loom and a penchant for sewing all her own clothes and making her own bread. Maybe she would have been happier if she'd had a goat?

In fact, as early as the 1800s, unhappy homemakers romanticized the strong, capable Colonial era woman, who was imagined to be much more wholesome and content with her lot in life. Magazines like *Ladies' Home Journal* featured stories of old-fashioned women impressing jaded Gilded Age millionaires with their virtue and hardworking spirit.

Hayes is quick to point out that homesteaders can develop the very same "housewife syndrome" Betty Friedan warned about in *The Feminine Mystique*. Hayes's recipe for radical homemakers is in three parts: renounce, reclaim, and rebuild. In the renouncing phase, homemakers turn their backs on mainstream American consumerism. In the reclaiming phase, they learn the skills necessary for their new lives—sewing, gardening, soap making. But in order to be satisfied, they must make it to the third phase—rebuilding—and begin to share their skills with the outside world by teaching, community organizing, or starting small businesses. If not, they'll risk becoming bored, isolated, and purposeless. Their activities, rather than becoming imbued with larger meaning and moral value, will begin to seem tedious and pointless.

Jenna, with her money-earning blog and her multiple memoirs, and Megan, with her blog, her classes, and her beekeeping book, both seem to have moved to the third stage. Saskia, with her blog and her future gardening classes, is on her way as well. Unlike nineteenth-century homesteaders, their labor is not done silently. On the contrary, all these women have multiple digital outlets for sharing their skills and receiving validation for their hard work.

Friedan thought the way for women to escape housewife syndrome was to share domestic duties with their male partners while pursuing engagement in the larger community. Though feminist activists like Friedan didn't "force" women into the job market, they did think it was one of the best and easiest ways to have a voice in the world (not to mention financial independence). For Hayes and co., having a voice in the world does not come through pursuing a career. Having a voice in the world, they say, comes through reclaiming your home—and showing others the path.

# Strange Bedfellows: How New Domesticity Brings Together Liberals and Conservatives, Atheists and Evangelicals, Mormon Moms and Radical Queers, the Rural Poor and the Urban Rich

New Domesticity makes for some surprising bedfellows. The interest in reclaiming old-fashioned domestic work crosses all kinds of political, religious, and economic divides. We see twentysomethings connecting with octogenarians over a mutual love of knitting. We see urban homesteaders swapping seeds with rural fifth-generation farmers. We see evangelical Christian moms trading homeschooling tips with lesbian unschooling parents on online forums. We see low-income families practicing frugal living to save money and affluent families practicing frugal living because it appeals to their eco-conscious sensibilities. We see Mormon stay-at-home-mom bloggers sharing recipes with atheist hipster foodies. Progressives have banded together with conservative libertarian types to denounce regulation in the name of freedom—to battle mandatory vaccines, to pull away from public schools, to fight food regulations. Liberal attachment parents can espouse pronatalist ideologies as rigid as anything Jerry Falwell ever cooked up.

The DIY movement appeals to people from both ends of the political spectrum, says UNC American studies scholar Marcie Cohen Ferris. "You could be a way, way conservative homeschooler in a military camp in Nevada and re-embrace domesticity because you're antigovernment," she says. "Or you could be a Carrboro-Durham [our little lefty bubble] young, educated locavore-hipster type."

In this environment, ultra-progressive attitudes can go so far that they start to resemble ultra-conservative ones. As a result, New Domesticity has spawned a fascinating, though sometimes frightening, alliance between extreme right and extreme left.

JJ, the thirty-two-year-old stay-at-home mom and writer in Los Angeles, says, "The friends I have from high school who are Mormon housewives are now completely aligned with my ultra-crunchy friends— forsaking the TV, forsaking birth control in favor of natural methods, giving birth at home in the bathtub."

"This movement can get claimed and co-opted or used by all these different people on different places on the political spectrum," says Minnesota philosopher Lisa Heldke, who has written about domesticity. Heldke jokes that when she brings her homemade bread to a party where she doesn't know the guests, she has to explain who she is and what the bread means. As in, is she a conservative farmwife or a liberal neo-homesteader? Does this bread symbolize her identity as a modern woman or that she is her grandmother all over again?

In this chapter, we'll look at some of the subgroups of New Domesticity—"crunchy conservatives," crafty Mormon homemakers, lesbian stay-at-home moms, right-wing homesteaders—to see how traditional labels like "modern" versus "traditional," "feminist" versus "antifeminist," and "conservative" versus "liberal" are melting together, or melting away entirely.


## FROM HIPPIE TO CONSERVATIVE
## CATHOLIC AND BACK AGAIN

Rachel is a fascinating example of how the same aspects of New Domesticity can be appealing for very different—even opposite—reasons.

The forty-year-old Indiana English professor and mother of two has done New Domesticity two ways: first as a "hippie radical," later as a conservative Catholic.

Raised in Kansas, Rachel grew up in a politically liberal home with two working parents. In college, she was definitely on the crunchy side, interested in a career in music or academia. When she first started thinking about having kids, she gravitated toward progressive ideas about child rearing, reading books about unschooling by left-wing educational theorist John Holt, and poring through 1970s-era tomes on natural childbirth.

But in her early twenties, Rachel fell in love with and married a Catholic man. She converted to Catholicism and quickly became a hard-line conservative, far more religious than her husband—"I didn't use birth control and I would pray before the abortion clinic," she says. Through her conversion, she maintained her beliefs about homeschooling, home birthing, and the like, which she discovered were also common in the conservative Catholic community.

Rachel found herself moving between two different worlds. On the one side were the women in her Kansas attachment parenting group, who tended to be the kind of political liberals she would have identified with in college. On the other side were her fellow conservative Catholic moms, who would have shivered at the idea of being called hippies or New Agers. Both groups were extremely family oriented and had romantic ideas about the home as a sacred space. Both saw themselves as rebels against the mainstream culture. The liberals were rebelling against the culture of consumerism and competitiveness, while the conservatives were rebelling against what they saw as a secularized, sinful world. Both groups were deeply involved in DIY—home birthing, homeschooling, growing their own food. It was only their reasoning that differed. When it came to homeschooling, for example, the liberal attachment parenting moms were concerned with maximizing their children's creativity and allowing them to learn at their own pace; the conservative Catholic moms were more focused on imparting Christian values. While a progressive woman who home-births might say something like "Nature designed my body to give birth without unnecessary medical intervention," an ultra-religious woman might say exactly the same thing, just replacing the word "nature" with the word "God."

"There are radical right-wingers and radical left-wingers," says Rachel.

"They end up doing exactly the same things, but they have different ideas motivating them."

When her first child was born, Rachel began practicing frugal living, a lifestyle equally common among both cash-strapped Christian housewives with multiple children and eco-conscious lefties concerned with living lightly on the earth. Frugal living, though not a set ideology, tends to involve a common set of strategies: not buying things you can make, reusing things until they fall apart, buying necessities secondhand, learning to do without things that most Americans consider necessary in order to stay out of consumer debt. For many, especially for women who are stay-at-home moms, the lifestyle becomes a major source of personal identity, with women challenging themselves to undertake ever-more-dramatic feats of frugality. Many of the people I've spoken with for this book practiced some form of frugal living, from living without a car to making their own reusable toilet paper out of old bedsheets (yes, this is really a thing).

At the time she got married, Rachel was planning on having five or six kids and envisioned having a big, rambling house of her own. But she and her husband were renting and had no way to afford a mortgage. So Rachel would peruse garage sales with a strict list, wandering from sale to sale until she found a perfect pair of children's size-four shoes, never allowing herself to buy anything not on the list. She made her own soap, and used that soap to make her own laundry detergent. She made all her food from scratch, right down to home-baked bread and yogurt.

Because her frugality served a greater goal—in Rachel's case, the ability to be a stay-at-home Catholic mother to six children—this challenging lifestyle felt purposeful. She was following in the Blessed Virgin's footsteps, raising babies to glorify God.

This sense of purpose is crucial, she says.

"If it's not in the service of a larger ideology that motivates everything you do, it doesn't often feel worth it, because it [frugal living and extreme DIY] is *so* difficult," she says.

But in her thirties, Rachel's ideology began to fall apart. After having two children, she realized she simply didn't want any more. Her vision of being the perfect Catholic mother to a massive brood crumbled. She was also having trouble stomaching some of the church's conservative political philosophy, and she found herself questioning her faith. In a short time, she abandoned Catholicism completely. Once again, she was a secular lefty "hippie"; she continued being interested in the same things—homeschooling, bread baking—but this time from a secular, liberal point of view again.

It was only once she found full-time work as a professor and began earning a steady income that her commitment to the frugal, from-scratch, home-based life waned.

Without financial necessity, her ideology of extreme frugality and DIY fell apart. It was so much easier to just buy the bread, she realized. She still bakes and makes yogurt when she has time, but only because she enjoys it. She no longer feels like her moral worth—as either a Catholic mother or a good liberal attachment parent—is contingent on her homemaking skills.

Rachel has observed the growing New Domesticity phenomenon with interest, noting that full-time stay-at-home domesticity seems to be increasingly romanticized. And now that she has some distance from her old way of being, she finds it troubling. "It's Angel in the House stuff," she says, referring to the nineteenth-century idea of the perfect, nurturing wife and mother. "It's a dangerous ideology for women."

## CRUNCHY CONSERVATIVES AND NEW DOMESTICITY

In the 1990s, the "culture wars" were pretty black-and-white. Liberals were tree-huggers with an unnatural affection for whales, while conservatives thought global warming was a conspiracy and SUVs a God-given right. Liberals bought tofu at the co-op, while conservatives ate nothing but frozen Hot Pockets from Walmart. Liberals grew organic kale in their backyards, while conservatives sprayed their lawns with Agent Orange. Liberals sent their kids to Waldorf schools to develop their "creative spirits," while conservatives homeschooled their kids so they wouldn't learn about evolution.

In reality, things were never quite that simple. But they've certainly gotten much, much more complicated.

While a majority of my interviewees considered themselves progressive or left-wing, many others were exactly the opposite. I talked with evangelical Christian home-birth advocates, conservative Southern organic gardeners, traditionally minded Mormon stay-at-home moms making extra money off Etsy, the Brooklyn-based indie crafting marketplace.

I'm not the first person to notice this odd alignment of extreme right-wingers and extreme left-wingers when it comes to the home and child rearing. Back in the early 2000s, conservative columnist Rod Dreher identified a growing movement: "crunchy conservatives." These "crunchy cons" included "gun-loving organic gardeners," "hip homeschooling mamas," and "right-wing nature-lovers"—in other words, people with conservative political and social beliefs but a fondness for the trappings of lefty liberal culture. But, as Dreher asked, why were these things—environmentalism, food-consciousness, DIY—considered liberal to begin with?

As Dreher sees it, the attributes of what I call New Domesticity in this book—eco-consciousness, family closeness, skepticism toward big business, an emphasis on time over money and people over things, a DIY spirit—are, in fact, the building blocks of a traditional, conservative society. Like the neo-homesteaders I interviewed, he waxes poetic about simplicity, community, and self-reliance. Like the attachment parents, he writes glowingly about the importance of family.

"We began to realize that even though we were conservative Republicans, this stuff made sense, and it didn't conflict with our moral or religious beliefs," Dreher wrote. "In fact, it flowed naturally from them."[1]

When it comes to new styles of ultra-time-intensive DIY parenting, crunchy secular couples and evangelical Christians often find themselves standing shoulder to shoulder.

Dr. Sears, the guru of attachment parenting, is also an evangelical Christian turned hard-core Catholic, a fact little known to many secular attachment parents. In his 1997 book *The Complete Book of Christian Parenting and Child Care,* Sears pontificates on godly marriage and child rearing in a way that would surely be unpalatable to secular readers—women should "submit" to husbands, fathers are the leaders of the family. Attachment parenting, Sears writes, is "the way God wants His children parented."

Most of the advice in Sears's Christian parenting book is fairly gentle and practical, a much-needed corrective to authoritarian "spare the rod and spoil the child" traditional Christian parenting advice. But there's a definite undercurrent of conservative gender essentialism. Women,

Sears writes, are designed by God to respond to babies' cries in a way that men aren't and therefore will naturally have a closer relationship to their babies, and so on.

Sears writes with something close to scorn for what he calls "detachment" or "convenience" parenting. Attachment families travel as a unit; detachment parents take selfish solo getaways. Attachment mothers trust their own God-given intuition; detachment mothers must rely on outside experts. Attachment mothers enjoy their children so much it fulfills them completely; detachment mothers need (gasp!) "alternative fulfillment."

Fifty years after *The Feminine Mystique,* the idea that women should be completely fulfilled and happy with a life of nonstop child care seems alarmingly retro. By the time *The Attachment Parenting Book* came out in 2001, "God" had been replaced by "Nature" to appeal to a secular audience. Sears is massively popular with both Christian and secular audiences.

## HIPSTER CHRISTIANS AND THE "FROM-SCRATCH LIFE"

Jessica, a twenty-nine-year-old mother of six in Calgary, Canada, takes equal inspiration from Jesus and the works of Michael Pollan.

A self-professed bookworm, she grew up in a conservative family in Halifax, Nova Scotia, where words like "environmentalism" would have been met with a funny look. But as a young mother, she began reading books like *The Omnivore's Dilemma* and *Animal, Vegetable, Miracle.* The books inspired her interest in DIY and sustainable living, which became increasingly important to her as her family grew—she and her husband believe in letting God determine the size of their family. So far, God has given them six children ranging in age from one month to eight years.

Jessica is now deeply involved in domestic DIY. She knits many of her children's clothes, cans her own fruit to later make into baby food, and tries to grow all her family's vegetables, though that's a difficult task in icy Calgary. She home-births, babywears, and homeschools, saying, "I decided I wanted my husband and I to be the biggest influence in our children's life for at least the first few years."

Though she and her family live in the city, Jessica and her husband, a computer programmer, have felt more and more drawn toward self-sufficient, off-grid living. "I want to someday be able to have a small family farm," she says. "Not necessarily something we would earn our income from, but something that would support our income in some ways and would provide our family with food so we could preserve stuff throughout the winter. We would love to be off the grid in terms of our usage of electricity."

Heather, a thirty-one-year-old stay-at-home Christian mother of three in upstate New York, sees what she calls her "from-scratch life" as part of her faith.

Her parents, both evangelical Christians, were environmentalists long before it was trendy to take reusable totes to the grocery store. Heather and her husband, a pastor at an evangelical Baptist church, are both ardent environmentalists as well. "If we really believe that God created the earth, we ought to take care of it," she says.

As an undergrad at evangelical Liberty University in Virginia, Heather studied adolescent and child development, and credits her education with her decision to stay home with her kids.

"I learned about how pivotal it was for my children, nurturing them and maturing them," she said.

Heather feels that, in recent years, there's been a growing respect for stay-at-home motherhood.

"Ten, fifteen, twenty years ago, because of the influence of the feminist movement, you definitely were seen as wasting your talents," she said. "I don't feel that pressure at all. In my generation, it's definitely not looked down on."

Unlike the stereotypical dutiful pastor's wife who considers her husband her shepherd, Heather says she has an egalitarian partnership with her husband. When Heather was young, her own mother went to medical school and became a physician while her dad stayed home, so she's used to nontraditional arrangements. She says the division of housework is a "nonissue"—her husband gardens, cares for the chickens, and does his share of the child care.

For conservative Christian women, New Domesticity can be a way of reconciling traditional lifestyles with the need for independence and creativity. For them, New Domesticity provides the perfect blend of the traditional and the modern.

Robin, a forty-three-year-old mother of two school-age kids in Silicon Valley, says her Christian faith is the main factor in her choice to live a simpler, downsized DIY life.

Just a few years ago, Robin and her husband were living the standard American Dream—suburban house, long commute to a corporate marketing job for Robin's husband, constant acquisition of more and more material goods. Then the recession hit. Feeling the financial pinch and unsure of what they really wanted, the family went away for a monthlong Christian spiritual retreat in Massachusetts.

After the retreat, their "desire to continue with that lifestyle just sort of unraveled," Robin says. "We wanted more time together. My son is eight, so he'll be leaving for college ten years from now. Right now, if my husband kept working in the Valley our kids wouldn't know him very well because he works so much . . . We didn't want the upwardly mobile thing. We joke that we're downwardly mobile. We have more freedom."

So the pair moved to a small farm just outside the city, where Robin began raising bees and chickens and gardening in earnest. Throwing out her childhood eating habits of "meatloaf and Hamburger Helper and Swiss steak," she started cooking organic, whole foods. She even tried to stop using paper products like toilet paper, instead having her family wipe with reusable cloth pads (she swears it's easy—a "nonissue," she says, though I must admit I'm dubious).

Robin's simple living has a very Christian flavor—she and her husband fast on rice and beans during Lent in solidarity with the poor, for example. At the moment, she's trying to launch a sustainable soap-making business that would source its ingredients from poor women in the developing world.

Robin admits that she and her husband have a very traditional division of labor—she does all the housework and most of the child care, including homeschooling. "It looks pretty June Cleaver right now," she says, laughing. But she hopes that if her husband gets a lower-key job and her soap-making business takes off, they'll begin sharing the work more equally.

"I come from an extremely traditional background," Robin says. "Me starting a business is departing significantly from my background."

While some women, as we've seen, use New Domesticity as a way to "opt out," women like Robin may be using it to "opt in."

For many ultra-conservative Christian women, the artisan economy of Etsy and its fellow online craft sites is a boon. Though the Brooklyn-based company was started by a trio of hipster men, it's become a place for conservative women to practice the traditional female economy of selling handmade items. Though these women may come from cultures where mothers are expected to stay at home no matter what, sites like Etsy are acceptable businesses because they seem to neatly combine work and domestic duties. After all, if you're already knitting and making soap, why not sell it? This is why Etsy is so popular in places like Provo, Utah, where nearly nine out of ten citizens belong to the LDS church; Provo has one of the highest concentrations of Etsy vendors in America, likely because Mormon women see craft-selling as a job compatible with being a stay-at-home mother.

Megan, a twenty-seven-year-old evangelical Christian mother of two in East Tennessee, is one of many conservative women who make "egg money" selling crafts on Etsy. Megan sells natural child care products like homemade herbal diaper rash cream, rosemary-mint organic baby shampoo, and hand-crocheted bath scrubbers. She also runs an online consulting business advising other women how to launch e-businesses. When she's not working, she sews, cans, gardens, and homeschools her two sons.

In a move that would certainly make any egalitarian-minded woman flinch, Megan thinks at-home businesses will help women avoid competing in the male world. Instead, they can use the Internet to monetize traditionally female tasks. To Megan, who thinks the mass entry of women to the workforce has been a failure, this kind of home-based business is the best of both worlds.

"My mom was born in the sixties and she grew up in the seventies—the whole women's rights movement and feminism and all that stuff was newer and more outspoken and stronger at that point, so a lot of women really felt that they needed to have a job and be independent," Megan says, though she notes that her mother was "definitely not" a feminist herself. "I think today with our generation, we know we have more options and a lot of women don't feel like they have to have a career to be independent. You can still be a wife and a homemaker and have your own business, like what I'm doing now."

## LDS ETSIANS AND MORMON MOMMY BLOGGERS: LATTER-DAY DOMESTICITY

Fans of lifestyle blogs have probably had this experience before:

You're perusing yet another cute lifestyle blog, admiring the young blogger's vintage teapot collection and Hipstamatic photos of chubby babies in striped leg warmers. But as you page through the blog archives, you notice certain "tells." The blogger is super-young (like, four-kids-at-twenty-nine young). She mentions relatives in Utah. She drinks a suspicious amount of hot chocolate. Finally, you see it: a subtly placed widget with a picture of a temple, or a hyperlink on the word "faith" or "belief." You click the link and up pops the official website of the Church of Jesus Christ of Latter-day Saints. Mormons and New Domesticity go together like (homemade) bread and butter. Family and motherhood are highly emphasized in the Mormon faith, and homemaking is seen as a spiritual calling. Mormons tend to marry young—Utah has the lowest average age of first marriage in the nation. After marriage, couples are encouraged to be fruitful and multiply—Utah's birth rate is nearly 50 percent above the national average.[2] Children are considered one of God's greatest blessings, and the concept of "childless by choice" is nearly unheard of in the LDS community. All this means that Mormon women have long seen motherhood and homemaking as a vocation, even as their secular peers were marching off to the workplace.

Mormon women also have a long history of DIY stretching back to their pioneer roots. For stay-at-home mothers of large families living out west, DIY homemaking like baking bread and sewing curtains was a simple matter of necessity. Per church teaching, members must keep at least three months' worth of food in their homes (and often keep much more). This has spawned a major culture of gardening, home canning, and from-scratch cooking. Mormons have also been growing and canning their own food since long before the term "urban homestead" became trendy in places like Brooklyn and San Francisco.

As these kinds of DIY have grown trendy in secular communities in recent years, Mormon women have been notable ambassadors of the crafty, homemade aesthetic. I was recently in the basement of a thoroughly non-Mormon household and noticed white boxes bearing a label reading "Church of Jesus Christ of Latter-Day Saints." It was the family's homegrown garden veggies, packed up and canned at the local Mormon cannery.

Mormon women are especially visible in the blogosphere. The reason for this is partly historical. Church elders have long encouraged members to keep regular journals for the dual purposes of historical record-keeping and promoting spiritual insight, and as a result Mormons are champion journalers and scrapbookers. In the 2000s, church elders began officially promoting new media technologies like blogs as a way of spreading the gospel, and the Mormon blogging community soon became so large it earned itself a punny nickname: the Bloggernacle.

Amy, a thirty-one-year-old from Salt Lake City, runs the popular blog *Progressive Pioneer*. She writes about knitting and crafting, posts mouth-watering pictures of homemade roast seaweed snacks and fig cake, links to recipes for DIY coconut oil shampoo. She's gone through a major raw-foods phase but now tries to eat lots of full-fat organic dairy and grass-fed beef in line with the popular Weston A. Price diet.

In other words, she's your typical New Domesticity–loving hipster. But she's also a faithful Mormon stay-at-home mom.

To Amy, DIY domesticity is a way of connecting with the pioneer women of early Mormon history, who came west seeking self-sufficiency and self-determination. To her, simple living is a spiritual calling.

"The doctrine of the church is very in line with environmentalism and whole-foods eating and gentle parenting," she says. "All that stuff is really supported scripturally and doctrinally . . . If you read Joseph Smith's [the founder of the LDS church's] writing, he is very much about stewardship of the earth."

When Amy talks about differences between men and women, she sounds remarkably like the natural mothers from chapter 6.

"There are obviously the physical differences, but then there are differences on a chemical and emotional level," she says. "When you nurse a baby your brain gets, like, bathed in oxytocin, which gives you really warm fuzzy feelings about that baby and helps you cope with the feelings that babies are really difficult. Men don't have that."

But while the natural mothers in chapter 6 felt like they were battling against a society that wants women to be like men, Amy feels completely supported as a mother by the LDS community.

"The prophet and the Quorum of Twelve [the leaders of the LDS church], they speak about motherhood so highly," she says. "There's a tenderness and an appreciation."

Amy sees New Domesticity as a sign that secular society is realizing what Mormons have known all along.

"I think it's super interesting that there is this resurgence [in domesticity]," she says. "I've always thought that it was a failure of the women's movement for, instead of celebrating the strengths of women, saying we can be like men and we can do anything men can do."

Amy sees the movement to revalue homemaking as a sign that people are coming to appreciate women's special talents. "We're sort of coming around now," she says. "I think that women who choose to stay at home sometimes feel like they are 'less than,' but it is coming around more that women can say with pride that I run the home and that's valuable. You do hear a lot about women leaving big Wall Street jobs to go home and be with their kids now, which I think is a good sign that the movement is strong to support domesticity and stay-at-home motherhood."

## PREPPERS AND URBAN HOMESTEADERS: CONSERVATIVE VS. LIBERAL IDEOLOGIES OF SELF-SUFFICIENCY

A few months ago, I found myself at a convention on self-sufficiency. There were talks on gardening and raising backyard chickens. There were young women selling home canning equipment from folding tables. There were workshops on DIY health care, such as using essential oils to treat anything from infections to insomnia. There was lots and lots of scoffing about the inertia and ineffectiveness of the government.

Where was I? Brooklyn? Portland? Austin?

Nope. I was in Greenville, South Carolina, at a convention of neo-survivalists. The majority of the five hundred or so attendees were conservative enough to make Rick Santorum look like Ralph Nader. Think "Don't Tread on Me" bumper stickers, John Deere hats (nonironic), babies dressed in camo onesies, and brush-cut dads, the waistbands of their khakis bulging with concealed handguns.

Yet they shared as much of the "the world's going to hell in a hand-basket so we better get ready to be self-sufficient" ideology as many of the people we've met in previous chapters. These "preppers," as they call themselves, store basements full of canned and dried foods, stockpile weapons and bullets, learn DIY first aid, grow their own veggies, and raise their own rabbits in suburban backyards.

Preppers are a rapidly growing subculture, mostly in Sarah Palin's "real America." What began as a fringe movement has grown enormously in the years since the Great Recession hit—now nearly every state in America has multiple preparedness conventions and expos every year, and an entire industry of prepper goods has sprung up to sell food-storage solutions, solar-powered radios, essential oils for first aid, and the like. There's even a popular reality show about preppers on the National Geographic Channel.

Unsurprisingly, these preppers tend to be further right than Joseph McCarthy. But replace those NRA bumper stickers with "Know Your Farmer" ones, and preppers become fairly indistinguishable from crunchy urban homesteaders. Their rhetoric of freedom and DIY is essentially the same, and the sense of antiestablishment distrust is identical.

As I listened to preppers talk about food storage and gardening and the importance of relearning our grandparents' Depression-era self-sufficiency skills, my mind flashed to book interviews I'd done.

Megan, the tattooed Brooklyn homesteader we met in chapter 8, had these kinds of fears. "If our food system were to collapse, which is not really that far-fetched, I can imagine people fighting over a bag of corn," she had told me. "If New York City was cut off from the rest of the world, there would only be enough food to eat for three days."

As I listened to an ex-military type with a brush cut scoff at the idea that the government could take care of us in case of emergency, I thought of "radical homemaker" Shannon Hayes, laughing at the idea of public schools and public emergency management.

As I watched a beaming redhead with *Cosmo*-perfect makeup demonstrate the health properties of doTerra-brand essential oils (company slogan: "Now you be in charge of your family's health") to a curious middle-aged woman with a blond pageboy—"I use lavender oil instead of Neosporin!"—I thought of all the liberal, educated mamas I've talked to who don't believe in vaccines or conventional medicine.

Most of us are neither preppers nor neo-homesteaders, of course. But the rhetoric of DIY and distrust is widespread.

Rod Dreher, the author of *Crunchy Cons,* is now busy writing a book about how conservative Christians should consider completely withdrawing from society. He advocates setting up self-sufficient intentional communities where people looking to live godly lives can set themselves apart from the wicked secular world. He calls this "the Benedict Option," after the sixth-century monastic Saint Benedict of Nursia. But it sure sounds an awful lot like off-the-grid radical homemaking to me.

Preppers are just one example of how people on both the right and the left of American politics are pulling away from communal solutions— government, school, health care—in favor of at-home, DIY solutions.

## "I'VE ALWAYS WANTED TO BE A STAY-AT-HOME MOM BUT BE REALLY QUEER"

It's easy to see why New Domesticity is embraced by those on the right who see it as a return to traditional values. But what about those who have long been accused of destroying traditional values: gays and lesbians? Do they find New Domesticity alienating? How do same-sex couples navigate modern gender roles?

Michie, a twenty-eight-year-old quilt-store employee and quilt maker in Asheville, looks every inch the twentysomething hipster: short blond hair, trendy lumberjack shirt, tweed cap. But she has a distinctly unhipster-like dream:

"I've always wanted to be a stay-at-home mom but be really queer," she says. "I wanted to be the one to be supported."

Now, I'd venture to say that most straight women my age, whether or not they describe themselves as feminists, would hesitate to claim they want to be supported by a man. But Michie, as a lesbian, operates outside the burned-over territory of male-female power struggles. She knows she doesn't fit into the "June Cleaver vacuuming in pearls" stereotype, she knows she won't be mistaken for some kind of Southern "submissive wife," and she knows she won't have to deal with a husband who claims he wears the pants in the relationship. She and her future partner will have no predefined gender roles, so even if Michie stays home with her kids, she won't necessarily fall into the role of "housewife."

This is not to say domesticity comes easy for the LGBTQ community.

Like so many other women today, Meaghan, a thirty-two-year-old university library employee from Washington, DC, is drawn to the trappings of old-fashioned domesticity—aprons, vintage tea towels, cakes, cross-stitch samplers. But as a young twentysomething navigating her sexual identity, Meaghan stayed away from all things crafty and feminine. It seemed too girly, she thought, and she didn't want to be pigeonholed as "too femme." But about seven years ago she got curious about knitting. "It felt like an accessible craft," she says. "A lot of guys were doing it." She, a gay male friend, and a straight female friend formed a knitting circle. Meaghan never looked back. She now spends much of her free time embroidering or baking, and she sells hand-stitched wall hangings on her Etsy site. Her work mixes the über-traditional with the very twenty-first century: felt pictures of tiny houses with hearts in the middle look like they could have been made by your great-grandmother, while her embroidery hoops decorated with military-style chevrons were made to celebrate the repeal of Don't Ask, Don't Tell.

Her partner, who identifies as transmasculine (basically, someone who is biologically female but dresses and identifies as a male), shares the domestic work equally.

"I truly believe my domesticity is a choice," Meaghan says. "I can say solidly that everything I do that is crafty or cooking related or home-care related . . . all of it is a choice because I truly enjoy it. I don't know if that's the same for people in a conventional hetero relationship."

NYU sociologist Kathleen Gerson thinks the increasing acceptance of same-sex partnerships will help break down traditional gender roles in the home. The degendering of domestic pursuits will be a "big step" toward equality, Gerson says, and the acceptance of gay relationships will help speed that process. "It's harder and harder to say what's naturally a man's domain or a woman's domain," she says.

Elizabeth and Sammy, the pair of Durham aspiring stay-at-home mothers we met in the introduction, feel being in a same-sex partnership allowed them a freedom their straight peers didn't always get to enjoy.

"When I'm cooking and cleaning and doing your laundry, it doesn't have the same weight as it would if you were a man," Elizabeth says, touching Sammy's hand. "Our heterosexual friends don't feel that way. The women feel more like they're the only woman in the house and their husbands don't give a shit what the throw pillows look like."

For Elizabeth and Sammy, choosing a domestic life feels truly radical.

"It's only one generation ago that to declare yourself a lesbian and not get married was a radical social act that alienated you from all institutions," says Sammy. "Lots of older lesbians have deep remorse for not having children. I feel so privileged that I'm part of the first generation that can do both.

"A lot of the angst I see around domesticity I see around isolation," says Sammy. Though she and Elizabeth live in the suburbs and work from home, their lives are far from isolated. For one thing, they have each other around 24/7. For another, they have a closely knit community of friends that functions in essence as a family. They're so close with one couple they have dinner together several times a week and often pick up the couple's young daughters at school. The friends recently installed several thousand dollars' worth of TV sound equipment in Sammy and Elizabeth's living room—they didn't have room for it and figured they'd just come over whenever they wanted to watch movies.

Though many of Sammy and Elizabeth's friends are not gay, the idea of the ultra-close "family of choosing" is a long-standing part of gay culture. Isolated from their biological families because of homophobia and often unable to have children of their own, gays and lesbians have long formed intimate social networks. Sammy and Elizabeth hope that being part of such a network will help them avoid the traditional pitfalls of full-time intensive domesticity—loneliness, isolation, exhaustion, boredom.

"We have the freedom to do whatever we want and we've picked something that looks like being a housewife," Elizabeth says, smiling fondly at Sammy. "We've come at it from a place of total freedom. This is the life of our dreams, and domesticity is really a part of that. I feel so privileged."

# CHAPTER 10

# Take-Home Points for the Homeward Bound: Lessons of New Domesticity

I set out to write this book because I wanted to better understand the fascinating, multifaceted phenomenon that is New Domesticity. I wanted to know where it came from and what it meant. I also wanted to know what it meant for me, personally. Was I the only one feeling torn about my love—nay, *obsession*—with glossy lifestyle blogs full of aprons and homemade jam? What did it mean to be ambitious in my career yet still sometimes fantasize about living on a farm in British Columbia? Was I a bad feminist for looking askance at the crazy-busy lives of the women of my mom's generation?

Writing this book helped me sort out some of these questions. First, it helped me realize that the domestic perfection on the Internet is often an illusion, and I should enjoy it without comparing myself ceaselessly to the gorgeous, serene, bread-baking, farm-dwelling domestic goddesses with perfect lives found therein. (Of course, I still compare, but I'm getting better.)

It helped me realize that so much of our choices around food are driven by guilt, and that this guilt is totally optional. Shopping at the farmer's market and baking bread and curing your own bacon are great, if you love those things, but they're not going to solve the world's problems. I like to shop at the farmer's market (when I can wake up in time!), but I also like to go to the megasuperjumbomart store at eleven P.M. and shop while wearing my headphones and talking to no one. I still eat Trader Joe's tortillas with melted cheese for dinner most nights, because my husband and I would both rather work than cook.

I've stopped feeling guilty about spending money or "outsourcing" work when I can afford it. As Rebecca in chapter 7 said, "Eating in a restaurant is not wasting money. That's a higher standard of living."

When this book becomes the next *Harry Potter/Eat, Pray, Love* bestseller sensation (as I have no doubt it will, of course), the first thing I'm going to do is hire a professional cleaning company for my house. I despise cleaning the kitchen. My husband hates dusting and cleaning the bathroom. We both detest doing laundry. We'd both rather work a bit harder at our jobs and make the extra money to pay the cleaners. That would be a higher standard of living for us. Why the guilt there? It's not the nineteenth century; I'm not meant to be judged on how good a housekeeper I am. Getting down on the floor with a lemon and a bucket of vinegar does not make me a better person.

I better understand my ambivalence about working long hours. We're right to question whether it's worth it, and what toll it takes on our family and personal life. But it's also reaffirmed why career achievement and financial independence are so important to me. Work is a major part of my identity, and making money is one of my major goals. That doesn't make me greedy, just pragmatic.

Also, researching this book has made me want to learn to knit. I wish I'd let my grandmother teach me before she died. I thought it was "boring" when I was a teenager. Now I'm sorry.

But instead, I can turn to YouTube, where a search for "knitting" nets me nearly twenty-five thousand results, from *How to Knit: The Basics* to complex video tutorials for knitting toy squids and octopi. And isn't this what New Domesticity is really about—sharing skills, connecting with others, reviving lost traditions, inventing new ones, working with our hands?

And yes, I'll be knitting at two A.M. in front of a Blu-ray, after working a ten-hour day and eating Thai takeout. But that's what makes New Domesticity different from Old Domesticity, right?

# LESSONS FOR THE FUTURE:
## TAKING THE GOOD, LEAVING THE BAD

So many of the values of New Domesticity are wonderful: an emphasis on family, a DIY spirit, a concern for the environment, an unwillingness to be beholden to corporations. But, as we've seen, there's also a dark side. An emphasis on DIY as a solution for social problems can disenfranchise those who don't have the time or money to DIY it. A privileging of individual rights over group goods can lead to serious problems, as we've seen with the antivaccination movement. An emphasis on what's "natural" can be sexist and can disenfranchise men. A negative view of all work as a soul-killing rat race can demoralize ambitious workers and can lead to women's exclusion from potentially promising career paths.

So what do we do? How do we take away the good of the New Domesticity movement and leave the bad? After researching this book, talking to hundreds of people, and staring at the pages of my manuscript, I've come up with five ideas that I think might help.

### LESSON ONE: ENFRANCHISE MEN

Young men don't want to be like their dads any more than young women want to be like their moms. They want to be more involved in their children's lives. They want to be more equal partners to their wives or girlfriends. They want to be freer to show their emotions and pursue their passions, whether those passions are cycling or baking or breeding ball pythons.

The big question for our generation is: will they be able to?

First, the good (even great) news:

Young men expect equality at home and at work. If you're a twenty-two- or a twenty-eight- or a thirty-three-year-old guy, you've grown up with the same "girls can do anything" mantra young women have, and you believe it just as much—if not more—than they do. You're used to women being doctors and lawyers and professors. If you went to college, likely half or more of your peers were female. If you're a twentysomething, college-educated city dweller, your girlfriend probably makes just as much or more money than you do, statistically speaking (if you're married or live in a small city or rural area, your female partner's probably still behind, financially).[1]

Men of my father's generation still routinely married their secretaries. Doctors married their nurses. Professors married their undergrads, then expected them to type up their papers.

Young men today want women with similar levels of education, intelligence, and ambition. Doctors tend to marry doctors and business execs marry other professionals. Professors who try to seduce their undergrads wind up the butt of jokes in academic satire novels.

These new, more egalitarian partnerships of the twenty-first century have produced a higher level of domestic equality than at any other point in history. Men don't expect their similarly educated, similarly employed wives and partners to do all the housework. Only the most unenlightened cretin would say, "Housekeeping is a woman's job," or "I don't do dishes" (and if he did, his wife would probably laugh in his face and hand him a sponge).

Younger dads are spending far more time with their kids. This is partly because employment patterns have shifted and mothers are working more. But young dads really *want* to be close and involved. In the recent (abysmally reviewed) movie *What to Expect When You're Expecting,* a pack of young dads roam Los Angeles playgrounds with their babies strapped to their chests in BabyBjörns. The fact that the scene was meant to be funny suggests a certain lack of progress, but the truth is that men caring for babies is no longer a novelty. From the teen dad I saw on a Minneapolis bus, tenderly feeding Cheerios to his toddler son, to yuppie-hipster dads carting their babies to Brooklyn beer gardens, fathers are more involved with child care than ever. When, in 2012, Huggies came out with an ad campaign based around the hee-larious notion that dads barely know how to diaper their babies, men were offended—and they weren't afraid to say so. After a dad-driven anti-Huggies petition and thousands of angry comments on Huggies' Facebook page, Kimberly-Clark (Huggies' parent company) admitted it had made a mistake and pulled the ad campaign.

Today men are questioning the "career comes first" dynamic of their parents' generation. They're not particularly interested in being the man in the gray flannel suit. Gen Y women *and* men are demanding workplace flexibility and making it clear to their bosses that they have personal lives and aren't willing to be in the office until ten P.M.

But the news is not all good for guys.

While women of my generation have unprecedented freedom and opportunity, men are still much more boxed in by societal expectations and mores. Talk of "Mommy Wars" aside, it is considered completely normal for women to work full-time, part-time, or not at all. Men are substantially more reined in. A stay-at-home dad is still a curiosity, paternity leave is even rarer than the already-rare maternity leave, and men who cut back on their careers to spend time with family or to pursue personal interests are tarred with the "slacker" brush far more easily than women.

While women have gone from being helpmeets to equal partners over the past forty years, things haven't changed as much for men. Dads my age are frequently asked if they're "babysitting" while caring for their own children. While women are generally applauded for trying "masculine" things—engineering, computer programming, carpentry—men are still looked at askance for doing "feminine" ones like teaching kindergarten or knitting.

If we're going to embrace New Domesticity, we need to make sure that the downsizing of career ambition doesn't continue to be a largely female prerogative. We need to make sure that the rallying cry of "take back the home" is shouted just as loudly by men as by women.

This will not be easy. While both men and women want to work less and have more balance, it's still largely women who actually try it. We have a preexisting cultural and historical framework for women to downsize, downshift, seek balance. It's widely acceptable for a woman to quit her job to stay home with her baby, take a lower-paying job to achieve better "balance," or work part-time as her kids grow older. But men are still very much beholden to their roles as breadwinners.

Thus, even when both members of a couple embrace the tenets of New Domesticity—tenets like time over money, people over things, homemade or local over corporate—it's still usually the woman who puts her money where her mouth is. Thus it's dangerously easy for an embrace of "simple living" or "voluntary simplicity" to turn into something that very much resembles the traditional man-breadwinner, woman-homemaker divide. So many of the women I visited throughout this book sought a simpler, more authentic life through downsizing their careers and focusing on their families and their personal passions. Their motivations for living these kinds of lifestyles were very twenty-first century: eco-friendliness, anticorporate sentiment, a deep belief in the power of DIY. But what they wound up with was a life that was, in many ways, not that different from their grandmothers'. They were entirely financially dependent on their male partners, who generally had conventional jobs. Their primary identity was through their children and their parenting philosophies. They spent most of their time engaged in repetitive domestic tasks.

We need to progress toward a culture where men and women care equally about work-life balance and both live their beliefs. There are some hopeful notes that this may be happening. Gen Y-ers, who are poised to be 75 percent of the American workforce by 2025, are already demanding the kinds of workplace flexibility and autonomy that working moms have been clamoring for since, well, forever. And though corporations have long been able to ignore mothers' needs, they can't ignore the needs of an entire generation of workers. So we're beginning, slowly but surely, to see changes in corporate culture. Some companies have implemented humane work policies like ROWE (results-only work environment), where employees are only evaluated on their productivity, not their physical presence. So if you want to go home early to catch your daughter's play or bake a cake for a friend's birthday, you can do it and catch up on your work at home later. Others have begun offering much more flexible time-off policies, since Gen Y-ers care more about vacation and sick leave than salary. I hope that in the future, we'll see even more of this, and that these liberal attitudes will spread toward non-white-collar industries too.

We need universal maternity-leave policies for women. But just as important, we need paternity leave as well, and we need to make sure men feel comfortable using it. Sweden had paternity-leave policies in place for years but found that few men were taking advantage of the benefit. While women felt comfortable taking time off to be with baby, men worried that they would look less dedicated to their careers if they did the same. So the Swedish government implemented a "use it or lose it" policy, mandating that the country's thirteen-month parental leave cannot only be used by one parent—the other parent must use at least two months of the leave, or both lose those months entirely. Today 85 percent of Swedish fathers take paternity leave. The policy has helped redefine notions of masculinity and femininity in the already-egalitarian country.

"Many men no longer want to be identified just by their jobs," said Bengt Westerberg, the country's former deputy prime minister.[2]

I hate to be the annoying liberal who brings up how great things are in Sweden, but there you have it.

We also need to continue to break down the stigma surrounding men doing "feminine" things.

We've seen huge cultural shifts in some areas of domesticity. Most young men are now perfectly comfortable rhapsodizing about their love for cooking, for example. But the changes are incomplete at best. We're still socialized from the earliest moments of childhood to consider the home a deeply gendered place, even if we don't realize it.

On a recent trip to Toys "R" Us, I was struck by the retro imagery still at play. In the food-toy aisle, I counted fifty different food toys and only *one* had a picture of a little boy on the package. The rest were pure XX: girls pouring imaginary coffee, girls toasting pretend toast in pink toasters, girls ringing up their plastic bananas at play grocery stores. There were pink and purple toy vacuum cleaners and toy shopping trolleys and toy high chairs. Little girls "fed" Little Mommy–brand dolls ("Help her emulate the nurturing role of today's mom with a Little Mommy™ doll!" rhapsodizes the Mattel website) and served tea with Tinker Bell tea sets.

These examples may seem trite, but these commercialized notions of what's "boy stuff" and "girl stuff" continue to haunt us as adults.

John, a thirty-seven-year-old quilter and quilt blogger in the suburbs of Raleigh, North Carolina, is a bit of a celebrity in the quilting world. He's regularly invited to speak at conventions and has even launched his own quilting magazine. But he keeps his hobby a secret from his coworkers at the software company where he works.

"There's all sorts of social and cultural stigma," says the married father of three. "I worry about the men at work, if they found out that I have a quilt blog."

Ryan, the homesteader in Charlotte, North Carolina, continually finds himself pushing against the barriers of what's considered "appropriate" male behavior. He sews, he cans, he cooks from-scratch dinners every night, and he doesn't give a damn if his friends and family think it's odd.

"Eventually, hopefully, we'll get to a lack of these divisions, but it's going to be forever," he says with a sigh. "I can't imagine that happening in a hundred generations."

LESSON TWO: QUIT OUR OBSESSION WITH ALL THINGS "NATURAL"
Lots of things are natural. Arsenic. Infidelity. Infanticide.

Yet we as a culture seem ever more entranced by the notion that what's "natural" is what's good. Though certainly not everyone involved in New Domesticity follows this line of thinking, it's dishearteningly common.

*It's natural for women to want to nurture babies because of oxytocin; it's unnatural for them to put their children in day care. It's natural to want to be in the garden; it's unnatural to be cooped up in the office. It's natural to breast-feed a toddler; it's unnatural to wean a baby in order to go back to work. It's natural to eat food you've cooked yourself; it's unnatural to rely on restaurants or pre-prepared foods.*

This kind of thinking has become immensely popular of late, partly as a result of our recent cultural love affair with pop-neuroscience and pop–evolutionary psychology. In the past decade, we've become enamored with writings and teachings that offer to explain why things are they way they are via simple Just So Stories that appeal to "nature" and "evolution." Books trumpeting the science of "natural sex difference" like Louann Brizendine's *The Female Brain* (2006) and *The Male Brain* (2011), Susan Pinker's *The Sexual Paradox: Men, Women, and the Real Gender Gap* (2008), and Leonard Sax's *Why Gender Matters: What Parents and Teachers Need to Know About the Emerging Science of Sex Differences* (2006) have sold thousands of copies and generated a huge amount of publicity in recent years.

The reason women don't achieve as much as men, these books say, is not because of sexism or the way society is structured. The reason is that women's brains are simply hardwired to be nurturing and family focused, not achievement oriented. It's science!

In Pinker's *The Sexual Paradox,* the developmental psychologist argues that since women apparently have equal opportunity now, the reason there are few women at the top of finance or politics or law or technology is simply that women aren't as interested in these things. Women care more about family than genius, she says. Because of their hormones, they're naturally more interested in babies than boardrooms. They're "wired for empathy" but have a hard time with math.

Despite the fact that this "emerging science of sex difference" is tenuous and contested by many scientists (the venerable science journal *Nature* angrily described Brizendine's *The Female Brain* as "psychoneuroindoctrinology"), this kind of thinking has become our new normal. It appeals to the side of us that loves the sexy-but-simple evolutionary explanation. It "just feels right." It's easier to believe that than to realize that we're still far, far away from gender equality and that to get there will take much more hard work.

New Domesticity is frequently guilty of this kind of "it's just natural!" gender essentialism. Throughout this book, we've seen a lot of praise for women's "primal" nurturing instinct and for women's "natural" ability and desire to care for the home. This kind of talk is often meant in the most positive way—"Isn't it wonderful that women are so caring! Shouldn't we support and encourage this?" It's often couched as "difference feminism"— "We're simply honoring what's special and distinct about females."

But this kind of thinking is extremely problematic for anyone who believes that women and men can and should be equally likely to achieve in their careers, and equally likely and able to care for children and the home.

The nineteenth-century Cult of Domesticity praised women for their supposedly unique virtues of submissiveness, piety, self-sacrifice, and motherly love. The best way to honor women, the thinking went, was to laud what made them naturally different from men.

Echoes of this thinking abound in today's new cult of domesticity.

In the words of popular "revolutionary housewife" blogger Calamity Jane:

> What could possibly be more feminist than to embrace the natural female quality of nurture? It seems to me that to truly honor "woman," we must also honor her biological role as mother.
>
>     . . . Let's not forget that we hold the ultimate power. Let's not forget to value and respect it. Let's not forget to kick some ass in our very own, uniquely female way. Because true revolution starts at home.

The problem of praising all things natural goes beyond gender inequality. In New Domesticity, the obsession with the natural plays out in the ways we eat, work, and raise our children. Writers and thinkers like Michael Pollan, Joel Salatin, Wendell Berry, and Barbara Kingsolver are heroes of the New Domesticity movement for their bucolic ideas of eating like your great-grandparents, living closer to the earth, aligning yourself with what's natural and normal and primal. A lot of this stuff is good common sense. But some of it strays dangerously close to an anti-intellectual nature worship, a privileging of all things rural and simple over all things urban and technological and complex. (Wendell Berry on airplanes: "[They] have nothing to recommend them but speed; they are inconvenient, uncomfortable, undependable, ugly, stinky, and scary." Really? That's *all* airplanes have to recommend them?)

New Domesticity needs to evolve without the senseless worship of all things perceived to be "natural." Women may produce oxytocin when breast-feeding, but contemporary men are more than equipped and eager to care for babies. Vaccines may be "unnatural," but they save millions of lives. Working in an office may not be what our ancestors did, but perhaps it gives us much-needed financial stability and a sense of self-worth.

A mother who puts her baby in day care at three months old is no less "natural" than a woman who stays home until he's in kindergarten. A woman who feeds her family takeout Thai food every night is no less "fully human" (I'm looking at you, Michael Ruhlman!) than one who revels in the earthy pleasures of baking bread. There's nothing inherently unnatural or bad about living in a city or working in an office building, and there's nothing inherently natural or good about living on a farm or growing your own veggies. We're modern humans, and we have a huge diversity of preferences. We're more than our biology. Just because our great-great-grandparents did something doesn't mean it's good. Let's not forget that.

## LESSON THREE: DON'T DOWNPLAY THE IMPORTANCE OF FINANCIAL INDEPENDENCE

Too much of New Domesticity is unfortunately couched as a rejection or reaction against "baby boomer lifestyles" or "our mothers' feminism."

Many of the people I spoke with conceived of feminism as being primarily about getting women into the workplace. Since these people didn't see the workplace as a good or valuable place, they thought this was a misguided goal. In fact, many of them accused the feminism of the 1960s and 1970s of having denigrated homemaking and forced women into the workplace. Many of today's problems, from childhood obesity to materialism to the loss of the hands-on skills of our foremothers, are said to stem from feminism's shortsightedness.

"With all the women's rights, where they fought to leave the home and go into the workplace, I know that was a pretty big movement for women, but I feel like it was the downfall," says Janelle, the thirty-three-year-old homeschooling attachment parent in the Philadelphia suburbs. "Right now we're reclaiming all this [domesticity]."

Janelle does her best to convince other women in her life that working is overrated. When her sister-in-law, overwhelmed with new motherhood, was considering leaving the workforce, Janelle strongly encouraged her to downsize her life and stay at home.

"She had her baby and went back to work, and, you know, was just miserable—horribly miserable!" Janelle says. "She took the baby to a sitter, and was just telling me she was so miserable and so sad. I said, 'Don't do it! What's your mortgage payment? You can cut cable!' So she did—she made the move to stay-at-home mom. I'm just so proud of people who walk away from their jobs to be with their families."

When asked about financial independence, Janelle takes a defiant stance.

"Who cares about the bills?" she says. "Who cares about what other people think of you? Who cares about the nitty-gritty stuff that isn't going to matter when we're dead?"

But let's be real here: Bills aren't the "nitty-gritty" details of life. Paying them is not optional. Not having the money to pay them can ruin your life.

The importance of financial independence often seems to get lost in our eagerness to ditch our boring jobs or pursue our passions.

To get a baby boomer take on New Domesticity and feminism, I call Leslie Bennetts, the prominent former *Vanity Fair* and *Newsweek* writer who started a firestorm with the 2007 publication of *The Feminine Mistake*, a polemic against mothers opting out of the workplace. Young women, Bennetts argued in the book, are putting themselves in a dangerous spot when they quit their jobs or take low-earning, secondary careers in order to care for their children.

Bennetts thinks young women aren't concerned enough about financial independence and that today's desire for slowed-down/downsized/part-time work will come back to bite us in the butt.

"These women are predicating their entire lives on the assumption that somebody else will always be there to do the heavy lifting when it comes to earning the income," she says. "And if they make a little bit of money, they feel they are income earners and they're contributing financially. Whether they're freelance writers or whatever, they consider themselves as having careers, they have dinner-party bragging rights about doing interesting things."

As a freelance writer myself, that last bit smarted just a tad. If I were a man, would I be content to work in such a low-paying, unpredictable field? If I have kids and cut down on my work hours, will I find myself making mere "pin money" ten years down the road, with no way to get back on track to a thriving writing career?

Bennetts says she understands what makes New Domesticity so popular. "I think there is a tremendous need and craving on people's parts for the kinds of comfort that domesticity at its best can provide," she says. "Nutritious, home-cooked meals; a peaceful and aesthetically pleasing home environment—all that stuff, it's wonderful."

But when you take on domesticity as a lifestyle at the expense of your moneymaking abilities, you're making a dangerous choice. Whether you're a stay-at-home mom or a lawyer who has quit her job to try her hand at homesteading, Bennetts warns, you'd better plan for financial independence no matter what.

"If the husband gets run over by a truck or says, 'I don't love you, I'm leaving,' or whatever, what is that woman who's been focusing on making jams going to do?" she asks.

Bennetts also thinks that young women in the first throes of nesting forget about the rest of their lives—the half century they're likely to live *after* their child rearing is done. And, given the spiking divorce rates among the middle-aged, it's quite possible they'll be single during the second half of their lives as well.[3]

"It's not like you have a four-year-old going, 'I love you so much, Mommy,' forever," she says. "You have a teenager who desperately wants to separate . . . If you don't have a career, these New Domesticity types are likely to find themselves standing in the kitchen with all these domestic skills and no outlet for them, no way to earn a living."

Plus, Bennetts says, with the characteristic acerbity that made *The Feminine Mistake* such a flash point, "at that point your kids are not thanking you for having made the hand-pureed baby food and for giving them homemade cookies. They don't feel you've done them a big favor; they say, 'Why didn't she ever grow up and take responsibility for her own life?'

"By the time women are in their fifties, it's carnage out there," Bennetts says. "These women are going to live another forty or fifty years, and it suddenly dawns on them they're totally screwed . . . You can't wave a magic wand and give them an exciting, challenging, lucrative career at fifty-five or sixty."

Bennetts then proceeds to tell me a succession of horror stories involving women she knows—a husband who announced he was gay after thirty years of marriage, a husband who "drops dead" on vacation, a husband who had a secret family with his mistress, a husband who had a backache and was dead of cancer six months later.

"I know a woman whose husband was struck and killed by lightning," Bennetts ends, grimly. "There are aspects of New Domesticity that are lovely, but it is no substitute for being able to support your family," she concludes.

By the time she's done talking, I'm ready to cancel the joint bank account I have with my husband and take out some major life insurance on him.

Jennifer Reese, author of the DIY cookbook *Make the Bread, Buy the Butter,* had a mother who smashed plenty of glass ceilings in her day. She was one of five females in her 1960s law school class but quit working in the 1970s to devote herself to the first round of "hippie organic home-making." She canned, she ground her own wheat, the whole shebang.

But when Jennifer's parents split, Jennifer's mother had to go get a job. "She basically never cooked again, and she sort of laughed at that phase of her life," Jennifer says. "My mom saw the downside of devoting her time to homemaking.

"I personally think it's really dangerous when women too happily give up their professional interests," Jennifer says. "Your husbands can leave you, and if you're just blissfully canning all the time . . ."

I think of all the women I've interviewed who see their choice to reject the traditional career path, whether to raise children or farm or start a craft business, as a form of rebellion against the Man. I think of my own friends, many of whom have mothers who were financially screwed after middle-aged divorces. As we embrace New Domesticity, we can't let it become just another way for women to do what they've always done: make less money than men.

And we need to get over the idea that feminism killed/destroyed/ ruined/denigrated/devalued homemaking.

Second-wave feminist activist Alix Kates Shulman (she of the infamous "Marriage Agreement" housework contract) practically vibrates with scorn when I ask her whether feminism killed domesticity.

"I am a great practitioner of the domestic arts, and I have never seen the tiniest contradiction between doing that and equality," says Shulman, who loves to sew, cook, and forage for wild food in the summer. "Feminism wasn't about prohibition at all; it was about expanding possibilities. What feminists objected to about housework was that they were assigned it, and no one else did it. Nobody was trying to abolish housework. That would be ridiculous! . . . We wanted men to take their share. That's all we wanted. That's everything we wanted."

## LESSON FOUR: UNDERSTAND THE CLASS ISSUES INVOLVED

In an era where free time is the ultimate luxury, time-consuming types of cooking, child rearing, and crafting speak to affluence and a wealth of choices. In the early twentieth century, a homemade quilt meant you couldn't afford linens from the Sears, Roebuck and Co. catalog. Today it means you have the time and money to indulge in an expensive hobby. In the 1950s, serving frozen and canned foods meant you were a cutting-edge homemaker indulging in the very best the Space Age had to offer. Today canned green beans symbolize cheapness, laziness, bad taste, a lack of giving a damn about your health. Convenience has become deeply associated with poverty, lack of education, and worse: think Walmart, McDonald's, TV dinners.

All this puts us in the weird and somewhat uncomfortable position of having privileged people proudly "reclaiming" the work that poor people have long done out of necessity.

Though most of the people featured in this book are not at all wealthy, the majority enjoy some degree of class privilege. Most have college degrees. Many come from professional families. This makes their experience of domesticity completely different from that of, say, a young Mexican immigrant who stays home with her kids because she can't find a job, or a Colonial-era knitter who had to make blankets or her family would freeze, or an 1850s pioneer smoking his own venison jerky to last through the winter because there was nothing else to eat.

My friend Beth thinks the current mania for jam canning is hilarious. A thirty-three-year-old writer, Beth was raised in a very traditional extended family in rural North Carolina, where stuff like canning was considered just another chore for women whose fingers were already worked down to the bone.

"I've grown up with that stuff, so I don't fetishize it," says Beth, who relishes her takeout dinners and often hires a maid service to clean her apartment. She thinks if more people understood the realities of old-fashioned homemaking, they might not find the idea of quitting their corporate jobs for life on a goat farm or an urban homestead nearly so charming.

"I remember my aunts' summer canning days, boiling all those tomatoes in the kitchen with the windows closed," she says. "It was so hot, and so much work!"

While most New Domesticity types are fairly well aware of their class privilege, it does create some uncomfortable, not to mention irritating, dynamics. When an educated mom refuses to "outsource" her children to day care or waxes poetic about the benefits of extended breast-feeding (smarter! thinner! better!), how can that *not* be seen as a judgment against her less-fortunate peers who work full-time, place their kids in day care and before-school programs, and don't have time to breast-feed for three weeks, let alone three years? Are their kids dumber, less attached? And when you don't believe in day care to begin with, why would you fight for the kind of universal free day care that might benefit your poorer neighbor? If you think "formula is the devil," why would you care whether or not other moms have access to it? Breast-feeding activists have even managed to remove the "goody bags" of free formula traditionally offered to new moms in hospitals. That's great for sending the message that "breast is best," but it doesn't mean much for the working-class mom who's going back to cleaning office buildings in a few weeks and might appreciate some free formula.

As JJ, the L.A. "natural parenting dropout," pointed out, the pressure to mother in a certain way is very much about class status. Breast-feeding, once seen as trashy, is now an absolute requirement among moms of a certain social class.

Joan Williams, director for the Center of WorkLife Law at the University of California Hastings College of Law, sees DIY homemaking as a way of "performing" class status. Williams thinks today's obsession with pure, homemade food is a way of showing that you're a member of the upper-middle class.

"Food has always been a class code, and since Alice Waters, the way to give an upper-middle-class act is with food that is fresh and local," she says. "The class code of the upper-middle class literally links morality and political virtue with certain forms of high-intensity food-preparation activities."

Since the recession, Williams says, people are "ever more frantic" to prove their class status. When you're baking bread, shopping at the farmer's market, and raising chickens, you're broadcasting more than "I like kale." Consciously or not, you're making a statement about your class status, your education, your concern for social justice, your good taste.

Kevin West, the writer behind the canning blog and cookbook *Saving the Season,* knows a thing or two about class. The former longtime European editor of *W* magazine, his life was spent jetting from Paris fashion show to Los Angeles film opening. Throughout the 1990s, West says, people were fixated on luxury and bling—Dior, Chanel, Louis Vuitton, "all those aspirational brands that promised some kind of fantasy of the unobtainable."

But in the early 2000s, those luxury goods became too widespread, too easy to obtain, in either real or knockoff form. Suddenly, fashion turned to obscure Americana heritage brands, half-forgotten companies of our great-grandparents' era like Filson and Red Wing and Woolrich. This is when we started to see every man in Brooklyn undergo a sudden lumberjack makeover.

"This was the new form of the unattainable," West says. "Not luxury goods like Hermès, but instead the incredibly arcane or obscure product that you yourself had identified and sourced. That was the new exclusivity. Likewise, in the food world, what we were seeing was the intensification of the ideas of organic and sustainable that have been around for the longest time now—since Alice Waters and Chez Panisse. Those ideas had become so widespread that foodie folks who were a little self-serious wanted to delve deeper—they wanted to look deeper into the past, to the thing that had not yet been beaten to death. So you began to see an interest in preserving and charcuterie."

Now, I doubt most people in this book are consciously trying to advertise their class status by making rhubarb preserves. But let's be honest—few of us are immune to the sway of fashion. And these activities have become widespread because they're considered fashionable. And the whole "there's value in the handmade" line tends to come from people who only make handmade goods by choice or as a hobby.

As Leigh Anne, the owner of an Asheville, North Carolina, indie craft shop, explains, her own mother was raised on a rural farm, grew up to become a nurse, and had "no interest" in handcrafting. "People saw it as being something you did because you didn't have money," says Leigh Anne, thirty-six, as she trims the threads on handmade waxed canvas bags that look like something a nineteenth-century miner would have carried his sandwich in. The bags are selling like gangbusters on Etsy.

Yet, despite all this, I see New Domesticity as a distinctly middle-class phenomenon, not a wealthy one. When I started researching this book, I was expecting to run into a lot of ultra-privileged people. Dropout corporate lawyers turned organic farmers. Wealthy homemakers obsessed with gardening and organic food. CEOs who gave it all up to practice DIY parenting.

Yet mostly what I found were middle-class people struggling with modern life. Underemployed recent college grads learning to knit because they got no satisfaction out of their temp jobs. Women who "just happened" to learn about attachment parenting at the end of their too-short maternity leaves from jobs they felt ambivalent about to begin with. Homesteaders who want to live off-grid because their experiences with mainstream life have been miserable—crappy health care, crappy jobs, crappy houses in crappy suburban neighborhoods. New Domesticity is most attractive to people who are removed enough from the horrors of rural poverty to find canning charming yet still struggle to find genuinely fulfilling careers and decent ways to balance work and life. For the genuinely rich, there's nothing to cry about. People at the very top of America's class structure, men and women alike, have options. They have the best educations that give them access to the best jobs. They can buy the best care for their children, whether that means a live-in au pair or a five-star day care. While a Yale-educated surgeon might knit for fun, she's not likely to "downsize" and start an Etsy shop. A couple of tech executives with thrilling, high-powered jobs aren't as likely to fall into the ideology of attachment parenting as a middle-class mom with an unfulfilling job.

New Domesticity is, at heart, a cry against a society that's not working. A society that doesn't offer safe-enough food, accessible health care, a reasonable level of environmental protections, any sort of rights for working parents.

## LESSON FIVE: DON'T NEGLECT THE SOCIAL GOOD

The DIY-mania we see with New Domesticity is wonderful in many regards, and I applaud its emphasis on creativity, community, and sustainability. But this same DIY-mania can lead to a troubling hyperindividualism. Worryingly, this hyperindividualism seems to already be a major characteristic of Gen Y. Despite all the young Occupiers we saw playing bongos in Zuccotti Park in 2011, Gen Y-ers are generally much less interested in collective political action than previous generations. And—perhaps because of their special-snowflake upbringing—Gen Y-ers put immense amounts of faith in the political power of individual choices. Worried about the food system? Grow your own veggies. Concerned with global warming? Buy a hybrid.

"Why is it we don't intervene in the bureaucracy?" asks Chris Bobel, the gender studies scholar, who has noted that many young activists prefer "DIY activism"—making art, changing their own consumer habits, making their own products rather than buying corporate ones. They tell her, "'We don't want to be in bed with the enemy,'" she says. "'That's not where change happens. That's old-school activism. We're all about DIY.'" Bobel sighs. "A lot of these activists weren't even registered voters."

Gardening and making your own soap and home-birthing your babies are fine, but these are inherently limited actions. If we want to see genuine food safety, if we want to see sustainable products, if we want to see a better women's health system, and if we want these things for everyone, not just the privileged few with the time and education to DIY it, then we need large social changes.

This is not to say that many DIYers aren't also fighting for social change—many are. But the overall attitude of "Screw the government, I'm going to grow my own food and shop at the farmer's market" is still dishearteningly common among the kind of educated progressives who might otherwise be the best advocates for large-scale social change.

While we want to believe that "all change begins at home," this is not necessarily the case; even if it were, all change needs to not end at home.

This is especially important to remember when it comes to women and the workplace. Some, like Shannon Hayes, liken the workplace to a wife-beater and question why women would want to get ahead in a "shitty" "rat race" that's destroying the environment. But unless you genuinely believe we're going to return to the days of yeoman farming, the workplace is here to stay. So either women are going to be fully in it or they're not. I for one would like to see them fully in it, equally represented all the way to the very top.

If women cut back on their ambitions en masse, institutional change will never happen and the glass ceiling will lower. We need to be there to demand equal pay, mandatory maternity leave, more humane hours. Leaving the "dirty work" of working to the men is a way of muffling our own voices.

New Domesticity comes out of a deep desire for change in the world. We don't want to trade our souls for our careers, and we don't want to live in a culture that encourages us to do so. We want to embrace the richness, creativity, and comfort that can be found in domestic life, and we don't want to fear that we'll be mocked or taken less seriously for doing so. We want to live in a more sustainable way, both economically and ecologically. We've realized that the consumption-crazy Standard American Lifestyle isn't good for the earth, and it isn't good for us. We want to focus on what really matters, and we've come to understand that what really matters isn't about accumulating possessions, and it's not necessarily about climbing the corporate ladder, either.

These desires are worthy and wonderful. But to achieve them, we need to embrace New Domesticity prudently. Focusing on the domestic realm isn't necessarily the best or the only way to change the world, and judging others (or ourselves) on how well we keep house is retrograde and ridiculous.

The key to making this all work, I think, is to be expansive rather than exclusive. Let's expand our definition of what constitutes work. Let's welcome men into the domestic realm without subtle jibes about their masculinity. Let's make child rearing about more than just being the perfect mom—let's make it about being a good village. Let's relax our dichotomies about "good food" and "bad food" and acknowledge that eating the occasional frozen dinner isn't going to kill you, just like eating nothing but local organic food is not a guarantee against ill health.

The world today is stressful and scary. But it's also exciting and wonderful and filled with more possibilities than our great-grandmothers could ever have imagined. Let's not retreat to our homes, the way the women of the original nineteenth-century Cult of Domesticity did. Let's invite the world inside.

# Acknowledgments

I am hugely indebted to my agent, Allison Hunter, for ushering this book from idea to, well, book, with skillful guidance, not to mention tolerance for all my neurotic questions. To my editor, Leah Miller, who totally "got" the project (often better than I did) and who worked so hard and with such skill to make it the best it could be, and to Millicent Bennett, for her immense talent and support. And thanks to the Free Press and Simon & Schuster teams, for all your hard work and skill.

I am incredibly grateful to all the people I've interviewed for this book, both the men and women who shared their life stories, and the professionals who generously gave their time to this project. I can't name you all, but the book wouldn't have happened without you.

A huge thank-you to the wonderful friends who gave me so much support, both personal and professional, during the often-challenging time of bringing this book into the world: Lindsey Alexander, Meredith Gringle Risk, Maggie Hood Bromberg, Marty Hebrank, Jeanne Queen, Christa Martin, Leslie Jamison, and Melanie Hibbert, as well as my brilliant sister-in-law, Maren Asay Stephenson. Thanks to my aunt, Deborah Shlian, for sharing her enthusiasm and wisdom. Thanks to my father, David Matchar, who always wants to read everything I've written. And thanks, above all, to my mother, Bobbi Matchar, who has always handled life, both the domestic and the professional, with enormous grace.

To Jamin, for everything and more.

# Notes

## INTRODUCTION

1. http://www.bostonmagazine.com/shopping_style/articles/fashion_masochist
_housewife_chic/.
2. http://www.nytimes.com/2011/02/03/fashion/03REPRO.html.

## CHAPTER 1. THE PULL OF DOMESTICITY IN AN ERA OF ANXIETY

1. http://austinurbangardens.wordpress.com/2011/09/19/no-grocery-store-
challenge-day-628/.
2. http://nccam.nih.gov/news/2008/nhsr12.pdf.
3. http://thechart.blogs.cnn.com/2011/05/20/home-births-at-highest-level
-since-1990/.
4. http://nces.ed.gov/pubs2009/2009030.pdf.
5. http://www2.ed.gov/about/offices/list/oii/nonpublic/statistics.html#homeschl.
6. gaia.adage.com/images/random/1109/aa-newfemale-whitepaper.pdf.
7. Sherrie Inness, *Dinner Roles: American Women and Culinary Culture* (Iowa City:
University of Iowa Press, 2001), 115.
8. http://www.nytimes.com/2008/06/15/magazine/15parenting-t.html?pagewanted
=3&ei=5124&en=1ca7f305ac138056&ex=1371182400&partner=permalink&ex
prod−permalink.
9. Ibid.
10. Ibid.
11. http://www.census.gov/newsroom/releases/archives/facts_for_features_special
_editions/cb11-ff11.html.
12. http://online.wsj.com/article/SB10001424052748704858304575498071732136704
.html.
13. http://www.nytimes.com/2007/12/01/business/01wall.html?pagewanted=all.
14. http://ncwit.org/pdf/NCWIT_TheFacts_rev2010.pdf.
15. http://www.newyorker.com/reporting/2011/07/11/110711fa_fact_auletta.
16. http://www.time.com/time/nation/article/0,8599,1983185,00.html.
17. gaia.adage.com/images/random/1109/aa-newfemale-whitepaper.pdf.

## CHAPTER 2. FROM ANGELS IN THE HOUSE TO CRUNCHY DOMESTIC GODDESSES: THE HISTORY OF "WOMEN'S WORK"

1. Dorothy Mays, *Women in Early America: Struggle, Survival, and Freedom in a New
World* (Santa Barbara: ABC-CLIO, 2004), 137.

2. Laura Shapiro, *Perfection Salad: Women and Cooking at the Turn of the Century* (New York: Farrar, Straus and Giroux, 1986), 138.

3. Gail Collins, *America's Women: 400 Years of Dolls, Drudges, Helpmates and Heroines* (New York: HarperCollins, 2003), 138.

4. http://www.masshist.org/revolution/non_importation.php.

5. Anne L. Macdonald, *No Idle Hands: The Social History of American Knitting* (New York: Ballantine Books, 1988), 31.

6. Ibid., 137.

7. Ibid., 41.

8. Glenna Matthews, *"Just a Housewife": The Rise and Fall of Domesticity in America* (New York: Oxford University Press, 1987), 9.

9. Dr. Charles Meigs, *Females and Their Diseases* (Philadelphia: Lea and Blanchard, 1848), 41, 47.

10. Virginia Woolf, *The Death of the Moth and Other Essays* (Harcourt Brace and Company, 1942), 237.

11. Matthews, *"Just a Housewife,"* 10.

12. Annegret Ogden, *The Great American Housewife: From Helpmate to Wage Earner, 1776–1986* (Westport, Connecticut: Greenwood Press, 1986), 88.

13. Abby Morton Diaz, *A Domestic Problem* (William B. Cairns Collection of American Women Writers, 1630–1900), 11.

14. Charlotte Perkins Gilman, *The Home: Its Work and Influence* (New York: McClure, Phillips and Co., 1903), 90-91.

15. Collins, *America's Women*, 296.

16. Shapiro, *Perfection Salad*, 39.

17. Ibid., 40.

18. Ogden, *The Great American Housewife*, 159.

19. Ibid., 160.

20. http://www.gilderlehrman.org/history-by-era/great-depression/essays/women-and-great-depression.

21. http://www.nejm.org/doi/full/10.1056/NEJMbkrev0809177.

22. http://www.prb.org/articles/2009/usrecessionandbirthrate.aspx?p=1.

23. Susan Strasser, *Never Done: A History of American Housework* (New York: Henry Holt and Company, 1982), 301.

24. Stephanie Coontz, *The Way We Never Were: American Families and the Nostalgia Trap* (New York: Basic Books, 1992).

## CHAPTER 3. JUNE CLEAVER 2.0:
## BLOGGERS AND THE RISE OF DOMESTIC CHIC

1. http://www.blogher.com/frame.php?url=http://www.slideshare.net/BlogHer/bh-social-media-0511-without-notes.

2. http://www.forbes.com/sites/larissafaw/2012/04/25/is-blogging-really-a-way-for-women-to-earn-a-living-2/.

3. http://uxscientist.com/public/docs/uxsci_5.pdf.

4. http://blog.nielsen.com/nielsenwire/online_mobile/buzz-in-the-blogosphere-millions-more-bloggers-and-blog-readers/.

5. http://www.blogher.com/files/2009_Compass_BlogHer_Social_Media _Study_042709_FINAL_0.pdf.
6. http://technorati.com/social-media/article/state-of-the-blogosphere-2010 -introduction/.
7. http://www.ncbi.nlm.nih.gov/pubmed/22094592.
8. http://pewresearch.org/databank/dailynumber/?NumberID=1031.
9. http://today.duke.edu/2006/06/socialisolation.html.
10. http://orangette.blogspot.com/2012/02/september-4.html#comments.
11. Betty Friedan, *The Feminine Mystique* (New York: W.W. Norton and Company, 2001), 76.
12. http://hipgirlshome.com/blog/2009/5/16/keep-the-apron-pitch-the-bra.html.
13. http://glenniacampbell.typepad.com/silenti/blogher/.
14. http://milkandcuddles.com/2011/03/blogher-2010-swag-bag-giveaway/.
15. http://www.forbes.com/sites/larissafaw/2012/04/25/is-blogging-really-a-way-for -women-to-earn-a-living-2/.
16. http://www.blogher.com/frame.php?url=http://www.slideshare.net/BlogHer/2012 -social-media-final-v2.
17. http://technorati.com/social-media/article/state-of-the-blogosphere-2011-part2 /page-3/#ixzz1wI7xnrdS.
18. Stephanie Coontz, *A Strange Stirring: The Feminine Mystique and American Women at the Dawn of the 1960s* (New York: Basic Books, 2011), 139.
19. http://pancakesandfrenchfries.com/.
20. www.remodelingthislife.com.
21. http://deadcowgirl.com/about/mistress-mommy-blogger/.

## CHAPTER 4. KNIT YOUR OWN JOB: ETSY AND THE NEW HANDMADE CULTURE

1. http://online.wsj.com/article/SB10001424052702304203604577394231271835046 .html.
2. http://twittercounter.com/pages/100.
3. http://www.alexa.com/topsites/countries;2/US.
4. http://trace.tennessee.edu/cgi/viewcontent.cgi?article=2169&context=utk _graddiss.
5. http://www.nytimes.com/2001/09/10/business/the-new-feminist-mystique -variety-of-brash-magazines-upset-the-old-stereotypes.html.
6. Craft Yarn Council (2002–2004).
7. Matthew B. Crawford, *Shop Class as Soulcraft: An Inquiry into the Value of Work* (New York: The Penguin Press, 2009), 7–8.
8. Rob Walker, *Buying In: What We Buy and Who We Are* (New York: Random House, 2009).
9. http://alt.coxnewsweb.com/statesman/metro/081205libs.pdf.
10. http://online.wsj.com/article/SB10001424052748704776304576253252673697210 .html.
11. http://www.guardian.co.uk/commentisfree/2011/may/28/suzanne-moore-back -to-1950s?commentpage=1#start-of-comments.

12. http://www.huffingtonpost.com/peg-aloi/tough-gals-do-they-still-_b_924507.html.
13. http://www.fastcompany.com/1795255/gen-y-entrepreneurial-rebels.
14. http://www.cbsnews.com/8301-505143_162-41841657/new-survey-gen-y-loves-entrepreneurship-but-lacks-resources/?tag=bnetdomain.
15. http://statinja.gov.jm/UnemploymentRatesByAgeGroup.aspx.
16. http://www.nytimes.com/2007/12/16/magazine/16Crafts-t.html?pagewanted=print.
17. Ibid.
18. Juliet Schor, *Plenitude: The New Economics of True Wealth* (New York, The Penguin Press, 2010), Kindle Edition location 1730–1731.
19. http://www.economist.com/blogs/freeexchange/2011/10/labour-markets.
20. http://www.entrepreneur.com/article/200450.
21. http://blogs.villagevoice.com/forkintheroad/2009/08/feeling_conflic.php.
22. Kellyanne Conway and Celinda Lake, *What Women Really Want: How American Women Are Quietly Erasing Political, Racial, Class and Religious Lines to Change the Way We Live* (New York: Free Press, 2005), 7.
23. https://prospect.org/article/part-time-bind-0.
24. http://www.doublex.com/section/work/etsycom-peddles-false-feminist-fantasy.
25. http://www.nytimes.com/2009/12/17/fashion/17etsy.html?pagewanted=all.
26. http://www.regretsy.com/2012/05/29/from-the-horses-blowhole/.
27. http://www.jstor.org/discover/10.2307/190176?uid=3739776&uid=2129&uid=2&uid=70&uid=4&uid=3739256&sid=21100827102011.

## CHAPTER 5. CUPCAKE FEMINISTS, HIPSTER JAM CANNERS, AND "FEMIVORES": THE RISE OF THE DIY FOOD CULTURE

1. http://www.industryintel.com/news/read/3286222056/Thirty-seven-percent-of-Americans-cooking-more-often-than-they-were-at.html; http://www.nytimes.com/2008/12/10/dining/10home.html?pagewanted=all.
2. http://www.cbsnews.com/8301-505245_162-57426508/whole-foods-profit-jumps-raises-full-year-outlook/.
3. Canning info via Lindsay at Ball.
4. http://www.npr.org/blogs/health/2011/09/08/140291032/poll-americans-concern-about-food-safety-drops.
5. http://www.goodreads.com/list/show/6011.Cupcakes_on_the_Cover_.
6. http://www.cbsnews.com/2100-500160_162-1060315.html.
7. http://www.prnewswire.com/news-releases/surprising-research-shows-men-like-cooking-more-than-women-1-food-site-allrecipescom-responds-with-new-cooking-site-exclusively-for-men-86864142.html.
8. http://www.foodchannel.com/articles/article/5-food-trend-for-2010-food-vetting/.
9. http://www.foodinsight.org/Resources/Detail.aspx?topic=2011_Food_Health_Survey_Consumer_Attitudes_Toward_Food_Safety_Nutrition_Health.
10. http://www.cdc.gov/listeria/outbreaks/cantaloupes-jensen-farms/index.html.
11. http://www.slowfood.com/_2010_pagine/com/popup_pagina.lasso?-id_pg=121.
12. http://www.bbc.co.uk/ahistoryoftheworld/objects/ryKLhLRqRF6MGhynjUCqjQ.
13. Otto Bettmann, *The Good Old Days, They Were Terrible!* (New York: Random House, 1974).

14. http://www.foodinsight.org/Content/3840/2011%20IFIC%20FDTN%20Food%20 and%20Health%20Survey.pdf.

15. Caitlin Flanagan, *To Hell with All That: Loving and Loathing Our Inner Housewife* (New York: Little, Brown and Company, 2006). 174–75.

16. http://www.nytimes.com/2009/08/02/magazine/02cooking-t.html?pagewanted=all.

17. http://www.oregonlive.com/foodday/index.ssf/2010/06/we_have_to_go_back_to _the_kitc.html.

18. http://www.huffingtonpost.com/marguerite-manteaurao/stirring-the-pot-with -the_b_147048.html.

19. http://www.dailymail.co.uk/femail/article-1313528/Feminism-killed-art-home -cooking.html.

20. http://www.huffingtonpost.com/michael-ruhlman/message-to-food-editors -w_b_555003.html.

21. http://www.oprah.com/health/How-to-Reduce-Exposure-to-GMOs.

22. Inness, *Dinner Roles*, Introduction.

## CHAPTER 6. DIY PARENTHOOD

1. Susan Douglas and Meredith Michaels, *The Mommy Myth: The Idealization of Motherhood and How it Has Undermined All Women* (New York: Free Press, 2004), 25.

2. http://pewsocialtrends.org/2007/05/02/motherhood-today-tougher-challenges- less-success/.

3. Ann Hulbert, *Raising America: Experts, Parents, and a Century of Advice About Children* (Vintage, 2004), 6.

4. Ibid., 13.

5. Coontz, *The Way We Never Were*, 225.

6. Ibid., 210.

7. http://today.msnbc.msn.com/id/48779186/ns/today-books/t/teach-your-children -well-shifting-focus-success/#.UFAkTd3ia1k.

8. Claire Dederer, *Poser: My Life in 23 Yoga Poses* (New York: Farrar, Straus and Giroux, 2011), 100.

9. http://abcas3.accessabc.com/ecirc/magtitlesearch.asp.

10. Kate Pickert, "The Man Who Remade Motherhood," *Time Magazine*, May 21, 2012.

11. http://www.llli.org/faq/advantagetoddler.html.

12. http://www.cancer.org/Cancer/BreastCancer/OverviewGuide/breast-cancer -overview-what-causes.

13. http://www.dallasnews.com/health/family-health/headlines/20110705-home -births-see-dramatic-growth-in-popularity.ece.

14. http://www.nytimes.com/2010/03/24/health/24birth.html.

15. http://www.thedailybeast.com/newsweek/2012/01/29/why-urban-educated -parents-are-turning-to-diy-education.html.

16. http://nces.ed.gov/pubs2009/2009030.pdf.

17. http://www.stanford.edu/group/reichresearch/cgi-bin/site/wp-content/uploads /2011/01/Reich-WhyHomeSchoolsShouldBeRegulated.pdf.

18. http://www.inewsource.org/2011/08/17/more-parents-opting-out-of-vaccines-for -children/.

19. http://www.nytimes.com/2012/04/20/us/measles-cases-rose-in-2011.html?
    _r=1&src=rechp.
20. http://www.inewsource.org/2011/08/17/more-parents-opting-out-of-vaccines-for
    -children/.
21. http://pediatrics.aappublications.org/content/123/1/e164.full.
22. Cordelia Fine, *Delusions of Gender: How Our Minds, Society, and Neurosexism
    Create Difference* (New York: W.W. Norton and Company, 2010), 87.
23. Jane Kramer, "Against Nature," *The New Yorker*, July 25, 2011.
24. Elisabeth Badinter, *The Conflict: How Modern Motherhood Undermines the Status
    of Women* (New York: Metropolitan Books, 2012).
25. Willian Sears and Martha Sears, *The Compleat Book of Christian Parenting
    and Childcare: A Medical and Moral Guide to Raising Happy Healthy Children*
    (Nashville, Tennessee: Broadman and Holman Publishers, 1997).
26. Pickert, "The Man Who Remade Motherhood."
27. http://www.smh.com.au/lifestyle/life/for-crying-out-loud-study-backs-baby
    -sleep-strategies-20120911-25p2a.html.
28. http://www.guardian.co.uk/lifeandstyle/2010/may/08/oliver-james-daycare
    -under-threes.
29. http://www.apa.org/monitor/mar00/childcare.aspx.
30. http://www.usu.edu/anthro/davidlancyspages/RW_Powerpoints/when_nurture
    _becomes_nature/index.htm.
31. David R. Tennant, ed., *Food Chemical Risk Analysis* (London: Blackie Academic
    and Professional, 1997).
32. Matthews, *"Just a Housewife,"* 151.
33. http://www.nytimes.com/2011/10/15/us/efforts-to-combat-high-infant-mortality
    -rate-among-blacks.html?ref=infantmortality.

## CHAPTER 7. THE EMERGENCE OF THE "HIPSTER HOMEMAKER": HOW NEW DOMESTICITY APPEALS TO A GENERATION OF MOTHERS UNHAPPY WITH THE WORKPLACE

1. http://www.pewsocialtrends.org/2012/02/09/young-underemployed-and
   -optimistic/.
2. http://familiesandwork.org/site/research/reports/genandgender.pdf.
3. http://www.washingtonpost.com/blogs/on-leadership/post/not-your-mothers
   -ambition/2011/03/03/AFf8cc2G_blog.html.
4. http://www.bpwfoundation.org/documents/uploads/YC_SummaryReport_Final.
   pdf.
5. http://www.theatlantic.com/magazine/archive/2012/07/why-women-still-cant
   -have-it-all/309020/.
6. http://www.inc.com/news/articles/200702/family.html.
7. http://fr.naalc.org/migrant/english/pdf/mgmexwpr_en.pdf.
8. http://www.cepr.net/documents/publications/nvn-summary.pdf.
9. http://thinkprogress.org/economy/2009/05/19/172785/sick-all-alone/.
10. http://www.unc.edu/courses/2006spring/geog/203/001/motherhoodpenalty.
    pdf.

11. Shelley J. Correll, Stephen Benard, and In Paik, "Getting a Job: Is There a Motherhood Penalty?" *American Journal of Sociology* 112, no. 5 (March 2007).

12. http://www.inc.com/news/articles/200702/family.html.

13. http://www.census.gov/newsroom/releases/archives/facts_for_features_special _editions/cb10-ff11.html.

14. http://hsb.sagepub.com/content/52/1/43.abstract.

15. http://www.nytimes.com/2010/07/01/world/01iht-poll.html?ref=thefemale factor.

16. http://www.washingtonpost.com/wp-dyn/content/article/2007/07/11/AR200707 1102345.html?hpid=topnews.

17. http://economix.blogs.nytimes.com/2009/10/01/revisiting-the-opt-out -revolution/.

18. Meghan Casserly, "Is 'Opting Out' the New American Dream for Working Women?" Forbes.com, September 12, 2012.

19. http://apronstringz.wordpress.com/reclaiming-housewifery/.

20. Elisabeth Badinter, *The Conflict: How Modern Motherhood Undermines the Status of Women* (New York: Metropolitan Books, 2012), 30.

21. http://www.worklifelaw.org/pubs/OptOutPushedOut.pdf.

22. Pamela Stone, *Opting Out? Why Women Really Quit Careers and Head Home* (Berkeley: University of California Press, 2007), 3.

23 Ibid., 3.

## CHAPTER 8. A WOMAN'S (*AND* A MAN'S) PLACE IS IN THE HOME AFTER ALL: THE RISE OF HOMESTEADING

1. Melissa Coleman, *This Life is in Your Hands: One Dream, 60 Acres, and a Family Undone* (New York: HarperCollins, 2011), 307.

2. http://www.theage.com.au/lifestyle/fashion/the-new-age-of-old-20111222-1p6sb .html#ixzz1vpN6daPQ.

3. http://faircompanies.com/news/view/downshifting-voluntary-simplicity/.

4. http://www.oprah.com/omagazine/Meet-Followers-of-the-Simple-Living -Philosophy/3#ixzz1vpTzlOFp.

5. http://www.oprah.com/omagazine/Meet-Followers-of-the-Simple-Living -Philosophy/4#ixzz1vpUM9Ed8.

6. Shannon Hayes, *Radical Homemakers: Reclaiming Domesticity from a Consumer Culture* (Richmondville, New York: Left to Write Press, 2010).

7. Ibid.

8. Jennifer Reese, *Make the Bread, Buy the Butter: What You Should and Shouldn't Cook from Scratch—Over 120 Recipes for the Best Homemade Food* (New York: Free Press, 2011), Introduction.

9. http://www.theatlantic.com/business/archive/2011/07/telecommute-nation-if -half-of-us-could-work-remotely-why-dont-we/242382/.

10. Jenna Woginrich, *Made from Scratch: Discovering the Pleasures of a Handmade Life* (North Adams, MA: Storey Publishing, 2008).

11. http://chronicle.com/article/From-Graduate-School-to/131795/; http://online.wsj .com/article/SB10001424052702303610504577418293114042070.html.

12. Hayes, *Radical Homemakers*.

13. http://barnyardbookworm.wordpress.com/2010/08/12/feminism-and-simple
-living/.

14. Joan Didion, *Slouching Towards Bethlehem* (New York: Farrar, Straus and Giroux, 1968), 113.

## CHAPTER 9. STRANGE BEDFELLOWS: HOW NEW DOMESTICITY BRINGS TOGETHER LIBERALS AND CONSERVATIVES, ATHEISTS AND EVANGELICALS, MORMON MOMS AND RADICAL QUEERS, THE RURAL POOR AND THE URBAN RICH

1. Rod Dreher, *Crunchy Cons: The New Conservative Counterculture and Its Return to Roots* (New York: Random House, 2006), 8–9.

2. https://jobs.utah.gov/wi/pubs/womencareers/factsheet.html.

## CHAPTER 10. TAKE-HOME POINTS FOR THE HOMEWARD BOUND: LESSONS OF NEW DOMESTICITY

1. http://www.time.com/time/business/article/0,8599,2015274,00.html.

2. http://www.nytimes.com/2010/06/10/world/europe/10iht-sweden.html?page
wanted=all.

3. http://www.nytimes.com/2012/03/02/us/more-americans-rejecting-marriage-in
-50s-and-beyond.html.

# Index

## ABOUT THE AUTHOR

Emily Matchar writes about culture, women's issues, work, food, and more for publications such as *The Atlantic, The Washington Post, Salon, The Hairpin, Gourmet, Men's Journal, Outside*, and many others. She studied English and Spanish at Harvard University. She lives in Hong Kong and Chapel Hill, North Carolina, with her husband.